SEATTLE
NOW & THEN

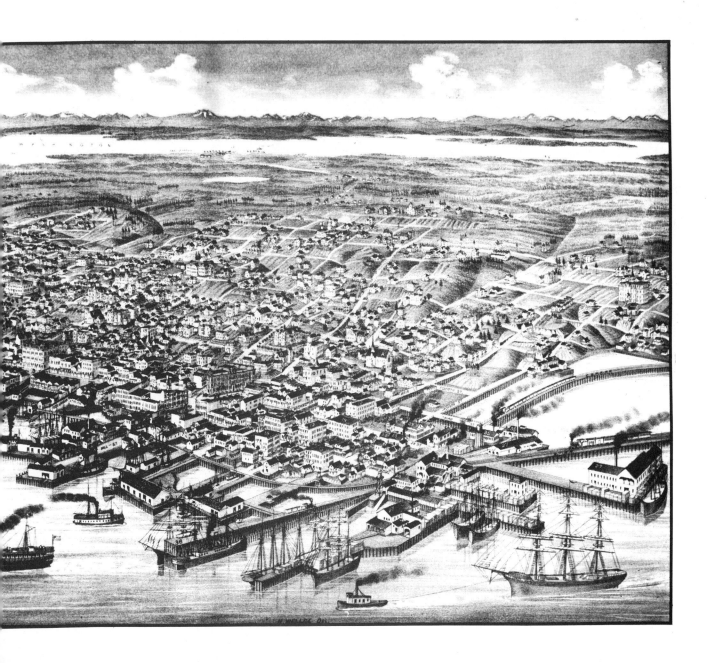

Introduction

I photographed my first "now" in 1978. My subject was the intersection of Second Avenue and Bell Street in Seattle's Denny Regrade. The story of that photographic act is this book's 52nd chapter — I call them "features."

Mine was not an original act. "Now and Then" is a photographic convention almost as old as the medium. Daguerre first introduced his "mirror with a memory" before the French Academy in 1839. That was 14 years before the settlement of Seattle was surveyed and platted, and, in the meantime, photographers were turning and returning for now-and-thens to street corners in Paris, Moscow, and Alexandria — years before there were any intersections in Seattle.

When photography did at last come to this city, it first came as an observance of now-and-then. The two oldest surviving photographs of Seattle are of the same subject, Henry and Sara Yesler's home, and were taken from close to the same place. The differences between the photographer E. A. Clark's "then" (circa 1859) and his "now" (circa 1860) are not dramatic but they are marked, if one takes the time to mark them. Their comparison is the subject of this book's first feature — "The First Photo."

Clark was not consciously exploiting this peculiar photographic capacity; I am. In the spring of 1980 I exhibited many Seattle now-and-thens at Cityfair. To the old convention, I added artists' and architects' renderings for buildings and parks that were never built and grand plans that failed to make it through the municipal elections. I called the exhibit, "Then, Now, and Maybe."

In the fall of 1981 I published 294 Glimpses of Historic Seattle. A few of those glimpses were now-and-then comparisons. Soon after, I came to The Seattle Times with this old idea and a fresh hope. I proposed a weekly column of now-and-thens in which this venerable reader-pleasing practice be given the advantages of good printing and good scholarship. Times columnist Eric Lacitis was my go-between and Pacific Magazine's editor Kathy Andrisevic, an advocate. Through them this proposal was met with consistent good will, and "Now and Then" is now in its third year.

It's desirable (perhaps even necessary, considering

the number of requests) that these features be gathered between the more permanent covers of a book. This is the result. All of the 112 stories collected here have appeared, in part, in Pacific. They will be familiar to Times readers, however, they will also be somewhat unfamiliar, for they have been changed. The stories here are all longer, and pictures have been added both in the book's main section and in its notes. Mistakes have been corrected, some of them from Times readers' suggestions; others I have uncovered and, no doubt, others are yet to be discovered.

But for all these changes, this book is still a collection — one I might have organized in any number of ways. My order does not follow that of their appearance, in part, in Pacific nor is it strictly chronological. Although chronology does figure, the book is arranged topically around events, neighborhoods, and institutions like the Great Fire, Queen Anne Hill, the waterfront the regrades, and the University of Washington.

I've chosen these historical photographs and their stories, using the rule of the "3 C's" — clarity, composition, and con tent. First, the picture should be in focus. Then, as a photograph, if its composition pleases or even excites me, I look for content. Content is the story or stories that lie within. If the story is wonderful, I'll even settle for bad focus.

However, to the "3 C's" readers have sometimes added a fourth — criticism. Some people don't like the oldest scenes. It's hard, they claim, to personally relate to a view from the 1880s. Others mildly complain that there's too much architecture in these cityscapes and not enough citizens. But, I reply, the clapboards and bricks have their human stories to tell as well.

My "now" photographs are not always scientifically shot from the precise location of the historical photographer. Often after considerable sleuthing, I return to the spot, as near as I can figure, of the original recording. Since this frequently leaves me shooting either underground (Pioneer Square) or in thin air (Denny Regrade), I move however far is required to record a "now" that can be compared in its features with the "then."

In the book, as in the column, the contemporary photos are usually printed smaller than the historical. If you wish to see them larger, you are urged to venture into the unpublished now itself. There may be some changes. I think of the short essays that accompany the articles as long captions. Consequently, the photographs have additional short captions beneath them only when something more should be said.

Acknowledgements

Every Saturday at noon on KUOW-FM radio, musician and humorist Sandy Bradley (or one of the twins in her Small Wonder String Band) introduces her Potluck Radio Hour by signing-on, "Live to you from the stage at Murphy's Pub in beautiful downtown Wallingford, the gateway to Ballard."

This book also comes to you live from Wallingford, and it reaches you after passing through Ballard, West Seattle, Queen Anne, South Park, Columbia City, and the Table of Contents and Index will list for you the rest of its itinerary.

But it was here, in Wallingford, that the book was created; the place which the merchants on 45th Street are now promoting—again on the radio—as "Seattle's friendliest neighborhood, nestled between I-5 and Aurora." The residents of Wallingford think this framing of their good nature somewhat fanciful, for there is nothing particularly nestling about the embrace of two smog and noise-spewing speedways. But Wallingfordians *are*, perhaps, friendly and inventive. For most of them the distant roar from the freeway can be imagined as Pacific surf crashing against Capitol Hill.

It was while sunbathing on a Wallingford deck and listening to that white noise spill off the I-5 bridge, that I made my first plans for this book. For five years I've lived in a modest bungalow on Eastern Avenue, and it was there—or here in the basement—that I wrote it—and am writing the last of it now. So, Wallingford is, indeed, the "gateway" to *Seattle, Now and Then*, and there are many connections here. I'll acknowledge a few.

First of all, I wish to thank Paulette Tippie and Sheila Raymond for moving their typesetting business, PJ's, away from the high rents and hard parking downtown to the lower rents and hard parking in Wallingford. It was a return, for Paulette and Sheila first practiced their skills at the old SeaGraphics when Stan Stapp was still the owner. So I thank Stan, once a friendly Wallingfordian

himself, as well. PJ's did all of the book's tyesetting.

I owe another Wallingford thanks to Jean Heuving for throwing a Labor Day party in *her* modest bungalow on 38th Street and inviting designers Marti Ehlers and Patt Emminger. In the kitchen they convinced me to have PJ's typeset the book with the hard-working and reliable Times Roman typeface.

Mark Vaccaro and Carson Fury helped with the book's layout. Both of them live in Wallingford; Carson on Corliss and Mark on 45th which *is* the gateway to Ballard, where lives Jean Emmons who also worked long hours on the book's construction. In its physics, the book needed skilled help from "outsiders" as well: Winky McCoy and Sam Garriott from Capitol Hill, Jessica Dodge from Queen Anne and Rand Howard from Paulsbo.

Celeste Franklin lives in "North Wallingford" on Phinney Ridge, and works at the Paradiso Cafe in downtown Wallingford. She did the final proofreading of the text, but is not responsible for the misspellings that remain. They were left purposefully as evidence that this is a self-published book and therefore not flawless. Another explanation is that these occasional mistakes are like the intentional flaws that are left in the Persian rugs to let the devils out of their otherwise perfectly closed designs.

A close reading of the book will show other imperfections. Some off them are trivial like the lower case "c" in every "courtesy" that introduces a picture credit. Others are conventional like the dirth of photographer credits for the historical photographs. Many of the photographers are acknowledged in the main text, but often I simply do not know who took the picture.

My old friend, Bill Burden, who lives on Meridian Avenue, is yet another Wallingford connection. I thank him now for helping with the book's distribution. (Well, this is actually an encouragement; for since I am still writing the book, it is obviously not yet distributed. When it is distributed, it will be Tartu Publications getting it to you. Tartu is not the name of a Ringling Bros. elephant; rather, if you look in the index of a very old atlas, you will discover that the Estonian town of Tartu was once also called Dorpat.)

My first two books, *294* and *494 More Glimpses of Historic Seattle* were distributed by Mother Wit. Mother Wit has not been seen for a year or so. She is apparently on an extended vacation. Her "daughters" are, however, still around and doing fine. And here, I thank them, Joyce McCollough and Kathleen Flynn for helping prove with all those glimpses that there is in these parts an extraordinary good humor for history. With Kathleen the Wallingford connection continues, for she is now the proprietor of Wallingford's 45th Street Books.

Now the Wallingford connection has almost run out,

for there are many others out of the neighborhood who have helped me in this, now and then. I'll mention a few.

Dick Moultrie got me started and Michael Wiater and Bob Royer encouraged me to keep going in this now ten-year study of regional pictorial history. Robert Monroe, the now retired head of the University of Washington Library's Special Collections, generously shared his wit and understanding of the subject early on, as did his assistant Dennis Andersen. (Andersen is now off in Iowa studying to be a Lutheran minister—a pursuit I dropped out of a quarter-century ago.)

The present staffs at the University of Washington Northwest Collection, the Museum of History and Industry, the Seattle Public Library's Northwest Collection, and the Municipal Library continue to share their time and understanding. A few of them are Howard Giske, Susan Cunningham, Glenda Pearson, Carla Rickerson, Richard Engeman, and Rick Caldwell. I thank them.

As the picture's credits testify only partially, a number of private collectors have also been helpful. I'll name a few. John and Lael Hanawalt, of the Old Seattle Paperworks in the Pike Place Market continue to uncover and share a wealth of local imagery and ephemera. Michael Maslan, Warren Wing, William Mix, and Fred Mann have also shared their resources and love for the subject with me—and so with you.

The Seattle Engineering Department's photography collection is, of course, public not private. Its keepers, Nick Cerelli and Bill Dahl have also given good service helping me search through the department's old nitrate negatives. This has also been a necessary project of preservation—systematically editing the collection for transfer to safety negatives.

Until the time of his death, now nearly two years ago, Lawton Gowey was a frequent collaborator. Now he still

is through his extensive collection which continues to be of use to researchers through the consistent cooperation of his wife Jean. She has elaborately extended his good works by turning the Gowey Collection over to the University's Northwest Collection.

Some people are helpful by disposition. While writing this book I have been fortunate to run into a few of them: Susan Gerrard, Dan Patterson, Sherri Ferguson, Kathy Hope, Doug and Judy McBroom, John Nonnemacher, Jim and Ann Faber, and Murray and Rosa Morgan.

Once a week I visit the Seattle Times with another "Now and Then." A weekly deadline is exhilarating, and I am thankful to Pacific Magazine's staff, Kathy Andrisevic, Ginny Merdes, Tom Stockley, Ed Walker, and Roy Scully, for the excitement.

I want also to acknowledge a type of ideal reader, persons whom I can count on to enthusiastically respond to almost anything I show them in the way of old photographs because they often remember something about the scenes within them. There are many of them, but I'll name Mrs. Herbert Coe who started taking her own photographs around 1900, Arthur Lingenbrink who is now 93 and still makes it to work at Link's Sign Company downtown; and Ivar Haglund, who is not so old, but who often also goes to work.

Finally, since this book is self-published it has needed a friend to stand by its side when it came time to go to press. Ed and Carolyn Littlefield have done that, and it is not the first time. Indeed, they have also stood behind me and even pushed. I am most thankful for their unanxious and timely generosity.

I dedicate this book to the Littlefields and to its first and last editors, Murray Morgan and Genevieve McCoy. They have had the most to do with the final shape of the book's text, although they may not wish to claim it.

Murray sat down with me (or sat me down) for a critical reading of my first seven features before Pacific Magazine got them. It was a single sitting, and the lesson was short but, I think, effective. Genevieve McCoy sat down not once, but hundreds of times at the round table in her dining room—and here we return to Wallingford and the cozy little bungalow on Eastern Avenue—reading, re-reading and transfering the features into her computer. Then she cut into and rearranged them with her merciless push-button efficiency. Without her friendly but elaborate criticism and help, *Seattle Now and Then* would have been Seattle sooner or later.

Table of Contents

1 The First Photo

Sara Yesler poses on her front porch for King County's first photographer, E.A. Clark. Her and Henry Yesler's home sat on the northeast corner of Front Street (now First Avenue) and James Street—the present site of the Pioneer Building. Behind them two and a half blocks of stump-strewn, clear-cut land extend to the line of virgin forest beyond Third Avenue. Most of that timber was no doubt planked in Henry Yesler's steam saw-mill at the foot of Mill Street—just a little ways behind and to the left of Clark's position.

The year was 1859 and, although this is probably not the first photograph Clark took of his community, it is the earliest to survive.

When Clark left Pennsylvania in 1850 and went to California, it was probably for gold. When he moved to Seattle in 1852, he came as a typical pioneer: poor of cash but rich in labor. He also might have come—uncommonly—with a camera. At least, he eventually got one.

Clark set an early claim on the shores of Lake Washington, but later moved into a Seattle home he either built or bought. He named it his "What-Cheer-House." Almost immediately Clark got into school, as a teacher, and into trouble, as the leader of a vigilante gang intent on hanging a native accused of murdering a white man.

Luckily for both Clark and the Indian, Sheriff Carson Boren arrived in the nick of time and stopped the lynching. The schoolteacher eventually became a justice of the peace.

As far as is known, only one other photograph of Clark's still exists. It also is of Yesler's residence and was taken less than a year after the first one. Both the scene and perspective are similar, except the town's first water system has been changed. The elevated flumes that brought the water rushing down James Street from a spring on First Hill have been removed. The Yeslers have also widened their home somewhat, and now Henry is there posing on the front porch with Sara, who is, perhaps, wearing the same high-buttoned and low-hooped dress in both scenes.[1]

The second shot is probably from the winter of 1859-60, and by the time the maples

E.A. Clark　*courtesy, Seattle Public Library*

that bordered the Yesler home on the south were beginning to bloom, E.A. Clark, the county's auditor-photographer was dead. (Twenty-two or three years later, three suspected murderers were lynched from these same maples.)

The Olympia newspaper, the Pioneer and Democrat, memorialized his April 27, 1860 passing with a few lines including: "He has been engaged in the Daguerrean Business for several years and leaves numerous traces of his skill in that art. He was about 32 years of age and leaves numerous friends to mourn his loss."

courtesy, Roger Dudley

2 How to get to West Seattle

Inquiries on how to get to West Seattle often concluded with the question of why go there. And for years, if there was no dugout canoe to be had or hired, the answer was "you can't get there from here."

These perennial questions of why and how to get to West Seattle were ones David Denny probably asked himself many times as he waited for his brother Arthur to find him at Alki Point. David had preceded the "Denny Party" to scout for a settlement on Puget Sound. When the rest of this party finally did arrive on a wet November 13, 1851, David

Denny, incapacitated with an injured foot and a fevered spirit, greeted them with a dismal "I wish you hadn't come."

Fifty-four years later to the day, a few survivors of this damp landing, in company with a large party of supporters, returned to that West Seattle beach. There they unveiled a pylon that memorialized themselves as the "founders of Seattle." It was a mildly controversial act. *(See feature 3.)*

But many others claimed Seattle actually "began" in mid-September, 1851, when the

area's first settlers, including Henry Van Asselt and Luther Collins, staked claims on the Duwamish River—in South not West Seattle. Others objected that the city was more properly "founded" in 1852 when the Dennys and others abandoned Alki Point and marked new claims on the protected east shore of Elliott Bay. From this Seattle site, Alki Point was hidden behind what the Indians called Sqwudux and the early settlers called Lamb's Point. Today we call it Duwamish Head.

And there were other names. In the 1860s it

was changed to Freeport, until 1877, when a Capt. Marshall spent enough buying up Freeport to call it Milton. A year later, in 1878, it was to the electrified citizens of Milton that another kind of transport was made, when a Colonel Larabee sang "Swannee River" over a telegraph wire converted for the first local demonstration of the telephone.

Milton was first called West Seattle in the late 1880s when the questions of why and how to get there were first seriously answered by the West Seattle Land and Improvement Company. This group of San Francisco capitalists bought a lot of land up on the bluff for view lots; they encouraged development along the waterfront with a yacht club, shipyard, boathouse and first regular ferry service from Seattle on the City of Seattle, and started the area's first community newspaper. And the news spread.

An 1890 issue of the Chicago publication, the Graffic, featuring Washington State, exclaimed, "Hundreds of spots of rare beauty may be found in the State of Washington, but surpassing all others, West Seattle easily stands out as the most attractive of them all." The Graffic's praise could not contain itself to this hemisphere. "Switzerland, despite the wealth of magnificent scenery has nothing comparable...the wild, rugged and imposing; the soft, harmonious and sublime; the beautiful, magnificent and glorious; all are here." These sentiments were calculated to first transport one to West Seattle rhetorically, and then physically.

Still, not enough buyers were moved. So the improvement company built a cablecar line that looped through 14 curves (the most, it was claimed, for any cable system) from the ferry dock to the top of the bluff and back. However, it ran only when the ferry arrived, and although Seattle was expanding, it was in other directions. In 1898 the capitalists abandoned their cablecars, and the few buyers they had attracted had to walk to their homes at the top of the bluff.

Our historical view of the City of Seattle landing and unloading its ferry passengers at the West Seattle slip date from about 1902, the year West Seattle first incorporated its 16 square miles. The new town also bought and converted the unused cable to an electric line, and proudly claimed the first municipally owned common carrier in the country. West Seattle was still a small bedroom community for Seattle—most of the city council's work was done on the ferry—but the boom was coming.

It arrived in 1907. The 1,200 citizens voted overwhelmingly for annexation to Seattle, because they were "plainly designated by

nature to form one community." It was, they asserted, their "manifest destiny." The two were now also linked by the West Seattle, a bigger and faster ferry.[1] However, the most encouraging connection was at last by land, or rather by trestle, along Spokane Street. *(See features 99, 100, 101.)*

West Seattle now offered in 1907 the modern suburban dream where one could, the promoters claimed, "fully enjoy the quiet of rural life combined with the comforts and convenience of the city, and feast on the soul-inspiring scenic charms which in matchless grandeur surround one on every side." In 1907, at last, the bedroom community was adding a living room and raising a neighborhood and answers to the questions why and how to get to West Seattle seemed self evident.

When in the mid-1960s West Seattle's density became higher than the city-wide average, the old questions returned. The living room had been converted into an apartment and "where two once lived now 80 do." Although they were not building 747s in West Seattle, the multi-unit construction reached its peak with the Boeing Boom.

In 1969 a citizen's group lobbied for resumption of the ferry service. It failed. In the spring of 1978, when the old dream of a giant bridge seemed to be fading, another citizen's promotion clamored for secession. Now the assured completion of the new super bridge dissolves the old question about how to get to West Seattle.

West Seattle ferry terminal   *courtesy, Seattle Public Library*

Posing in the foreground are a number of Ivar Haglund's relatives. Those he can identify are left to right, Knud Olson, Mrs. Belle Teig and her son Clifford, her husband Jacob Teig and another son Ralph and Mrs. Linda Olsen.

3 The Smith's Stockade

In the early 1900s the Stockade was a popular summer resort on Alki Point. Its owner and builder, Alfred Smith, would drive his surrey to the ferry and return with guests ready to enjoy the combined country and seaside pleasures of hiking, boating, riding, clam digging, and eating the resort's famous chicken dinners.

However, it wasn't summer pleasures that attracted these snugly attired visitors to the Stockade's veranda and front lawn on a cool November 13, 1905. This was exactly fifty-four years since the city's first settlers, the Denny Party, landed here and huddled under a roofless log cabin.

A few of these originals (including Rolland Denny and Carson Boren) gathered here with their well-wishers to dedicate a pylon commemorating their settlement's damp beginning on November 13, 1851.

The pylon was donated by another Denny, Lenora; but the land was given by the Stockade's host, Alfred Smith. And although Alfred arrived in Seattle as a teenager with his father and future Seattle mayor Leonard Smith not until 1869, still an odd story told by pioneer Cornelius Hanford suggests that the Smith family can make a visionary's claim of having come to this city before anybody, including the Dennys, Borens, Terrys and Bells.

Hanford's second-hand tale goes like this. In 1835 Alfred Smith's whaler uncle Daniel Smith "anchored in this harbor, and finding good water flowing to the beach...replenished the ship's casks." Then, "as in a daydream, he seemed to see many vessels in the harbor surrounded by the buildings, towers and streets of a glorious city." Thirty-two

years later, in 1867 Daniel Smith followed his vision and moved to Seattle. His younger brother Leonard and nephew Alfred followed soon after. [1]

Alfred did his courting at Alki, and by-and-by married Lorena Hanson the daughter of Hans Hanson who purchased Alki Point from Doc Maynard who got it from Charles Terry who stepped ashore here with the Dennys in 1851.

In 1902 Alfred and Lorena hired Norwegian ship carpenters to build their Stockade out of Alki Beach driftwood. It was constructed on the site of the settlers' original log cabin. However, this log cabin was fort-like—its timbers were set upright, hence the name Stockade.

Lorena died in 1920 and Alfred two years later. Their children kept up the Stockade's popular traditions—including the chicken dinners—and started a few of their own.

Beginning in 1929, Founders' Day was celebrated every November 13 with a luncheon at the Stockade. Rolland Denny was the perennial guest of honor at these events, and the program was dotted with recollective speeches, and old songs by local soloists.

Ivar Haglund, folksinger

In 1936 the Stockade failed from a combination of poor ferry service and the Great Depression. The Founders' Day festivities were moved to the Alki Fieldhouse and the music part of the 1937 program featured a young West Seattle tenor named Ivar Haglund.

Ivar is a relative of Lorena Hanson Smith and so by marriage is also related to the visionary whaler Daniel Smith who in 1835 had his Elliott Bay premonition of "towers and streets of a glorious city." Now, appropriately, 149 years later Ivar collects clams from Puget Sound and gathers rents from his Smith Tower.[2]

The first cabin on Alki

Dedication of founders' pylon   *courtesy, Historical Photography Collection, University of Washington*

4 Princess Angeline's Shack

The Indians of the West were actually shot twice: first by the cavalry and then by touring photographers. In 1889 the Northern Pacific Railroad capitulated in its hostility towards Seattle and began giving the city regular service at rates comparable to Tacoma's. A year later the railroad sent out its official photographer F. Jay Haynes in his own plush car to record Seattle's progress. His subjects included the city's harbor, its mansions, churches, parks, and one shack. For many years Princess Angeline, Chief Seattle's eldest daughter, was the most photographed subject in Seattle, and Haynes in his search for the photogenic city found her resting beside her shack in the neighborhood of what is now the Elliott Bay side of the Pike Place Market.[1]

One year later a Post-Intelligencer reporter accompanied by a pioneer who helped him translate Angeline's Chinook jargon into his own English journalese, visited the "humble palace of this wizened aboriginal princess." This time Angeline was inside sleeping. While his guide stirred her, the reporter paused outside to begin his report. His paragraph and Haynes' photograph "read" somewhat alike.

"Her cabin or shack is about 8×10 feet in size, with a roof of split cedar shakes. Half of one of the gable ends has the clapboards put on diagonally... At one corner of the house is a huge pile of driftwood, gathered from the ruins of fallen cabins in the neighborhood or picked up from the Bay near by. In the front yard are half a dozen tin and wooden buckets rusty and dirty... A narrow, dwarfed door, and a little dirty pane of glass constitute the means of getting into the palace. A horseshoe and mule's shoe are nailed immediately above the entrance. The door stands open all the time."

The window and shoes had been added to the door since Haynes' visit, but it was still open, and the reporter followed his guide inside, where "the only space in which the floor was visible was about three feet square. Two low bunks and a shorter one, covered with remnants of dirty blankets, a rickety little cook stove and a few rude cooking utensils and a wagon load of rags, old shoes, pans, boxes etc. were stacked upon the beds, under the beds and on the

courtesy, Frederick Mann

floor . . . When Mr. Crawford (the guide) asked Angeline how long she had lived in her present house, she held up her two hands, spreading out her fingers to indicate ten years."

Despite the reported attempts of "various benevolent ladies to move her to more comfortable quarters," here Princess Angeline stayed until her death at 86 in the spring of 1896. The door to her shack was then closed and draped in black crepe. She was moved to Lakeview Cemetery and buried in a canoe-shaped casket with a paddle resting on the stern. Princess Angeline was carried there in a black hearse drawn by a span of black horses and followed by the funereal company of what was then left of Seattle's pioneers.

Princess Angeline crossing Seneca St. on First Ave.   *courtesy, Lawton Gowey*

5 Yesler's Mansion

In 1882 Seattle pioneer Henry Yesler made the national news. The Harper's Weekly story was about the mob lynching of three accused but untried murderers. The hanging was done from a stanchion braced between the forks of two maple trees on the James Street side of Yesler's backyard. The Harper's reporter either interviewed Henry or overheard him say, "that was the first fruit them trees ever bore, but it was the finest." The artist's sketch accompanying the article shows the outlaws hanging between Yesler's maples, and beneath them in the crowd stands Henry Yesler busy at his favorite avocation: whittling.

Yesler continues to whittle in this week's smaller historical photograph. His wife Sara poses with him in front of their home at First Avenue and James Street, the present site of the Pioneer Building. To their left are the hanging maples. Although hidden by the leaves, the stanchion is still in the picture, left there as a morbid warning to visiting hoodlums.

The year is 1883 and the street is decked out in lanterns, bunting, and bordered with evergreens. It is either the Fourth of July or the brief September visit of the Northern Pacific's Henry Villard and his entourage who were then on a grand tour celebrating the completion of the railroad's transcontinental connection. Whatever the festive occasion, the Yeslers were also celebrating their good fortune of being the largest taxpayers in King County, and having survived in prosperity nearly 30 years in their little home in the center of town. (The $92,000 assessment of Yesler's King County properties in 1881 had risen to $318,000 by 1883.)

So Henry and Sara Yesler decided on a larger extravagance, and hired an architect named Bowman to design it. In place of their modest one-story, five-room corner home they would have a three story, 40-room mansion which with its surrounding grounds filled an entire city block between Third and Fourth Avenues, and James and Jefferson Streets.

Construction began on the Yesler mansion in 1883, but later that year so did the depression. Both Henry's prosperity and his home building faltered. By 1885 the Yeslers were nearly bankrupt. When, at last, in July of 1886 they moved into their showpiece, it was still not finished. The planned ornate white oak, ash, and redwood paneling was missing. Most of the rooms were empty, so Henry promptly leased many of them as unfurnished office spaces.

By all accounts Sara and Henry were a robust couple, with an exuberant habit of dancing into the late hours at public balls. When Sara died suddenly on August 28, 1887 of a "gastric fever," she was only 65. Flags in the city and on ships in the sound were hung at half-mast; many businesses closed and the great house could not hold all the mourners. When the funeral services were over Henry was alone in his home with 40 rooms and a few renters.

Soon, and wisely, Henry Yesler decided to leave town. Ten days after his wife's death, in company with James Lowman, his nephew who since 1886 had been managing Yesler's business affairs, Henry headed east on the Northern Pacific. He carried two lists: one of friends and relatives to visit, and the other a shopping list of furnishings for his mansion.

The 77-year-old Yesler was an intrepid traveler and soon exhausted his 33-year-old nephew who, in early October, excused himself from the full itinerary and returned home. Yesler kept going until November 26 when he returned to his mansion with the flu and a swollen ankle he had sprained in San Francisco. The injury, illness, and memory of his whirlwind tour were, perhaps, enough stimulation to fill the void in his big house left by Sara.

It is possible that Henry's mourning was diverted by his second cousin, Minnie Gagle, a "good looking girl with expressive grey eyes" and 56 years Henry's junior. Minnie lived in Leitersburg, Maryland, Henry's birthplace and one of the spots on his tour. In 1888 the Gagles moved to Seattle. By 1889 Minnie was living in the Yesler mansion, and on September 29, 1889 she and Henry were married in Philadelphia while on another trip east. Returning home, Henry now more than ever stayed in his mansion. But his marriage seemed either so scandalous or bizarre to his old cronies that many were alienated and stayed away.

In 1892, at the age of 82, Henry Yesler, accompanied by Minnie, left his mansion for the last time on a tour to both Alaska and Yellowstone Park. Soon after his return his robust health slipped away. In the early Friday morning of December 16, in the company of two doctors, two nurses, his nephew, his wife, and the entire family, the bedridden Yesler wondered aloud if he was about to die. Minnie answered, "Are you afraid of dying?" He replied, "No, I don't care anything about it. The mere dying I don't like, but the rest I don't care anything about." Then, after some nourishment, he added, "That's all I care for."

The Yesler's first home on Pioneer Square   *courtesy, Seattle Public Library*

Henry's death was followed by all "the rest." And although he now could not "care anything about it," everyone else in town did.

More than 3,000 mourners crowded the Yesler mansion and its grounds for the largest funeral in the city's first forty years. A scandal as big as Yesler's estate ensued. Henry's young nephew accused his younger wife of destroying the will. And the city was involved, for it was claimed that this "father of Seattle," who had built Puget Sound's first steam sawmill, been mayor twice, payed the most taxes and much else, had left the bulk of his estate, including the $100,000 mansion, to his city. Now the citizens' repressed resentment for the scandalously young interloping Minnie broke loose. However, neither this prejudice nor legal charges were supported by evidence sufficient to convict her.

In seclusion and guarded by her family, Minnie Gagle, Yesler continued to reside in the mansion until 1899 when the Seattle

Public Library moved in. Sara Yesler, as the Public Library's first librarian in 1868, would have approved the change. Now it was librarian Smith who had his office in one of the bedrooms. The bindery was in the kitchen; another room held periodicals, which left more than thirty rooms for stacks and storage. Our view of the Yesler Mansion as Public Library was taken in either 1899 or 1900; for on the morning of New Year's Day 1901 the library burned down taking twenty-five thousand volumes with it.

In 1903 the Coliseum, a barn-sized theater, "the largest west of Chicago, seating 2600," was built on the grounds. Then on May 4, 1916, the "immense pile of granite and terra cotta" still standing there was dedicated. Our view of the King County Courthouse, as of the library, looks across Third Avenue. Henry Yesler's bas-relief bust is part of a commemorative plaque at the entrance.

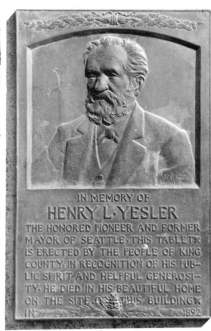

IN MEMORY OF
HENRY L·YESLER
THE HONORED PIONEER AND FORMER
MAYOR OF SEATTLE. THIS TABLET
IS ERECTED BY THE PEOPLE OF KING
COUNTY. IN RECOGNITION OF HIS PUB-
LIC SPIRIT AND HELPFUL GENEROSI-
TY. HE DIED IN HIS BEAUTIFUL HOME
ON THE SITE OF THIS BUILDING
IN   1892

courtesy, Lawton Gowey

6 Salmon Bay Charley

Indian Charley and his wife lived in a disheveled cedar shack on the south shore of Magnolia's Salmon Bay. For a half century Charley, also known as Siwash Charley and Salmon Bay Charley, sold salmon, clams and berries to the first settlers and later to the soldiers at Fort Lawton.

The historical view shows Charley's house at the turn-of-the-century taken by the photography firm Webster and Stevens. Any attempt today at a "scientific" recreation of its exact perspective would have put us literally in the bay. We are close enough. The Army Corps' early-century deep water dredging erased the natives' promontory and thereby briefly revealed the many layers of discarded clamshells that had piled up over the centuries of native settlement.

Charley's native name was Hwelch'teed, and he was probably the last of the Sheel-shol-ashbsh (hence Shilshole) group that centered here around this once narrow Shilshole-Salmon Bay inlet to the fresh water interior. ("Sheel-shol-ashbsh" translates "threading the bead" which was descriptive of the canoe trip to Lakes Union and Washington.)

These Shilsholes were one of eight or nine principle native groups whose habitat was what we now call "Greater Seattle." Local historian David Buerge has determined that this Salmon Bay site was once the center of a large community whose area extended from Mukilteo to Smith Cove.[1] Here long before Charley's shack was built there were three long houses, the largest of them big enough for potlatches and a ritual dance house.

These Sheel-shol-ashbshs went into a sudden decline a half-century before white settlers grabbed their land. Sometime about 1800 their numbers were ravished by a "great catastrophe," probably an attack by one of the slave-taking, booty-hunting and beheading Northcoast tribes. By the time the local ethnographer and pioneer doctor Henry Smith settled Smith Cove in 1853, the tribe had dwindled to a dozen families at most. *(See feature 48.)* By the late 1880s there were only two families left, and they lived separately.

Steady white settlement started in the 1870s when German immigrant Christian Scheurman moved here, cleared the timber, and married a native woman who had ten children before she died in 1884.

*The shack and Salmon Bay
from the opposite direction.*

In 1895 Seattle boosters organized to attract a military post and acquired the acreage that is now Fort Lawton and Discovery Park. The little area that is now Lawton Wood (the part in our "now") was part of those military plans but Christian Scheurman withheld it.

Soon after the military moved in "next door" this protected enclave was itself improved with the mansions of what were advertised as Seattle's "most successful citizens." In 1925 these neighbors—about 30 homes sparingly distributed about a generous 30 acres—organized the Lawton Wood Improvement Club. Their purposeful motto was "to beautify and develop Lawton Wood." When the last of the Scheurmans, Ruby Scheurman Wells, moved out in the late 1970s this "beautifying" had been congested by the developing."[2]

Now the salmon are returning to the bay and the lakes and the Indians of All Tribes have returned to the Day Break Star Center at Discovery Park, just south of the Lawton Wood woods.[3]

courtesy, Historical Photography Collection, University of Washington

7 The First Panorama of Seattle

The Gazette, Seattle's first newspaper, reported in 1865, that E.M. Sammis, the town's first resident photographer, had just returned from a stay in Olympia and would "be ready in a few days to take pictures of everybody at his splendid new gallery over Kellogg's Drug Store."

Although not "everybody" responded, the number of citizens who did was probably more than the seven or eight whose portraits have survived—including those of Doc Maynard and Chief Seattle—and are in the University of Washington's Historical Photography Collection. These few preserved traces of Sammis' work also include cartes de viste (small view cards) of the young town's two architectural showpieces, the Territorial University and the Occidental Hotel, and a card of Sammis' "splendid new gallery," which was where the Merchant's Cafe is now near First Avenue and Yesler Way.

Perhaps the most extraordinary image in these few remains is one lovingly described by Dennis Anderson, formerly in charge of the collection, as "a bent, torn, soiled, little rag of a photograph but the earliest surviving original panoramic view of the city." The original measures 2½ × 4 inches.[1]

Sammis took his panorama from Snoqualmie Hall, above the southwest corner of Commercial (now First Avenue S.) and Main Street. The view is north and extends from the still-forested eastern slopes of Denny Hill on the left to the residence and barn of an original settler, Charles Terry, on the right—near the site of today's Municipal Building.

On the horizon at center left, the Territorial University looks down from Denny's Knoll—at the northeast corner of Fourth Avenue and Seneca Street. (Denny's Knoll is not Denny Hill. The southeastern forest slope of the latter can be seen on the far left.) The little "White Church" in the center of the photograph was Seattle's first, and directly below it is the Masonic Hall near the southeast corner of Front (now First Avenue) and Cherry. A bit less than a block farther south and across James Street is the white Occidental Hotel. (A flagpole reaches another thirty feet or so up from its roof.)

The normally busy Commercial Street is void of human activity not because Sammis requested everyone to stay inside. Rather, the film in his camera required such a long exposure that busy persons on the streets would not hold still long enough to be recorded.

Therefore, loggers heading for McDonald's Saloon, in the lower right corner of the photograph, riders moving up the street to Wyckoff's Livery Stable, the only two-story structure on the east side of Commercial, and even the idlers that commonly hung out around the flagpole where Commercial ran into Yesler's mill are all invisible.

Because of cash-poor times, paying customers were usually invisible to Sammis. A year earlier, in 1864, Sammis was in Olympia advertising his photographs at "six dollars a dozen or fifty cents each."

With his return to Seattle in the spring of 1865 he surely brought with him into his new studio a hope that business would improve. However, the editor's announcement in the August 12 issue of the Gazette reveals that by mid-summer Sammis was relaxing his cash-only policy: "E.M. Sammis, photographer, wishes to say to the farmers and country people in the vicinity of Seattle that he will take all kinds of country produce in exchange for pictures. He says, "There is no excuse now. Come one come all.""

Within a year Sammis would be gone, but he left his panorama and those few other dog-eared traces of his photographic art that survive.

Sammis' studio, upstairs—at present site of Merchants Cafe.

Snoqualmie Hall at Southwest corner of First and Main.

8 Commercial Street

This historical scene resembles a set for a Hollywood Western. The empty street and the waiting "extras" scattered down the sidewalks seem suspended just before the director's command releases a desperate gang of outlaws or a stampeding herd of longhorns from behind either the camera or the distant corner.

Actually, this now century-old scene is only deceptively idle. These were the two busiest blocks in the gaslit commercial heart of Washington Territory's largest town. This was Seattle's Commercial Street (now First Avenue S.).

In these two blocks between Main and Mill (now Yesler Way) Streets, most businesses opened at six in the morning and stayed that way until nine or ten at night. Laboring here were two jewelers, four hardware merchants, a tailor, a sign painter, a fish merchant, five tobacconists, a bill collector and a ship chandler; there was also a combination gun and toy shop, a hotel, four bars, an opera house, two barber shops, two banks, two restaurants, and four clothing stores, And, as the newspaper ads then often exclaimed,

there was "much more than there is room here to tell."

The year is probably 1881. That's the dating ascribed by Thomas Prosch in his pioneer photo album of Seattle. And Prosch would likely know, for in 1881 he was just around the corner on Mill Street editing either the Intelligencer or the Post-Intelligencer. On October 1, 1881 the Daily Post consolidated with Prosch's Intelligencer, and he came along as editor and part owner.

Unlike the first, our second and somewhat earlier view of Commercial Street is not deceptively still. Rather, it has been silenced by the "Big Snow" of 1880. It began to fall on January 6 and within a week was piled in six foot drifts. On January 8 John Singerman, unwilling to wait for a total meltdown, dug a channel across Commercial and, as the Intelligencer reported, "began removing the extensive stock of the San Francisco store into its new rooms in the Opera House building."

The two across-the-street locations of the

San Francisco store (and its sign) can be compared with these two Peterson Brothers photographs. Business was good and the "new capacious and elegant quarters in the Opera House were the largest in the city." With this move the San Francisco Store became the city's first department store, keeping its boots, shoes, and clothes in one room, with dry goods, fancy goods, and general merchandise in another.[1]

Squire's Opera House (on the right) was put up in 1879 by the future governor and senator Watson C. Squire. Its biggest night came in 1880 when Rutherford B. Hayes, the first president to visit the West Coast, shook 2,000 hands in a reception there. The highlight of 1881 was the five night stand of Gounod's Faust by the Inez Fabbri Opera Company. To save voices this touring company carried a "double cast of star performers" who sang on alternate nights.

Across the street (on the left) the New England House, as an 1881 Seattle Chronical ad claimed, was "eligibly located and its accommodations for families unsurpassed." Actually, the city directory of 1882 reveals that it was mostly single men like George Elwes, music teacher; J.H. Morris, stonemason; J. Jasques, shoemaker; William Downing, spec-

WATSON S. SQUIRE.

courtesy, Seattle Public Library

Front Street (now First Avenue) south from Columbia Street, 1888.
Pre-fire site of Toklas and Singerman.

ulator, and J.D. Leake, compositor at the Chronical, who lived there and boarded on the European plan.

The Miners Supplies down the street was most likely one of the few businesses on this commercial pay streak whose 1881 profits were petering-out. The Skagit River gold rush of the previous year was by now a disappointing bust, and there was not much call for outfits, although there was for beer next door.

Throughout the 1880's Commercial Street was the stage for many parades and one riot. The "Anti-Chinese Riot" of 1886 flared at this Main Street intersection in the scene's foreground. Three years later the great fire of 1889 scattered Commercial Street with the remains of its flattened commerce. Within three years it was rebuilt wider, higher, sturdier, and into the neighborhood of brick we now have the wise urge to preserve and enjoy.[2]

courtesy, Seattle Public Library

9 The Big Snow of 1880

When Washington Territory's Governor Elisha Ferry sent off his 1879 "state of the territory" report to Secretary of the Interior Carl Schurz, it included the obligatory recital of the comfortable and fertile advantages of Puget Sound's temperate climate. Ferry wrote: "When the statement is made that ice and snow are of rare occurrence and almost unknown in Western Washington, it appears to be so incredible to those residing many degrees south of this on the Atlantic Seaboard that it makes no permanent impression on the mind."

The governor's warm report was featured front page in the Seattle Intelligencer's first Sunday edition for 1880. But the night before, the weather began to write its own report. The wind had blown so hard and cold that it pushed into homes "through cracks not before known to exist." That night the rain froze, and the next day, Monday, January 5, the snow began to fall.

Two days later, on Thursday the 8th, the paper exclaimed: "There's no telling the depth of snow a few hours ahead. We tried it and wretchedly failed. The prophesy and the actual measurement do not jibe... We'll be safe this time and suppose this morning's snow depth at ten feet."

It was only a bit less than half that. The Friday edition confessed that "we shall have to admit hereafter that snow does occasionally fall in this country.... The average citizen walks nowadays as though he were drunk."

And the snow, like the citizens, kept falling. Saturday the paper threatened "if anyone has anything to say about our Italian skies... shoot him on the spot." And more snow fell on Sunday the 11th.

In eight days of falling, the 64 inch total of the Big Snow of 1880 was and still is a local record. Normally the horizon line of our landscape separates a moody gray above from a contemplative green below. But the Big Snow of 1880 covered this typical scene with a white excitement that had parents pelting their children with snowballs, boys and girls sharing the same sleds, and seagulls walking—not floating—on the snow-fattened waters of Elliott Bay. Schools were closed, telegraph wires downed, railroads stopped, shipping stalled, and a few photographs taken—including the two shown here.

Both were photographed by the Peterson Brothers from or near their studio at the foot of Cherry Street. The one view looks out from the back of their studio across Yesler's wharf and Elliott Bay towards West Seattle, then named Milton. The other view looks east up Cherry Street towards First Hill.

In 1879 Yesler's wharf, and the many businesses including the sawmill that were on it, were consumed by fire. In 1880, rebuilt, it is covered by a snow heavy enough to collapse the roof of the small business shed in the center of the scene. The windjammers parked between it and the King Street coal wharf beyond are a few of what the Puget Sound Dispatch, another Seattle paper, reported as the "fourteen ships, barkentines, and schooners in our harbor awaiting cargoes."

The King Street coal wharf was the lucrative terminus for the Seattle and Walla Walla Railroad—the one stopped by the snow—which carried the coal from Newcastle and Renton and supplied principally San Francisco and the Central Pacific Railroad with Seattle's largest export. By 1881 this scene would be regularly filled not with sail riggings but with the steam colliers of the Oregon Improvement Company which bought the railroad, coal mines, coal wharf, and ships.[1]

On the Monday night the deluge began, the Royal Illusionists slid into town two days early for their Wednesday night performance at Yesler's Hall. The snow-encased pavilion,

View up "Cherry St. Canyon," 1910.

First Ave. north from Cherry St. during 1880 snow.

which was since the mid-1860s the Seattle center for touring performers, lecturers, and local meetings and celebrations that required a few hundred seats and a roof, is on the right of the view up Cherry Street.

On Tuesday night, "150 ladies and gentlemen" braved the snowstorm to enjoy the operetta, "No Song and No Supper" performed by the all-amateur cast of Mrs. Snyder's music class. The Intelligencer review noted that "despite the fact that none of the singers and actors had ever appeared on stage before...it was a decided success."

The next night, however, the Royal Illusionists' professional tricks were not sufficiently artful to get them and an audience through the growing drifts to their scheduled Wednesday night performance in Yesler's Hall. Instead, they took their illusions off to Victoria where the snow was only a foot deep.

On Monday January 12, it began to rain. On Wednesday afternoon the Intelligencer weather reporter would walk to work not through snow but mud. That evening he wrote for the Thursday edition: "The snow is about gone in town. It disappeared as fast as it came."

1890 etching of Seattle waterfront from the King Street coal wharves.

10 Seattle 1880

In 1880 Seattle had more saloons, churches, wholesalers, theaters, and secret societies than were needed by 3,533 citizen consumers. While Walla Walla was a one industry town up to its suspenders in produce, and Tacoma was a company town anxiously waiting for the Northern Pacific Railroad to complete its long-promised transcontinental connection, Seattle was a buzzing center of urban opportunists busy making "mosquito fleet" connections around the Sound.

This 1880 scene has two centerpieces. One is the modestly monumental Territorial University on the horizon, right of center. In 1880 it had 11 instructors teaching 150 students a curriculum that included chemistry, French, botany, elocution, Greek, telegraphy, plain and ornamental penmanship, drawing, and commerce. The other dominating landmark is the spreading mercantile confusion of Yesler's wharf which fills most of the photograph's lower half. In 1880 it was still being rebuilt after a July 26, 1879 fire that destroyed not only Yesler's sawmill but also one schooner, a great deal of lumber, and ten other businesses.

Behind the wharf and running through the entire photograph is the long and gently rising Front Street (now First Avenue, north of Yesler). In 1876 it was subjected to the engineering and political sweat of Seattle's first large regrade. Much of the cribbing supporting the smoothed-out street can be seen in the photograph, which extends from Columbia Street on the right to mid-block between Union and Pike Streets on the left.

1880 was also the year President Rutherford B. Hayes came to town, Henry Villard bought the Seattle and Walla Walla Railroad and sensibly changed its name to the Columbia and Puget Sound, the Sisters of Holy Names built their first school here, and one of Duwamish Valley's first settlers Samuel Maple died at 53.

The 1880 photo is deceptively quiet, for the local hustlers were moving. That year 38 licenses were issued for selling liquor and 17 were issued for pool and pigeon hole tables. In 1880 this town already had that invigorating mix of virtues and vices that is part of city building.

The 1879 Seattle City Directory described the town as "built on a terraced plateau, giving to every house and street a panorama of the lower and upper Sound...The houses number 1356 and are extremely picturesque, displaying great taste in their gardens and having a general air of thriftiness and comfort."

Sometime in 1880 a now unknown photographer recorded a five section panorama of this city-on-a-slope from the end of the King Street coal wharf. The entire spectacle extends from Smith Cove on the north to Beacon Hill on the South.

The one-fifth part printed here reaches, left to right, from the top of Denny Hill at Third Avenue and Stewart Street (now some 100 feet lower) to the Talbot Coal dock at the foot of Washington Street. (The photograph's right border meets the horizon line at about Sixth Avenue and Madison Street.)

In 1880 the town, although quilted with rural patches, was busy planting the seeds for a city. That year the local census enumerator and Central School principal E.S. Ingraham counted 3,533 inhabitants. Walla Walla counted 55 more, but this was the last year that Seattle would be the second largest town in the territory.

Actually, in 1880 Seattle was less intent on passing Walla Walla than in getting to it on the Seattle and Walla Walla Railroad. By that time track had been laid only as far as the Newcastle coal mines east of Renton. Seattle boomers expected more from the railroad than coal. The city directory whooped: "This road's completion (to Walla Walla) is absolutely necessary. It will not be long before it will bear to the ships in our harbor the golden grain from the prairie land of Eastern Washington." But it never did, nor did it ever have to. *(See features 38-40.)*

Another 1880 statistic tells why. Enumerator Ingraham counted no less than 29 manufacturing establishments, including a brass foundry, sash and door factory, boilermaker, soap factory, tannery, boot and shoe factory, flour and grist mill, cigar factory and soda water factory. This was the germ of that diverse, self-reliant, and exporting economy that would soon enough forget Walla Walla and concentrate, to quote the directory again, "on becoming what Nature had made her: the Queen City of the Northwest."

courtesy, Historical Photography Collection, University of Washington

11 The King Street Coal Wharf

The biggest thing in Seattle in 1881 was the King Street coal wharf. The Lilliputian pair in the foreground gives the pier its scale. It was both a favorite perch from which to photograph the city and a popular subject itself for photographers throughout the 1880s and 1890s.[1]

In this view the camera looks east towards Beacon Hill, or what is really the ridge that once ran continuously from Beacon Hill to First Hill. The two were not separated until 1909 when work began on the Dearborn cut just a little left of the hump that appears at the photographer's center horizon. To the right of the railroad's right-of-way is the beginning of Seattle's first industrial neighborhood. Most of these manufacturer's sheds are on pilings driven into the sand. The systematic filling of these tidelands would not begin until 1896.[2]

The sheds just behind the water tower are parts of a planing mill for the manufacture of sash and blinds. Behind that is a box and furniture factory, and, further on, the long sheds that cross the center of the scene are the repair shops for the Columbia and Puget Sound Railroad.

The C.&P.S. was originally the Seattle and Walla Walla Railroad, the narrow-gauged line this city completed in 1878 to the coal deposits east of Lake Washington. The first coal-filled gondolas pulled out of Newcastle on February 5 of that year, and for another half-century delivered it here.

Another pioneer landmark, the Felker House, is on the scene's left. This glossy white clapboard with the dark shutters and second floor veranda was built in 1853 when it shined like a temple amidst the rough log cabins of the year-old settlement. It was Seattle's first hotel and often called Mother Damnable's after its quick-tempered manager, the profane Mary Conklin, who was as salty as her patrons.

There were 54 marriages in King County in 1881. Seattle got its first foreign language churches (the German Reformed and the Scandinavian Baptist), a city-wide water company, and a telephone franchise, even though there were no telephones. Other 1881 highlights included the first local demonstration of electric lamps aboard the Willamette, which was one of the 42 steamers licensed that year for business on Puget Sound.

It was also in 1881 that the two newpapers the Post and the Intelligencer came together as something you can still hold in your hands 103 years later.

The still forested Beacon Hill one year earlier in 1880 from the King St. coal Wharf.

The King Street coal wharves with West Seattle in the distance.

The waterfront from Denny Hill, circa 1885.

12 Skid Road

A few Seattle streets are landmarks. Yesler Way is one. Through the years the condition of its surface and the character of the structures lining it have changed radically. Yet, Mill Street, its first platted name, has always been the centerstrip of first a settlement and later a city.

Local legend has it that while Henry Yesler was searching Puget Sound for the right spot to build its first steam sawmill, he knew instantly he had found it when he took that first step from his rented dugout canoe onto the shores of Seattle. To his north were the cliffs and to the south the tidelands, but this spot in between was perfect. It was level enough ashore to build a mill and deep enough off shore to dock and load lumber schooners bound for San Francisco, which was always burning down.

Everywhere Henry Yesler looked there was virgin timber, including the horizon which conveniently dipped directly to the east of

this preferred landing spot. This meant Henry could build a skid road up that hill, on a grade sufficiently gradual for cattle teams to skid logs over and down to his mill from the forests above.

So Henry Yesler decided to stay. Doc Maynard and Arthur Denny were pleased as pulp products to have Henry and his machinery in town. They drew him a spatula-shaped claim whose handle included his preferred spot and that forested hill in a narrow strip along the future Yesler Way to near the present-day 20th Avenue where it widened to a spread of virgin timber large enough to feed his saws for a few years.

The long shed and stack of Yesler's mill can be seen at the western end of his street in the oldest of these three photographs; all look to the west down Yesler Way from between Second and Occidental Avenues. This is one-half of a stereoscopic view made in 1874 by an itinerant photographer from Olympia named Huntington.

Another landmark is the Occidental Hotel on the right. In this picture it is still the "leading house in town" although it is now a

decade since it was first opened on May 28, 1864. And that was 12 days too late to host the May 16th arrival of that first coterie of single women traditionally named the "Mercer Girls."

Occidental Place, the area in front of the hotel and today's Pioneer Square, was the scene of many a circus and celebration. It was described by Sophie Frye Bass, an Arthur Denny granddaughter, as a "place for wrestling matches and political rallies or the swapping of yarns, and there too a group of young blades styled themselves 'the pluguglies', and at Fourth of July celebrations dressed as jesters, they would ride in a lumber wagon, drawn by four horses, wear masks or blacken their faces, and carry on crazily."

Although Seattle here looks like a somewhat cluttered set for the 'pluguglies', or a Hollywood western after the shooting is over, 1874 was long remembered as the start of a much bigger production: the birth of the "Seattle Spirit." Another Denny granddaughter, Roberta Frye Watt, wrote about this transition in her book *Four Wagons West*: "That day—May 1, 1874—when the citizens

courtesy, Seattle Public Library

took pick and shovel and as a community went out to build a railroad by hand, that day, they turned their backs upon pioneer days forever...On that day they wrote the name of Seattle in the annals of history and in the list of great world cities."

A less heroic description of what those citizens started that 1874 May day was a fight against Tacoma and the Northern Pacific Railroad with a narrow gauge line that reached Renton three years later. Renton is where the coal was.

The second historical view of Yesler Way is from about 1912. In the intervening years the street had been first planked in 1879, and then bricked-over in 1901. The part we see here was also consumed by the great fire of 1889, and then raised nine feet on the rubble and widened by 18 more.

The years also turned the old Mill Street into a dividing line between a proper business district to the north and a neighborhood to the south variously called Maynardtown, the Lava Beds, the Tenderloin, and Down on the Sawdust. However, this lowland's most popular name, which would be adopted worldwide, was simply Skid Road: a seamy place for men who were often transient, single, and on the skids, or married and on a shady retreat from respectable family life.

Most of the cityscape in the 1912 view is also in the contemporary scene. Regrettable exceptions are the western end of the Yesler cable tracks which run out of the picture's bottom border, the interurban tracks just

beyond which turn from the center of Yesler onto Occidental Avenue, and the Seattle Hotel on the right. The Yesler cable line was pulled up in 1940; the electric Tacoma interurban, whose station was in the still standing Interurban Building on the far left, was closed down in 1928; and the Seattle Hotel was razed in 1962.

Of all the Pioneer Square casualties, the hotel's destruction was most responsible for stirring citizens to organize and save this neighborhood. The grotesque architectural reminder to maintain this preservationist struggle is seen, in the place of the hotel, on the right of our contemporary view. It's called the "Sinking Ship Garage."

13 John Collins' Occidental Hotel

A century separates this "now" and "then." Both photographs were precariously shot leaning out of the second-story windows of Henry-Yesler-built buildings at the southwest corner of what was once called "Yesler's Corner."

The angle of the contemporary scene is purposely wider so that the changes between the pre and post-fire intersection can be more readily seen. In the lower righthand corner of the historical scene, Commercial Street (now First Avenue S.) jogs east at Mill Street (now Yesler Way) before it continues on north as Front Street (now First Avenue). On the left, the lavish Yesler-Leary Building passes over the contemporary First Avenue and extends into what is now the sycamore, pergola, and totem pole-adorned Pioneer Square "triangle." The wider-angled "now" shows the irregular Yesler Corner straightened and a jogless First Avenue S. continuing north across Yesler Way, past the recently renovated Mutual Life Building. (The photo was taken during the renovation.)

A century ago plasterers and masons were putting the finishing touches on the Occidental Hotel in the heart of Pioneer Square. The structure with its beautifully detailed facade was claimed by its builder, John Collins, to be

the "leading Hotel in the Northwest." And for a few short years it probably was.[1]

On February 27, 1884 one of its first occupants, the Puget Sound National Bank, moved into its ground-floor room lavishly lined in ash and black walnut. The then-eight-page Daily Intelligencer announced, "no banking concern in the Northwest can boast of finer quarters."

Even before Collins came to town, the site held a hotel. In 1864 the original Occidental, a clapboard house with 30 rooms, was constructed. One year later Collins arrived in Seattle, unstrapped the $3,000 in gold dust tied to his waist and bought one-third interest in the ivory-white Occidental. As he said several years later with confident hindsight, "I was sure Seattle was the coming city on the

Sound, and its history verified my belief." *(See features 7, 12.)*

Collins' own history had something to do with that. In the 20 years between the construction of the old and new Occidental, Collins not only took on its sole proprietorship, but also helped write the town's first charter; served on its first city council; signed in the incorporation of its first railroad, the Seattle and Walla Walla; developed the Renton coal fields; started the Seattle Gas Light Co., another first; and served a term as mayor.

During 1883-84 while building his new Occidental, Collins also found time to sit in the territorial legislature.

The new Occidental was so successful that by 1887 Collins increased its capacity to 400 guests by joining a new addition to its thoroughly renovated and refurnished "old" part. He also added an elevator. Then, suddenly, everything crashed.

Around four o'clock in the afternoon of June 6, 1889, John Collins made a rushed attempt to buy the wooden houses across James Street. He wanted desperately to blow them up. The owners refused, and within a few hours both the firetrap houses and the brick and stucco decorated hotel were consumed by the great fire.[2]

While the bricks were still smouldering, John Collins stood in the midst of his warm ruins and proclaimed in words that were often repeated in the coming weeks, "within a year we will have a city here that will surpass by far the town we had before the fire." Collins was hot with the Seattle Spirit.[3]

John Collins cooperated with his vision by building on the site a third Occidental Hotel which he later renamed the Seattle Hotel. As many will remember, in the early 1960s it was torn down and replaced with a parking garage that is popularly imagined as resembling a sinking ship.

First Avenue north from Cherry Street in the 1870s.

14 Yesler's Corner

In 1883 the Seattle Post Office sold $133,000 worth of stamps and envelopes. Many envelopes were stuffed with letters from new residents to relatives back home. They came mostly from single men who wrote of the just-completed transcontinental Northern Pacific Railroad and the statistics of Seattle's outstanding growth that year.

That year some of the young city's citizens were cutting a canal for logs and small boats between Lakes Union and Washington. Others were building a toll road through Snoqualmie Pass, grading 43,000 feet of city streets, and setting up uniform house numbers and a grid of telephone poles and wires. That year Seattle got its first kindergarten, day-care nursery for working mothers, its first news stand, its first foreign language newspaper, Die Puget Sound Post, and its first local union of Christian Temperance Women.

Besides writing lots of letters, the city's 7,000 inhabitants—then twice that of Tacoma—transacted 2,570 real estate transfers and built 600 homes. Henry Yesler and John Leary built one elegant three-story landmark with a monumental corner tower that immediately became the showpiece of Seattle's booming 1883.

That symbol of the new Seattle civic vision, the Yesler-Leary Building, is seen on the left. Across the street is the old Seattle, that of the clapboards and frontier town facades. The view looks north up Front Street (now First Avenue) across Mill Street (now Yesler Way).

In 1883 this intersection was not called Pioneer Square but rather "Yesler's Corner." Since its first irregular platting in 1853, it was a clumsy corner where commerce was required to jog a half-block west before continuing south on Commercial Street (now First Avenue S.).

For 30 years there had been a civic urge to cut through this interference but the city could never afford Henry Yesler's asking price. But now in 1883 this awkward interruption of trade was adorned with the city's most earnest symbol of its metropolitan ambitions—the Yesler-Leary Building.

Only six years later the city council would decide to get rid of Yesler's Corner and establish Pioneer Place. This did not require plundering the Yesler-Leary Building, for the Great Fire of 1889 had done that and much more. Indeed, everything in this mid-1880s scene would be either gutted or flattened by the fire. Now it was not difficult for the civic spirit to imagine more radical transformations, like the widening and raising of streets and the cutting through of odd corners.

However, one of Seattle's by then 40,000 residents did not share this popular vision. That was Henry Yesler. Suing the city for the loss of his little corner, he was eventually awarded $156,000 or $12 a square foot. He also received the rancor of every other property owner in the burned-out area. They got only 66 cents a square foot for the widening of streets over their old holdings.

The second historical view, photographed in the spring of 1890, shows the beginning of these alterations. The remnants of the corner foundations of the old Yesler-Leary Building are evident in the hole on the left. (A contemporary well-placed core sample drilled beneath the pergola would probably come up with some of that old brick.)

Here the street grade is being raised with the replatting. (Note the boardwalk on the far left.) The bulk of the Starr-Boyd Building on the left and just beyond it the Merchants Bank Building are now gone—the former in the 1950s to the 1949 earthquake, and the latter in the 1960s for the eight-story parking lot seen in the contemporary photograph.

On the far right, to either side of the telephone pole, sit the two cornerstones to the corner entrance of the Pioneer Building. Beyond that, the still-standing Howard Building is already up, and further on at First Avenue's northeast corner with Cherry Street, the still-standing Scheuerman Building is also evident.

courtesy, Historical Photography Collection, University of Washington

The contemporary view was photographed from the top floor of the building housing the Merchant's Cafe. In its basement is a bar built, in part, under the sidewalk along Yesler. This sidewalk is still skylighted with the tablets of concrete and cut glass which were set there in 1890. Those sidewalk skylight panels can be seen at the bottom right of the 1890 view, some little distance beneath the Pioneer Building's cornerstones.[1]

courtesy, Historical Photography Collection, University of Washington

15 The Great Fire of 1889

The Wednesday, June 5 edition of the Seattle Times ran beneath its masthead an enthusiastic advertisement for a sale on summer parasols. It had been an unseasonably hot spring and the sun that beat on the city also fanned forest fires in the Cascades. Burning unchecked, they glowed by night and sprinkled ash on Seattle by day.

The Times also reported front page that across the continent wetter weather continued on the ruins of Johnstown, Pa., where cold and heavy rains helped spread diphtheria. Six days earlier, May 31, a dam that spanned the Conemaugh River burst and in the time it took a wall of water to rush 12 miles downstream, the flood devastated Johnstown, killing 2,200.

The Wednesday Times also printed an ad for Frye's Opera House. Its "coming Friday night only appearance of the Cecilian Opera" also featured "new scenery and

magnificent stage effects."

A story inside continued the compliments: "Theatre goers during the past few weeks have observed a wonderful change in the stage settings at Frye's Opera House. Since the first of the year Frye has put in ten new sets, including one fancy gothic city, one chamber, a very elegant garden setting, a woods scene." Indeed, Frye's theater (at the present site of the Federal Building) was a local landmark of distinction with its mansard roof, 1,400 seats, and stage with seven trapdoors. The feature article concluded with assurances that "there are five large exits which provide against any danger of a panic in case of fire or an accident."

Soon enough the fire came. There would be no Thursday Times, no summer parasols, no "elegant garden setting," no "fancy gothic city" and no Seattle business district.

The fire photograph looks south down

Front Street (now First Avenue) from Spring toward Madison and the intersection where the "Great Fire of June 6, 1889," first ignited in a basement wood shop across the street from the Opera House. The crowd stands well back from the heat: there is no defending the theater, which although brick is still ablaze and soon will be consumed.[1]

This excitement was captured by William Boyd, a professional photographer who had migrated from Iowa to Seattle a year earlier, and whose studio, near what is now Pioneer Square, was on the far side of the fire he photographed. The scene was shot around 3 o'clock in the afternoon shortly after the fire began. It is one of the few images of the fire itself. Most local photographers were probably too busy saving their equipment to use it.

Although many thousands of prints and negatives of the pre-fire city were lost to the flames, it is not known whether Boyd made it back around the fire and to his studio in time to rescue his. Within two hours it was cinders and by 7 o'clock the fire had eaten its way to Main Street. It continued on through the

evening past King Street to a wet death in the tideflats where the Kingdome now stands.

The fire moved north as well. By sunset the spot from which the photograph was taken, near Spring, and all of the picture's subjects, including one of Boyd's competitors, the Minneapolis Art Studio, were also consumed. And in that direction another casualty is noted in Murray Morgan's classic of local history, *Skid Road*:

"It climbed east up the hill toward Second Avenue from the Opera House. So great was the heat that the fire pushed backward against the wind across Madison Street and into the Kenyon block which housed, in addition to stores, the press of The Seattle Times."

And The Times was stunned until Monday, the 10th, when its first postfire edition announced that "the Times is still on earth. It is slightly disfigured but still in the ring...The Times office went up in flames, nothing being saved except the reporters, the files and a few other implements of the trade."

This dauntless report was preceded by a rhyming headline which read: "SEATTLE DISFIGURED, but still in the ring, this is the song Seattle will sing, New buildings, New hopes, New streets, New town, there's nothing that can throw Seattle down. She goes thru adversity, fire and flame but the Queen City gets there just the same.

This Queen City also got a lot of press attention nationally. But it wasn't the leveling of 30 central-city blocks that was news as much as the human interest it discovered in the frontier town's steadfast generosity. Before the fire, citizens had pledged $576 in relief to the Johnstown disaster. After their catastrophe, they decided still to keep the faith and send that pledge along to the flood victims.

The Monday Times reported: "Everywhere confidence in the future of this city is maintained...The heaviest losers are the most cheerful."

This booming optimism was encouraged in the eventual finding that no human lives were lost. However, thousands of rats and at least one horse died that day. As the Monday Times reported: "The men who left a dead horse in a vacant lot off Madison near Broadway on the day of the Fire: If they do not remove the carcass, they will be reported to the police as the stench arising from the animal is sickening."[2]

The post-fire view of First Avenue from Columbia Street.

Frye's Opera House

courtesy, Lawton Gowey

16 Brick Buildings and Box Houses

It was close to sunset when the fire first crossed Mill Street. It was four hours since an incendiary mix of boiling glue and wood shavings ignited on a carpenter's floor at Madison and Front Streets. There was no wind but there was also no water, so while the fire moved slowly, it moved steadily—about a block an hour.

When, at last, it reached Skid Road and vaulted the 66 feet of Mill Street into the clapboard tinder of the Tenderloin District to the south, most of the fire fighters stayed north. The futile heroics of throwing dynamite and wet blankets in the fire's path were surrendered to the sensation of one hundred acres of a burning city mixing its pyrotechnics with the setting smoke-filtered sun sliding into the Olympics. Thomas Prosch, editor of the Post Intelligencer in the late 1880s, described the effect. "For a couple of hours after the fire crossed Yesler, the spectacle was a magnificent one, the flames rising high in the air, and covering almost the entire burned area, while the noise of falling walls, the crackling, the occasional explosions, the shouts, added to the glare and heat in making the scene a memorable one."[1]

The Great Fire of June 6, 1889 was left to burn itself out in the tideflats south of King Street. That night the local version of the myth of the phoenix was born; the city would re-create itself from its own ashes.

Prosch continues: "Hundreds of tents went up as by magic, and newspapers, den-tists, professional men, merchants moved into them at once.... The business quarter was alternately dusty and muddy. The conditions, in fact, seemed to be fascinating, and the experiences of those days will always be remembered by those who passed through the fire scenes and rebuilding events, as among the most interesting in their lives. It is, perhaps, enough to say that within two years Seattle's business quarter was finer and more convenient than that of any other place of like population in the world."

One of the 130 new brick buildings built during the year 1889 was John Cort's New Standard Theatre at the southeast corner of Occidental Avenue and Washington Street. It is the fancy structure right of center in the 1889 post-fire panorama taken by the photographic firm Boyd and Brass. Renamed the Lyric, it is also the centerpiece of Ashael Curtis' photograph which dates from 1912.

While Seattle was rebuilding and Washington Territory was politicking for statehood, John Cort was temporarily producing his variety shows in a big tent on First Avenue near Madison Street. There he waited the five months it took to build his New Standard, the first post-fire brick theatre in town. When it opened on November 18 it was only one week late for President Harrison's November 11 proclamation granting Washington statehood. This delay was unfortunate, for thereby Cort was not required to lift his normally bawdy entertainment to the heights of patriotic sentiment.

Cort was forced out when the difficult times that followed the crash of 1893 were made harder in 1894 by a local ordinance revoking the license of any establishment that both employed women and sold liquor. He returned in 1900 to build the Grand Opera House, then the "finest theatre in the city" and today the Cherry Street Parking Garage. Here, north of Skid Road, the consumption of Cort's theatrics did not require a whiskey chaser delivered with feminine encouragement.[2]

However, his old boxhouse theatre south of Seattle's "sin-line," Yesler Way, did. Since 1896 the Standard had been named and renamed the Orpheum, Wabash, Mascot, Clancy, and then in 1907, the Lyric. It was the Lyric that real estate sensation Henry Broderick remembered as "the home of below-the-belt burlesque, a rendezvous for robust rowdies of both sexes. The stage was more or less a blind for the real curriculum of boy meets girl. Overlooking the stage at the rear of the balcony were a series of loggias, each equipped with chaise lounge and opaque curtains where waitresses offered shenanigans at market prices. In short, this showplace, in the very center of a then vibrant skid-road, was a brazen bagnio...It was the only place in town where one could be in a theatre and a bordello at the same time."[3] (See feature 30.)

151-53 Washington St.

courtesy, Lawton Gowey

17 The Fire Boat Snoqualmie

While the ashes were still cooling over the 130 burned-out acres of the city's central business district, Mayor Robert Moran assembled the stunned citizens at the Armory on Union Street at Fourth Avenue. It was one of only two surviving auditoriums that wasn't a church, and it wasn't big enough to contain the sleepless crowd that had spent the previous night watching their city burn.

The usually dour looking 34-year-old machinist-mayor, with the prematurely drooping mouth and moustache to match, was a paragon of the Western American self-made male: ingenious, efficient, and a bit imperious. He was the type to systematically rebuild a city. *(See feature 24.)* Moran's first directive was to deputize 200 volunteers to both keep the peace and keep strangers out of the piles of rescued valuables that now cluttered the streets, sidewalks, and front lawns at the rim of the devastated area. Practically everyone had lost something, including His Honor whose machine shop on Yesler's wharf was now a scarred mess in the bay.[1]

The fire of June 6, 1889 had disgraced both the city's fire department and its privately owned water system. There was neither pressure enough in the pipes to conjure a flood against the flames nor hose strong or long enough to reach the fire with saltwater pumped from the bay. In the midst of this fiasco the mayor took control and tried fighting the fire with fire, or rather dynamite. Moran attempted to clear a path in the fire's way by flattening its fuel. It didn't work, but the try was typical for the slight-figured but large-mannered engineer.

He proclaimed to the inflamed citizens assembled at the armory that rebuiding a city should also include a fire department that could keep it rebuilt. Within a year the city had five new firehouses, an electric alarm system with 31 boxes, and the first fire boat on the west coast, the Snoqualmie.

The Snoqualmie was designed by New York naval architect William Cowles to be a coal burning, tug-shaped ship of 91 feet with a 23 foot beam that would do 11 knots and shoot 6,000 gallons of saltwater per minute. When the bids were accepted the low one entered was from Mayor Moran.

Construction began in April of 1890, and the Snoqualmie's first trial run was a celebrat-ed affair witnessed by the city council, curious citizens, and, most auspiciously, Mr. T. J. Conway, assistant manager of the Pacific Insurance Association. When the trial was over, the pleased Conway announced to the press, "She did very well. Splendidly, in fact, and I shall feel justified in recommending a liberal reduction in insurance rates here."

This was the kind of fire protection that the businessmen on the waterfront wanted. More than 60 wharves and warehouses with a frontage of more than two miles had been put up since the fire flattened everything south of Union Street. With the presence of the Snoqualmie, insurance rates did drop by 20 percent.

The Snoqualmie's slip was next to Fire Station Number Five at the foot of Madison Street. From here for 37 years the fire boat wandered up and down the waterfront looking for small fires to put out or big ones, like the Grand Trunk Fire of July 30, 1914, to contain. The fire boat was also used to rescue ships in the sound and even salvage them, using its strong pumps to raise sunken vessels.[2]

The Snoqualmie fought its last fire on Elliott Bay in 1927, the year it gave up its slip

to the new fire boat in town, the Alki. For the next 47 years the Snoqualmie helped lower insurance rates on Lake Union, aided in the construction of the Mercer Island Floating Bridge, and served as a small freighter between here and Alaska.

The last fire the Snoqualmie attended was her own—in 1974. It burned for 36 hours off shore of a fuel dock at Kodiak Alaska.

Fire Station Number Five
at the foot of Madison Street.

18 Harrison's Royal Entrance

At 1:15 in the afternoon of May 6, 1891, the steamer City of Seattle enroute from Tacoma and accompanied by the Greyhound, Bailey Gatzert, T.J. Potter, and City of Kingston were met off Alki Point by 30 more steamers, all of them blowing their whistles, strung with patriotic bunting, and packed with passengers in their best attire. This was the proper way for the 23rd president of the United States to enter Seattle: on board its namesake steamer and surrounded by its "mosquito fleet."

That "grand day's" final edition of the Press-Times reported, "As the steamers get nearer shore the din becomes deafening. It is 1:28 o'clock. The City of Seattle is only 300 yards away from Yesler's dock. The band is playing and the people on the docks are waving their handkerchiefs to those on deck. It is 1:30 o'clock. A great cheer goes forth from the people, for the president can be seen on the upper deck, bowing and smiling."

Since April 18 Benjamin Harrison had made 200 entrances. The routine was for the presidential party to arrive in town on its special train and pause long enough for an exchange of protocol pleasantries with favored citizens and a brief speech to the euphoric

crowd gathered at the station. These inspirational messages always emphasized the peculiar merits of whatever fine place he was rushing through. Occasionally, in the bigger towns, the presidential party would disembark from its five posh coaches for a whirlwind tour of the town.

So it was with Tacoma. Harrison arrived there at eight in the morning, made a speech, took a tour, and by late morning was on his way again, this time to Seattle. However, Harrison's entrance into Seattle was not typical. With his debut, not on rails but across water, the whooping and hollering was spread out across an entire waterfront. This nautical procession with a flotilla of 40 tooting steamers resembled an imperial entourage accompanying the emperor's annual visit to one of his provincial capitals.

The Press-Times account continues: "At 1:36 today President Harrison and party walked down the gang of the City of Seattle and stood in the Queen City of the Sound.... An immense concourse of people were gathered on all the docks and steamers around...A mighty cheer went up and the whistles and bells of the steamers and factories added to the clamor."

This scene was captured by the photographic partnership Boyd & Brass within a minute or two of that 1:36 p.m. presidential disembarking.[1] The steamer City of Seattle, its sternside showing, lays beside Yesler's wharf just to the left of the puff of white steam in the center of the scene. The sternwheel of the Bailey Gatzert is evident just this side of the presidential steamer. Another City of Seattle, the ferry that serviced West Seattle, is in its slip near the foot of Marion Street and is seen this side of the Gatzert. In the distance the Oregon Improvement Company's King Street coal wharves are topped with a line of coal gondolas.

Most everything was lavishly decorated in red, white, blue and green—fir trees were the decor of the day. The Press-Times reported that "Yesler's wharf looked like a miniature Puget Sound forest being studded with young evergreens."

Before boarding the Yesler Way cable cars, the presidential party paused beneath a welcome arch constructed in Pioneer Place and covered with patriotic streamers and fir boughs. Here a chorus of high school girls delivered a specially composed welcome song which included these lines: "Hark! the air is

thrilling with the song we sing. Hear the music echo loud our voices ring. Would you know the meaning of our triumph song? Tis the song of welcome of the joyous throng!''

Standing in the rain, this joyous throng watched Harrison's party disappear over Yesler's hill on its way to Leschi. *(See feature 77.)* There the steamer Kirkland was boarded to toots of ''Yankee Doodle,'' and a fast ride through the rain was made to Madison Park. Here the entourage boarded cable cars for the return trip whose highlight, the Press-Times reported, were the 2,400 children assembled at Central School, ''waiting with expectant hearts and bright eyes, all looking to catch a glimpse of the president.''[2]

While the president's party was touring, the largest assembly in the history of this young city was crowding the grandstand erected on the old University grounds. The Press-Times was ready with five long-hand reporters and three stenographers. The paper's detailed report continued: ''At 3:55 o'clock the crowd began to yell for no apparent cause and kept it up for a full two minutes.... The crowd surged forward, pressing the soldiers against the stand and several women fainted in the jam...President Harrison and party ascended the stand at exactly 4 p.m. When the stout figure was seen on the stand, a roar went up that split the

heavens.''

These ''split heavens'' responded with a rain so hard that most of the speeches, especially Harrison's, were cut short, and before the faint could be thoroughly revived, the party was over and the president off to his special train. There he appeared with a crumpled hat, a cigar in his mouth, a smile on his lips, and a farewell to Seattle: ''The peo-ple of Seattle have treated me very kindly.... My reception has been a royal one.''

And it was; for many who attended the presidential procession across Elliott Bay it seemed more like a royal ritual than a democratic celebration. When Harrison at last left town at six that evening, he had a copy of that day's Press-Times in his hands and was reading the full report.

19 The Rainier Hotel

The Great Fire of 1889 encouraged the city to rebuild bigger and in brick. But its first response was a huge hotel which was constructed quick and cheap, and entirely of wood. The Rainier was ready for occupancy only 80 days after the first lumber was unloaded at the building site. This effort was the kind of manic community labor we associate with instant barn raisings. The result was the somewhat barn-like fortress we see filling the center horizon of our historical scene and the entire block between Columbia and Marion Streets, and Fifth and Sixth Avenues.

While flattening the city's business district, the June 6 fire also consumed most of its halls and hotels. The thousands of "floating strangers" who began flooding these "ashes of opportunity" to help rebuild the city and themselves often had to sleep in tents or under trees. Since the grand brick hotels of the 1890s, including the Denny, Seattle, and Butler,[1] took awhile to build, the Rainier was put up in a flash by a collection of the "moneymen of Seattle" led by Judge "He

Built Seattle" Thomas Burke.[2] The Seattle Press-Times reported that "its construction was made possible by public spirited capitalists stepping forward regardless of whether it would be a paying institution or not." It wasn't.

In its five years as a showy hotel with a breezy view of the bay from a wrap-around veranda, the Rainier lost $100,000. The Great Crash of 1893 had its sad effect. On August 16, 1894 the Press-Times reported "in all probability the handsome sightly Rainier Hotel will be closed in the near future.... What will be done with the Rainier Building is not known." The gold rush of 1897 came too late to save the Rainier. Then the miners, coming and going, dropped their tired bodies into the beds of hotels down by the waterfront. These included the Rainier Grand Hotel at First and Madison, whose furnishings—beds included—were moved in from the abandoned and bankrupt Rainier up on the hill.[3]

The historical scene was photographed not in the hard times of 1893-94 but in

1891-92—good times still for both the Rainier and the Seattle-Press Times. The newspaper was published in its offices at 214 Columbia Street, just kitty-corner from our photographer's perch at the southwest corner of Second Avenue and Columbia Street. (The top of the newspaper's sign can be seen at the lower left-hand corner of the photograph.)

Arthur Churchill Warner took this photograph[4] which includes other landmarks as well. The James Colman mansion survived at the southeast corner of Fourth and Columbia for the 55 years between 1883 and 1939. Its boxish cupola just barely breaks the horizon line on the far right. *(See feature 94.)*

Another tower is seen just above and to the left of the Colmans. Standing six stories at the corner of Ninth and Columbia, Coppin's Water Works supported a holding tank for water drawn by an adjoining windmill from springs beneath Charles Coppin's combined home and business. Throughout the 1880s his water works supplied users down the hill, the Colman's included. The water was delivered through bored logs, some of which were uncovered during the early 1960s excavation of Interstate-5.

This 20th-century freeway also cut through the site which for 59 years supported

courtesy, Lawton Gowey

the brick towers of Central School. Kitty-corner across Sixth and Marion from the Rainier, the school was also completed in 1889. However, it was made of brick, more than two million of them. Central School was Seattle's only high school until 1902 when Broadway High was built "way out on Capitol Hill." The Central's weakened towers were prudently razed after the 1949 earthquake. The rest of the building was leveled in 1953. Many of its alumni still display their souvenir bricks atop their fireplace mantels.[5]

The Warner photograph is dappled with many other lesser landmarks. The Eureka Bakery, just left of center, was for years run by the pioneer Meydenbauer family. They are remembered by their namesake bay on Lake Washington and their creek which runs under Bellevue. *(See feature 80.)* Today, the Meydenbauer property on Columbia Street is filled by the old Central Building. Kitty-corner across Third Avenue, the Seattle Chamber of Commerce occupies the spot which in 1892 housed Bonney and Watson, the city's oldest mortuary.

The Rainier Hotel was converted into apartments and survived until 1910. In 1896 the Seattle Press-Times became the Seattle Times and has survived.

20 Wildlife Along Bridal Row

In 1888 young Dr. Frantz Coe came west from Michigan looking for a practice and found one in Seattle when ex-mayor Gideon Weed, who was also one of the oldest and most respected physicians in town, invited Coe to share his offices. So the 32-year-old doctor sent for his wife, Carrie, and soon they were settled into 606 Pike Street—one of the six newly built and joined abodes that together were called "Bridal Row."

The Coes, however, were not on an extended honeymoon, for Carrie had brought with her their three children, Frantzel, Harry and their first-born Herbert. Within a year the Great Fire of 1889 would destroy the Weed and Coe medical offices but not the domestic peace along Bridal Row, which was described by Sophie Fry Bass in her book *Pigtail Days in Old Seattle* as "an attractive place with flowers in the garden and birds singing in the windows."

Sophie also lived on Pike Street with her pioneer parents, George and Louisa Frye, just across Sixth Avenue from the Coes. The Fryes had moved there many years before when Pike was a path and their back door opened to the forest. In 1890 the corner of Sixth and Pike was no longer at the edge of town, but it was still largely residential. While the central city was loud with the noises escaping from its booming efforts to rebuild itself after the fire, the residents along Pike were still listening to birds sing, sniffing flowers, and some of them like the Fryes were even milking the cows and gathering eggs.

However, around 9:30 on the Saturday morning of September 20, this settled peace was interrupted by what the next day's Post Intelligencer called the "Panic on Pike Street." Both Sophie Fry and young Herbert Coe were witnesses to a wild event that had "passers-by scattering in terror and women relieving themselves with piercing screams."

Sophie Fry Bass recalled how "I heard the chickens cackle loudly and...I shuddered when I saw the cougar cross Sixth Avenue; I could hardly believe my eyes." The cat had killed a chicken in the Kentucky stables a short distance from the Frye home. There it was also shot in its behind and, quoting the newspaper's account, "enraged and uttering a terrific yell, it bounded the sidewalk and rushed down Sixth Avenue."

It turned up Pike Street and as "the panic spread to the thronged thoroughfare and all pedestrians made a rush for safety, with two great bounds the cougar landed in the yard of Dr. F.H. Coe's residence." Nine-year-old

courtesy, Seattle Public Library

The view east up Pike Street, across Fifth Ave. "Bridal row," just left of center at Sixth, has been raised one story for retail storefronts at the street level.

courtesy, Mrs. Herbert Coe

Herbert, who was playing on the porch, heard the warning shots and fled inside behind the fragile safety of the front room window. The big cat went to the window and looked back at him with his claws upon the pane. For one long transfixed moment they stared at one another until a man with a 44-caliber revolver emptied it into the cougar. Eight feet and 160 pounds of wild cat lay still in the flowers along Bridal Row.

In this view of the "Row," Herbert sits atop the fence post. Behind him is the window that kept the cat from him. In front of him is the wooden planking across Pike Street, which Sophie Frye Bass remembered as at times "mighty smelly like a stable, owing to the horses...In summer the water wagon went down the dusty planks each day. There was a street sweeper too, and when it came all would rush frantically to close the windows."

By 1895 with the encouragement of a very good practice and the steady conversion of Pike Street into a commercial thoroughfare, Frantz Coe and his wife Carrie left Bridal Row and took their children up to a bigger home on First Hill. There an older Herbert recalled he no longer needed to check under his bed each night for the lurking cougar. By 1902 they moved again to Washington Park and into a new home with a view out over the lake.

In 1903 Pike Street was regraded all the way to Broadway Avenue, and Bridal Row

put up on stilts and a new story of storefronts moved in beneath.

Dr. Frantz Coe died suddenly in 1904, two years before his son Herbert graduated from his father's alma mater, the University of Michigan Medical School. On July 15, 1962 the Seattle Times published a feature article titled "Seattle's Four Grand Old Men." One of these was the "beloved" Dr. Herbert Coe who by then had for 54 years been an essential part of the Children's Orthopedic Hospital, in-

cluding 30 years as its chief of surgical services and ten years as chief of staff.

Herbert Coe died in 1968 at the age of 87. He is survived by his two sons and widow Lucy Campbell Coe, daughter of pioneer hardwareman James Campbell. Mrs. Coe recalled for us the details of young Herbert's confrontation with the cougar and supplied the photograph of Bridal Row. She was born here in 1887 or one year before her future husband's family settled into Bridal Row.

21 A View from Profanity Hill

In 1890 a photographer, unknown to us now, set his tripod near the present site of Harborview Hospital and recorded the Pioneer Square area. The panorama extends from Cherry Street, on the right to the King Street coal wharves on the left. The most revealing division in this photograph is between its upper and lower halves which are two sides to the boundary line of destruction from the fire of 1889. All the masonry structures to the west of that line were built after the fire and on its ashes. All the clapboard buildings below that line were there during the fire and escaped it.[1]

The most lavish of these wooden survivors was Henry Yesler's residence: the dark mansion center right, now the site of the King County Courthouse. Directly behind this Gothic showpiece is the five-story Butler Hotel at the northwest corner of Second Avenue and James Street. *(See feature 5.)* To its left and in the center of the photograph

shines the Occidental Building in whose top floor the Library Association opened its first reading room in 1891. *(See features 31-33.)*

Another landmark is the long dark shed in the lower left. Built in 1886 as Turner Hall, it was one of two auditoriums that survived the fire—the other being the Armory at Fourth and Union. In 1890 George Frye, who lost his Opera House at First and Madison to the fire, leased the Turner and renamed it the Seattle Opera House. Its standard repertoire was minstrel shows.

This still photographic record of a quiet harbor with a single steam schooner belies the city's extraordinarily noisy activity in 1890. For this was one step past the starting line for the ambitious post-fire Seattle of 42,000. With regular transcontinental rail connection, the city received an average of more than 100 new citizens every week for the next 20 years.

In 1890 more than 2,000 new buildings were put up and a new city charter created almost as many new bureaucracies. Favorite pastimes included the first year of professional baseball with high-priced imported players, and steamboat racing. In November of '91, the Victorian, racing the Flyer over the 28 miles to Tacoma, set a new record of one hour and nineteen minutes. The Flyer came in at 1:31.

Another kind of urban noise gave its name to that part of First Hill from which our anonymous photographer took his panorama. It was called "Profanity Hill" because, even for those without bundles to carry, it was such an "expletive" to climb. Cameras and tripods were much heavier in 1890, and we can imagine that the photographer, whoever he was, concurred.

22 Trinity Church

On the Sunday afternoon of January 20, 1902, Edmonde Butler gave his first recital on Trinity Episcopal Parish's new organ. Since the instrument was declared to be the finest north of San Francisco, the church's pews were crowded long before organist Butler took his place behind the console. There, his fingers electrically linked through 4,500 valves to the 1,243 speaking tubes before him; he played a program which the P.I. reported as "carefully selected with a view to contrast and to show off the capabilities of the instrument."

Later that night when Butler and his satisfied audience were fast asleep, the organ performed an encore of its own. Two days later, after sifting through the ashes, Fire Chief Cook concluded that it was the organ which had burned down the church. A short circuit in the wiring ignited the chancel and then spread to the nave. There hidden behind stone walls and dark glass and fueled by Christmas decorations still hanging for Epiphany, the heat built up under the high roof until the windows exploded and the roof fell in with the organ's last crescendo. Only the rock walls remained.

And they remain today as the granite shell for the rebuilt Trinity which we see in both of these sightings west down James Street and past the parish at Eighth Avenue.

This was not the first time that fire had figured in the building plans of Seattle's original Episcopal congregation. Trinity's first church was built by its parishioners in 1870 at Third and Jefferson. This cozy gothic clapboard covered a floor of only 24 by 48 feet and was not adorned with a tower until 1880. However, it then rang with the largest bell in Washington Territory.

In 1882 the sanctuary was lengthened 22 feet to make room for the Territory's first pipe organ and a growing congregation which preferred a Protestant service with a little more liturgical style. In 1889 the rector, George Watson, bought property up on First Hill where many in his congregation were building lavish homes. The motivation to begin building the stone church was ignited on June 6 of that year when most of the city's business district burned down. The old parish went with it, the only structure destroyed on Third Avenue north of Yesler Way.

On the third anniversary of this "Great Fire," the congregation gathered in its new

The first Trinity parish and rectory at Third and Jefferson

home to make a "thank-offering to Almighty God for the good that He hath brought out of evil." Some of this "good" was remarkably profitable. The congregation sold for $25,000 the old Third and Jefferson lot it had bought for $200. The church's "good" move up the hill was also an ascent from the saloons and moral potholes it left behind "down on the sawdust."

As a pioneer parish, Trinity had grown into a family church serving the often uppercrust residents on First Hill. However, by the early years of this century, this distinguished society was moving out of its mansions as the apartment houses and hospitals moved in. Trinity was then faced with the difficult decision of whether to follow the flight or stay and serve the central city. It stayed.[1]

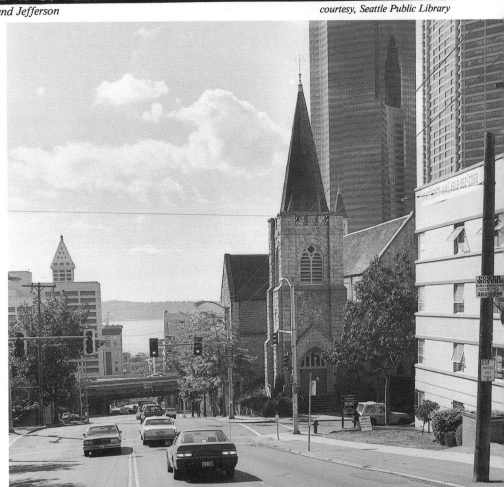

23 Courthouses and Castles

The two most evident structures in the photograph above, taken about 1906, were both once King County Courthouses, and each was called a "castle." Their somewhat eccentric histories, though quite different, both border on the grotesque.

The frame construction in the center was built in 1882 at the southeast corner of Third Avenue and Jefferson Street—the present site of City Hall Park. It had two careers, the first as the modest home for the county's courts. But soon after the county moved out in 1890 and up to its new imperious courts overlooking the city (the dome on the horizon), the city moved in.

In the 18 years municipal government was managed from that corner, Seattle's population swelled from 40,000 to more than 200,000. City Hall swelled as well into an odd collection of clapboard additions aptly renamed the "Katzenjammer Castle."[1] When, in 1890, King County gave in to the monumental urge to recommend itself with a

castle-on-a-hill, it also set off a chorus of complaints.

From the start it was called the "Gray Pile," the "Tower of Despair," and the "Cruel Castle." This poetic invective often fell to expletives less literary when lawyers in a hurry were forced to sprint the long and steep steps on Terrace Street to reach their litigation and pant out the abuses that gave the hill its popular name, "Profanity."

In 1914 a local landmark of both mass and scale was completed: the Smith Tower. Less than one relatively level block away, ground was ceremonially broken, beginning construction of a new courthouse: the one still with us.

The Town Crier, a local tabloid, announced: "In a city and county possessing such structures as the Smith, Hoge, and Alaska buildings and the Washington, Savoy, and other fine hotels, the old Court House has long stood as a silent and dingy bit of sar-

casm....Fifteen years of effort by county commissioners to reduce profanity in King County to a minimum is now triumphantly consummated!"

Now, although lawyers—and judges—no longer needed to climb the hill, that did not end the profane career of the malformed castle on the hill. The Times of January 17, 1926 reported that after 35 top-heavy years "King County's old Courthouse, rearing its imposing bulk atop steep, slippery Profanity Hill, is in danger of collapse. Beneath its 200-foot tower of tons of crumbling brick...are more than 200 human beings—prisoners—locked behind bars. The jail is a relic of barbarism. The danger of collapse is no mere fancy."

The Times writer added to this grave description a dark and ironic revelation: "In the west wing, under the statue of Justice who has lost her scales, is the execution chamber, where records show at least two condemned prisoners have been hanged." (The closer photograph of the old Courthouse is of this west wing. The scales are still in place.)

Not until January 8, 1931 were 36 holes bored into the crumbling brick pillars still

Seattle City Light at 7th and Yesler

courtesy, Historical Photography Collection, University of Washington

tentatively supporting the old Courthouse cupola. They shared 200 sticks of dynamite. In the moment it might take an exhausted barrister to mouth a monosyllabic indecency, the old embarrassment was leveled. And now fully revealed behind it and braced against a modern sky, the new King County Hospital appeared ready and waiting for its February dedication.[2] In 1931, the prisoners were moved into their own "penthouse" in the top floors of the new addition to the King County Courthouse.

Our contemporary view of Harborview Hospital shows that it has its own imposing brick bulk, but that it is also finely touched with modern art-deco detailing. The picture was taken from such a position—on Seventh just north of Alder—that if the old Courthouse were still there its dome would have blocked our view of Harborview.[3]

KING COUNTY'S NEW COURT HOUSE, SEATTLE. Cost, $225,000.

TWELVE YUKON RIVER STEAMERS
BUILT BY MORAN BROS. COMPANY
SEATTLE WASH.
1898
Length 175' Beam 35'
Depth 6½

24 Moran's Five Challenges

At the normally tender age of 14, Robert Moran quit school and went to work. Soon thereafter he came West and, as a young man of 17, he wound up in Seattle. "I was dumped out without breakfast on Yesler's wharf at 6 o'clock in the morning of November 17, 1875."

It was but eight years earlier that Horatio Alger published *Ragged Dick*, the popular novelist's first of a series of stories about poor boys who rise from rags to riches, having faith that "in this free country poverty is no bar to a man's advancement."

Young Robert fit this script perfectly. He had a precocious engineer's aptitude to build things, and only 10 cents in his pocket. Like a good entrepreneur, Moran decided to keep the dime in his pants and take his first meal on credit in the Our House Cafe at the foot of the wharf he only seconds earlier was "dumped onto."

Young Robert Moran's 10-cent introduction to Seattle was the first of the five auspicious events that would make of his life the most clearly sculpted model of capitalist virtue in this city's history. As Moran himself characterized it at the age of 80, "it is a

history that would record an industrial self-made life from a breakfast on credit to the construction, complete in all parts, of a first-class battleship."

Robert Moran's second great challenge came after he was elected mayor of his city and it was flattened by fire in 1889. As the weekly Argus later explained, "after the Great Fire his was the mastermind in the work of reconstruction, for Robert Moran's soul is the Seattle Spirit." This identification of the hero with his community is at the center of the Moran epic.

Each of these five events involves a victorious response to some grave challenge. The first was to youth and poverty; the second to fire; and the third to the arrival on July 17, 1897 of the steamer Portland with that "ton of gold." This time Moran responded by building 12 riverboat steamers and leading their perilous procession over the Gulf of Alaska to service on the Yukon River.

These 12 light-draft riverboats were built, all in a row, on tideflats south of town. Construction began January 15, 1898 with the labor of 2,100 men and continued until June 1, when the ships sailed out of town on a high

tide. What followed were two months of stormy seas, suffered not always in silence by frightened crews in sometimes mutinous moods. One of the 12 boats, the Western Star, was wrecked in a storm off Cook's Inlet, but the crew was saved. The dramatic journey's climax came July 26 when Moran and his battered ships reached the port of St. Michael near the mouth of the Yukon River.

When Moran returned to Seattle in September he reported to the press: "You may say that the tonnage of the Moran fleet, that is, the Seattle Fleet, has insured fully double the amount of freight to points in the Yukon this season."[1]

Robert Moran's fourth challenge was the battleship Nebraska. This $4 million floating fortress was launched in 1904 with a civic subsidy of $100,000 from 536 pledging citizens. Many more Seattle residents had posters of this dreadnought decorating their family sitting rooms.

While the city was consummating its identification with Moran, the not yet 50-year-old symbol of success was preparing to die. This was his fifth and last great challenge. In 1904 with the launching of the Nebraska, Moran

Moran's Nebraska, 3 views

abandoned shipbuilding, saying he was a "nervous wreck." "The doctors had me ticketed for Lakeview Cemetery, due to organic heart disease," he said. "There was none." Instead of the six months the doctors were giving him, the high-pressured engineer survived another 40 years by becoming an artist-engineer.

After buying a large part of Orcas Island, Moran designed and built a home on the island in the San Juans. He named it Rosario and many of its 16 bedrooms were outfitted with ship's bunks. From the comfort of these berths, Robert Moran's guests, staff, and family were aroused early every morning by the mighty sounds of a great pipe organ which Moran played in a combination morning concert and alarm clock.

Then, before the day's work and sitting together over a breakfast he could well afford, the old master engineer would repeat in detail to his guests some of the stories that together built the epic of Robert Moran's five great challenges.[2]

25 Outfitting the Argonauts

In its first issue for 1898 Frank Leslie's Popular Monthly, a national magazine, included an article about Seattle. It was the tenth installment of its "American Cities Series," and reads in part: "The eyes of the civilized world today are turned upon two points—namely the gold fields of Alaska and the City of Seattle. To speak of one is to mention the other."

"At no point in the world's history has there ever been such an awakening, such an irresistible spirit of adventure. People in every walk of life have caught this adventurous spirit and are pouring into Seattle to prepare for the journey northward." The lead paragraph then concludes with a food metaphor that is unusally hard to swallow: "And like a little leaven it has worked the lump into a large loaf spreading from the Atlantic to the Pacific, from the Arctic to the Antarctic."

The food for thought "Seattle equals Alaska and Alaska equals Seattle" was the regular diet served up world-wide by a distinguished local huckster named Erastus Brainerd. In the fall of 1897 this onetime curator, art critic, and newspaper editor was hired by the Seattle Chamber of Commerce to concoct the promotion that would alchemically line the muddy streets of Seattle with gold and goldseekers.

Brainerd brewed up the international epidemic he named "Klondike Fever." (It was Seattle's first infection of a kind of "Husky Fever.") The Popular Monthly caught it, and so did thousands of other publications. The only route of relief was through Seattle.

The same issue of Popular Monthly included another and more sober Seattle promotion: an advertisement for the Pioneer Outfitters, Cooper and Levi. It reads: "If you must go to the Alaska goldfield, you must have a good outfit properly packaged in specially prepared packages. If not it will be ruined while in transit. We have sold more outfits than any other firm in Seattle. Probably it is because we have the reputation of furnishing the very best goods and employ professional packers."

The advertisement also included a free offer to receive and hold all mail for the goldseekers—who were called Argonauts after the Greek myth of Jason and the Golden Fleece—and to send a "supply list for 'one man for one year' showing weight and cost of articles and an excellent map of the Alaska route."

The source of this "excellent map," and its starting point, is shown in this historical scene at 104 and 106 First Avenue South, in the Olympic block (which since the building collapsed in 1972 is the "Olympic hole" at the southeast corner of First Avenue and Yesler Way.)[1]

Overflowing onto the sidewalk in front of the Cooper and Levi storefront are a few of those "professionally packed" supplies, including yellow corn meal, whole peas dried, lentils, lanterns, lye, summer sausage, sleds, and one dog. (Actually, dogs, although in demand to pull the sleds, were not part of this Pioneer Outfitter's 'Supply List.')

Aaron and Esther Levy came to Seattle in 1889. Soon thereafter, Isaac Cooper arrived, married Elizabeth, the Levi daughter, and in 1891 joined Aaron in a business partnership. They supplied a variety of bulk goods from rolled oats to corn cob pipes to lumber camps, rural retailers, and the slim but steady stream of gold seekers heading into Canada and Alaska throughout the mid-1890s. When at last the Rush came in 1897, Cooper and Levi were ready.

When Seattle's ecstatic morning news-paper announced the July 17 arrival of the steamer Portland with its "ton of gold," Cooper and Levi alertly managed to slip an ad into the same edition warning: "Don't get excited and rush away half-prepared. You're going to a country where grub can be more valuable than gold, and frequently can't be had at any price. We can fit you out quicker and better than any firm in town. We have had lots of experience and know how to pack and what to furnish." And they did.

Within the first month of the arrival of the Portland, local merchants sold $325,000 worth of supplies to the miners. A good percentage of this came out of Cooper and Levi's store. By the fall of 1897 about one thousand locals, including most of the fire and police forces and the town's newly resigned mayor, had left for the gold fields. Through the coming months and years many thousands more arrived from all points south and east on the Northern Pacific and Great Northern Railroads.

Actually, it has long been a local habit to sensationalize the significance of the gold rush, its Argonauts, and its promotional Jason, Brainerd, in bringing in the Golden Fleece of civic greatness to Seattle. Probably the diversified economy of Seattle would have continued to grow without the "Klon-dike Fever." As Roger Sale suggests in his fine history, *Seattle, Past to Present*: "Tacoma could have had five Brainerds and would have gained little from them."

In 1901 Cooper and Levi sold out to the Bon Marche. In the ten years of their partner-ship they had not only outfitted lumbermen and miners, but were also leaders of local philanthropy through their Cooper and Levi Trust. Mrs. Esther Levy was the first presi-dent of the Hebrew Ladies Benevolent Socie-ty, the precursor of today's Jewish Family Service. Her daughter Elizabeth Cooper suc-ceeded her. Both families were also involved in the founding of Temple de Hirsch.

In the contemporary photograph only the stone column which supported the southwest corner of the now-collapsed Olympic Build-ing remains. The shape of its individual stones can be identified in both photographs.

The Levi residence on First Hill   *courtesy, Jewish Archive, University of Washington Library*

26 Road to Nome

In one of our two historical scenes of the same disembarking steamer, someone (we normally assume the photographer) has conscientiously inscribed on the original negative: "S.S. Victoria leaving Seattle Dock."

However, captions to historical photographs are notoriously unreliable.[1] I was able to correct this misnomer with help from Jim Faber. He's the author of the 1976 *Irreverent Guide to Washington State*, founder of the Washington State Ferry tabloid Enetai, and is now putting the finishing touches on a history of water transportation on Puget Sound.

Faber knows his steamships, and the S.S. Victoria especially. He crewed a few trips on the Old Vic between here and Nome in the mid-1930s. Faber says the steamship pictured here is not the Victoria; it's the Ohio. When it was first put in transatlantic service in 1873, it was the largest liner ever built in the U.S. A single crew could drive its 360-foot iron hull

up to 13 knots. Here nearly 40 years later, it's heading for Nome, sometime between 1907 and 1909.

If it's 1907, it will strike an iceberg between St. Michaels and Nome, and 75 of its panic-stricken passengers will jump overboard. Four of these (and perhaps one or two of those we see on deck) will drown. But if this is the photographic record of the Ohio's first trip north in 1908, then its passengers will be tormented by the freakishly long and frustrating journey ahead.

One of them, 26-year-old Seattle resident Max Loudon will keep a log which begins: "My Dear Mother, As you know Earl and Mabel saw me off June 1st. We only went out 1,000 yards when the boat stopped to put ashore a man who had got on board by mistake." (By the time the journey ended, most of the passengers who stayed on board considered themselves also there "by mistake.") Like many others paying lower-class steerage

fare, Max Loudon was enroute to Nome for work to support his family.

Since the first strike in 1899 and the rush in 1900, the beach in front of Nome had been panned over six times and nearly exhausted. Now it was the common dream of the passengers in steerage, on the dozen or so ships heading north, that when the ice cleared they be the first to step ashore and claim the best paying jobs. In 1908 that meant working for a wage on the heavy equipment dredging the permafrost in back of Nome.

Lower-class passengers could normally expect 19 or so bathless days and nights of boiled potatoes and fitful sleep in anyone of 144 identical bunks made of coiled spring wire stacked with three tiers to the seven-foot ceiling. "When we go to sleep we simply take off our hat, coat, and shoes, lie on the mattress and pull our blankets over us." Twenty days and nights later, after traveling 2,400 miles out of sight of land, Max Loudon woke up to see "in every direction nothing but snow-covered ice. All the captains say they have never seen so much ice before." Then the gathering flotilla of steamers with anxious passengers and crews "hovered around Norton Sound waiting to make a dash as soon as the ice opens."

Not until July 11 could Max Loudon mail his log home to mother. "I arrived this morning after being 40 days and 40 nights on the Ohio. We were among the first to leave Seattle and the last to arrive. Our captain was certainly cautious enough to suit even you. Everytime he saw a cake of ice he turned and ran for open water. The passengers were the angriest lot of men you ever saw."

When the Ohio's Captain Conradi returned with his Ohio to Seattle on July 30, the Times reported both the news of the passengers' "ridiculing mood" and the captain's reply. "I carried them safely to their port and I pay no attention to what they say or think about me. . . . There has been, and there is, only one master on this ship and that is the captain, as the passengers all found out before they got through."

This was more than the captain could say for the Ohio's 1909 trip to Nome. If the passengers in our pictures are beginning that run, they will come upon a grim surprise in Swanson's Bay, British Columbia. There, the Ohio struck a rock. Its skipper managed to beach her and save 209 of its passengers. But four were lost and the Ohio, too.

Jim Faber poses before the Goodtime II.

courtesy, Old Seattle Paperworks

27 AYP's Arctic Circle

In 1907, a decade after the first rush north for gold, workers started transforming the wild University of Washington campus into a civilized stage for celebrating the decade of Seattle's success in outfitting and exploiting Alaska, the Yukon, and eventually, it hoped, Asia.

When the Alaska Yukon and Pacific Exposition (AYP) opened on June 6, 1909, the centerpiece was the Arctic Circle, shown in our "then" image by the AYP's official photographer, Frank Nowell.[1] Here a semicircle of seven structures surrounded the Cascades and Geyser Basin. These were temporary structures designed in a variation of typical exposition style: neoclassical colonades supporting great arching roofs decorated with profuse baroque details. The seven buildings were named, from left, the Agriculture, European, Alaska, U.S. Government (the domed centerpiece behind the fountain), Philippines and Hawaii, Oriental, and Manufacturing. Under this cosmopolitan cover was exhibited a cornucopia of mostly local enterprise combined with products from the trans-Pacific region Seattle hoped to exploit.

The Hawaii Building, in the photo just to the right of the fountain, advertised the fertility of the Islands with, what the Times reported, were "gigantic piles of fruits including a pyramid of coconuts, and a pineapple 30 feet high composed of small pineapples cunningly arranged." The centrally placed U.S. Government Building featured at its entrance a marine hospital operating room with masked, life-sized, wax figures so real that the 'scene sent shivers up the backs...of the bewildered visitors." The Alaska Building, to the left of the Federal, included a somewhat predictable display of one million dollars in gold dust, nuggets, and bricks. Security measures taken for the display were advertised as much as its dollar value.

The Agriculture Building on the far left included the "first display of clams ever shown at an exposition." And across the Arctic Circle in the Manufacturing Building, the Times reported, was a "telephone switchboard and four pretty girls who are doing real work handling the telephone company's business on the Exposition grounds." The building also displayed the "disappearing bed which, the inventor asserts, will revolutionize domestic architecture by making bedrooms unnecessary."

Many visitors preferred to stroll the grounds or on clear days just sit around and watch the crowds mill around the Arctic Circle. And some, like those relaxing in Nowell's photograph, would look (past the photographer) across the formal gardens and down the Rainier Vista to what the AYP's publicists promoted as "the only real mountain such an exposition has ever had."

But the Arctic Circle was not the whole show. It was the side of the Exposition meant not so much to entertain as to edify. It was the center of elegance intended to raise the standards of popular taste. Meanwhile the popular taste was satisfying itself down at the sideshow of primitives and exotic carny attractions called the "Pay Streak." This second exposition center was less intentionally designed than instinctively assembled to pander to a variety of tastes that often paid extra not to be elevated.

Exposition visitors went back and forth between the crowded excitement of the Pay Streak and the meditative pace of the dazzling white city that surrounded the geyser basin. At night this bright model of civiliza-

tion instantly crystalized into the heavenly city on the hill when the elaborate covering of electric lights were turned on.

The Arctic Circle, and the entire AYP, had its beginning in 1905, when Godfrey Chealander, Seattle citizen and Grand Secretary of the Arctic Brotherhood, returned home from Portland's Lewis and Clark Exposition with his Alaska exhibit and a desire to find a Seattle showplace for it. With help first from Seattle Times City Editor James Wood, and then from every talent that the well-rehearsed "Seattle Spirit" could lend it, Chealander's modest urge was transformed into a 108-day grand affair that attracted nearly four million paid admissions. Unlike most expositions before it, the AYP, its organizers were fond of repeating, "opened on time and paid for itself."[2]

In the contemporary scene the geyser basin is the same, but is renamed Frosh Pond. (Here it is enjoyed by a different species of sitter.) The very temporary classical plaster of the Arctic Circle has been replaced by a more permanent brick architecture of academic gothic.

courtesy, Old Seattle Paperworks

28 The Pay Streak

The popular center of the 1909 Alaska Yukon and Pacific Exposition (AYP) was a two thousand foot strip of gaudy amusements and carnival concessions called the Pay Streak. The Arctic Circle's cool arrangement of snow-white classical monuments encouraged meditative strolling and edified sitting but down on the garish Pay Streak the crushing crowd moved from novelty to novelty, generating human heat.

The Pay Streak ran parallel to the western border of the campus, one block east of Fifteenth Avenue. At its northern end was the Klondike Circle, a ring of buildings near the exposition's main gate at the 40th Street entrance to the University.[1]

The still standing Architecture Building filled the northwest corner of the circle and housed the AYP's fine arts exhibit. Across from it was the not-so-fine art of the Battle of Gettysburg. Here in a two-story coliseum, Civil War aggression was regularly reenacted, and although the sounds escaped the building, the pyrotechnics did not. For the full effect

there was a modest admission price, 25 cents.

From this point a line of mixed attractions extended a long and sensational way to the Gondola Landing on Portage Bay. This southern end of the strip was the site of the lighter-than-air flights of the "world famous airship the A-Y-P," frequent fireworks displays, and "fish dinners with prices the same as downtown."

In between the Battle of Gettysburg and Portage Bay, the crowd's choices were as varied and sensational as the concession names suggest. One could ride the Magic Swing, Fairy Gorge Tickler, Vaccuum Tube Railway, or the more predictable Ferris Wheel. Or one could take one's taste for adventure into the Streets of Cairo, (seen at the left of our photograph), on a Trip Down the Yukon, or visit the Live Game Exhibit. The crowd's more bizarre interests were encouraged by the Upside Down House, Temple of Mirth, Theatre of Sensations; and one could pay a little extra to have Albert the Educated Horse answer questions.

The price of admission through the Main Gate of AYP was 50 cents for adults and 25 cents for children. The Pay Streak's attractions cost from 5 to 50 cents, and there were many complaints that these added costs were more than a working man could provide for himself and his family. The Times and every other local periodical answered these anxieties with an unrelenting campaign of publicity for all that was "free at AYP."

The Times reported that "all of the exhibit buildings around the Arctic Circle are free as the air and one is not compelled to pay out a cent after entering the gates to see anything which is not in the line of pure amusement or refreshment....Of course, if the visitor becomes excited at the sight of the electric lights and the crowds of people and listens too intently to the siren voice of the barker on the Pay Streak it will certainly cost him more."

The concession proprietors did their own excavating, designed and built their own fanciful structures, hired their performers, and

courtesy, Historical Photography Collection, University of Washington

then through the 108 days of the AYP barked for the crowd's patronage. This view of the Pay Streak looks toward its northern end. On the right is the jungle compound that featured what was, perhaps, the most popular attraction of the entire AYP: the Igorrotes. A few of the loinclothed primitives from the Phillipines stand beneath the Igorrotes sign as a tease for the packed crowd. The barker encouraged the crowd to pay up the admission price and enter behind the thatched front for a complete view of native habits.

The Igorrotes stirred two local commotions. First, they were dog eaters. It was rumored that at night they roamed the streets of the city looking for strays. Second, the loincloths, for all their ethnic authenticity, were for those properly bundled in the Edwardian costume a shocking display of the human body. A special committee of local leaders, including Judge Thomas Burke and the Presbyterian minister Mark Matthews, was formed to determine the moral status of the scanty covering. Either the exhibitionist or the cosmopolitan spirit of the Pay Streak prevailed, for the loincloths were declared proper clothing for primitives.[2]

The contemporary photograph was taken from the fourth floor of the genetics wing of

the University's Health Sciences complex. The view is to the north and in line with what was the Pay Streak. If the Igorrotes were still with us, their compound would be on the front lawn between the Genetics Building and Pacific Avenue, or in the immediate foreground of our "now" view.

29 Temple of Timber

The Alaska Yukon and Pacific Exposition officially opened at noon on the first day of June 1909 when President William Howard Taft, pressing a golden key, sent a telegraphic signal from Washington D.C. Soon after the doors of the Forestry Building swung open. Then while the popular Pop Wagner's band played the Stars and Stripes Forever from the bandstand outside, "the crowds surged through the great structure admiring its massive architecture and its varied assortment of exhibits." Actually, this building overwhelmed the exhibits inside it.

There were two ways to describe this out-sized "temple to timber": with poetry and with statistics. The favorite numbers recited were of its 320-foot length—"as long as a city block"—and the 124 logs that supported its roof and two towers. The 80 on the outside were an average 5½ feet thick, 50 feet high, and "left in their natural clothing of bark." Those inside were stripped of theirs; but all 124, "selected for their symmetry and soundness," were unhewed and weighed about 50,000 pounds each.

The poetic response to this building saw it as a "taming of the wild forest where the forest is yet seen." It also was likened to an artistic arrangement of wild flowers into a bouquet. The more popular poetry repeated over and over again on postcards and from park benches was that here was "the largest log cabin in the world!"

Giant Fir Pillar · Forestry Bldg. Seattle

courtesy, Old Seattle Paperworks

The building's architects, Saunders and Lawton, had with substantial grace shaped Washington State forest products into the AYP's classic revival architectural style. From the outside the Forestry Building looked "like a Greek temple done in rustic." However, on the inside it was a lumber sideshow, filled with the freaks of forestry—like a pair of giant dice six feet thick, cut from a single block and captioned "the kind of dice we roll in Washington." Also on show was the "Big Stick" which, at 156½ feet long, was "one immense piece of milled timber," and the 19-foot thick stump with a winding staircase to a cabin built on its top.

With this kind of preparation it was expected that when the fair was finished its Forestry Building would become the woodsy quarters for the University's Department of Forestry. Instead, it became home of the Washington State Museum and a growing family of hungry wood-chewing beetles. The latter ultimately pushed out the former, and by 1931 this "temple of timber" was razed to sticks.[1]

Now in its place is the brick HUB, or Husky Union Building.

30 The Priest and the Prostitute

Washington Street was once a thoroughfare; the way both to Rainier Valley and a "good time."

This sighting, taken around 1900, looks west down Washington Street from between 4th and 5th Avenues S. Up the street's center the Seattle Renton and Southern Railway made its electric way to Columbia City and points south. The climb between 4th and 6th Avenues was steep enough to require the aid of a mechanical counterbalance—Seattle's first. (The slot through which the streetcars attached themselves to the counterbalancing underground weight can be seen just left of the right-hand track.)[1]

On the picture's left is the Montana Livery Stables. Its two floors could accomodate 120 horses, and some were for rent. It advertised, "the stables are prepared to respond immediately to demands for carriages, hacks, etc. for weddings, receptions, entertainments, funerals, and other requirements demanded."[2]

Occasionally, Washington Street businesswoman Dorothea Georgine Emile Ohben required a rented carriage. She needed the conveyance to show-off her merchandise through the streets of Seattle, and Ohben's "goods"

were "bad women."

Mrs. Ohben was stockly built with blue eyes, black hair, and the extraordinary social skills required of a successful madame. Her professional name was Lou Graham, and throughout the 1890s she ran, at the southwest corner of Third Avenue and Washington Street, Seattle's plushest parlor house. (The house is just left of center in the historical view where its little tower is topped by a flagless flagpole.)

A parlor house was a high class whorehouse. At Lou Graham's you were expected to come in well-dressed, and later you were sent home that way. A parlor house was neither a box house or a crib house. The former was a kind of theater with loges arranged for privacy into three-sided boxes with the open end facing the usually bawdy stage. The latter were low class brothels sectioned into little no-frill rooms, or cribs. Seattle had its big city monopoly on sin with plenty of boxes, cribs, and parlors.

Immediately kitty-corner to Lou Graham's house for ladies of the night was Our Lady of Good Help. Seattle's first Catholic Church,

pictured right of center, was dedicated here in 1870. Its builder, Father Francis Xavier Prefontaine still lived and preached here in 1900. It was, wrote Seattle's real estate czar Henry Broderick, a case of "piety and prostitution on the same corner."

Broderick told this story often. "The pioneer priest would one day be summoned across the street to offer spiritual consolation to a dying girl in Lou Graham's resort. He asked her to join him in prayer. She demurred. Considering her trade, she thought that heaven would have nothing to do with her . . . the good father raised his hands and said, "My child, let's put it this way. I know a fraction of your life which is not good. But the Man at the Gate knows your total life, and I'm sure he will find something on which to base mercy. Let us pray." There was time left only for the girl to say "Thanks, Father, for the lift."[3]

Father Prefontaine was lifted to his eternal reward in 1909; Lou Graham went to hers a few years earlier. Our Lady of Good Help was razed in 1904 for the southern access to the Great Northern's tunnel under the city. However, Lou Graham's four-story brick bawdy house is still in the "now." *(See feature 47.)*

Father Prefontaine

Our Lady of Good Help, looking southeast across Third Ave.

courtesy, Old Seattle Paperworks

31 Pioneer Square Candor

The Pioneer Square Historic District is today a nationally prized preserve of architectural integrity because of the fortuitous fire on June 6, 1889.

When the smoke had dissipated over the 30 business blocks flattened by the fire, the normally cloudy city council also saw clearly for the one political instant needed to prescribe wider streets, sturdier structures, and new grades. When these new and nobler buildings began to grow like mushrooms from the loam of woodash, they came up mostly Victorian Romanesque. The old wood-frame "cradle of Seattle" was being reborn in varied colored stone and brick with fine terracotta detailing and decorations.

Since many of these new structures were designed by an imported and prolific architect from Massachusetts named Elmer H. Fisher, this consistency of architectural style was given a personal continuity as well.

This grand showpiece neighborhood brought people out of the buildings and into the streets, where as much wheeling and dealing was done as behind the desks and counters.

Indeed, at the turn of the century, Pioneer Square was one big street scene for posing and promenading. Unlike many contemporary malls and business districts which seem designed to entice the anxious consumer inside for a fast sale, the ornate facades about Yesler Way encouraged gregarious milling, sophisticated dickering, and dignified gazing.

Our old scene (the tableau of five businessmen) dates from 1900 or 1901. It is one of about 100 happily preserved negatives whose principal subject was the street activity around Pioneer Square at the turn-of-the-century. The photographer, Walter P. Miller, supplied the Seattle News-Letter, a local weekly with a brief history, with candid shots which were then included in a regular front-page column of gossipy bits and brief anecdotes, titled "Stories of the Streets and of the Town."

Most professional photography at the time was aimed at landmarks, ceremonies, or promotions. If people were the subjects, they were conventionally idealized in carefully produced and retouched studio portrait work. By comparison, the consistently can-

did values of Miller's series for the Seattle News-Letter is peculiarly straight forward. In looking at the sculpturally pleasing grouping of the street bull session and the relaxed but conventional poses, it is not possible to determine if the subjects are aware of Miller's presence.

Throughout the 1890s most of the big deals were struck either within or in front of the stately victorian structures that lined Pioneer Square. And when gold was struck in Alaska, the sidewalks were congested with outfittings for the "rushers" as well. (See feature 25.) But when the taste for glass-covered skyscrapers, like the Alaska Building built in 1904, began to move the business and commercial centers of Seattle north along Second and Third Avenues, the style of the street scenes around Pioneer Square got seedier.[1]

By World War I it was depressed, and when everything else took a long economic bath through the 1930s, Pioneer Square simply continued its prolonged dive. The mania for the modern which so impoverished the post-World War II building boom with tacky prefabrications hardly touched Pioneer Square. This was most fortunate for Pioneer Square was lying in wait for the 1960s and

'70s and the fight for preservation.

Walter P. Miller's scenes of Pioneer Square street life were saved for us because they were recorded on flexible negatives rather than on glass. Light and compact, they managed to survive and eventually surfaced through the good services of Roger Dudley, another local professional photographer.

Many years ago another long active professional, Loomis Miller, acquired the Webster and Stevens studios. The large collection of historical images that came to Miller with the business included our second candid street scene on Pioneer Square. The view is through the Pergola, and the same arched corner entrance to the Pioneer Building can be seen in all three photographs. The Webster and Stevens image dates from about 1912.[2]

The reader can decide what parts of the "now" image are candid, if any.

courtesy, Old Seattle Paperworks

32 Hub of the Past

Here are two views of the elegant neighborhood which architect and preservation activist Victor Steinbreuck described in 1966 as the only regional location "where a significant group of older buildings of one period remain to form a cohesive whole...buildings whose real value lies in their historical association, visual delight, and potential use to the community."

The elevated view looks across Pioneer Place to James Street. The year is 1910, the date of the Pergola's completion. On the left is Henry Yesler's pride, the Pioneer Building, with its tower still intact. To the right, across James Street, the classic front of the flatiron-shaped Seattle Hotel is largely obscured by the crowded hatchings of a telephone pole. The corner of the Olympic block, on the far right, is seen again on the left of the other historical photograph.

The date of this second image is 1904. It was on April 1 of that year (as the white sign running beside the sidewalk at eye-level forecasts) that the insurance firm of Calhoun, Denny, and Ewing moved into the then brand-new Alaska Building: the city's first

structural steel skyscraper. This was an early move in a business migration that would ultimately bring some long economic hard times to Pioneer Place.

In 1966 local preservationists were in the midst of the long struggle to save Pioneer Square from decay on the one hand and the forces of urban renewal on the other. In 1966 the threat came down from city hall when Mayor Braman joined a promotion that would have converted the historic district into a modern model of parking lots and highrises. Steinbreuck asked rhetorically, "Is Seattle's past worth saving?" Bill Speidel continued the alarmed inquiry, "Old Seattle, is it doomed?" and columnist Emmett Watson answered intimately, "I swear, my friends, progress is going to be the death of this city yet!"

The forces of preservation prevailed. The parking lots were never built, and in 1970 all those thick-walled Victorian structures were officially named by the city council as precious parts of the Pioneer Square Historical District. The old neighborhood

was now also protected by the Pioneer Square Historic Review Board.

From 1971 to 1983 the person most responsible to this sensitive business of preserving and renovating Pioneer Square was the city's historical preservation officer, Earl Layman. Here, in our contemporary view, he stands before the green pastoral screen of sycamores that effectively hides most of the scarred hole that was once the Olympic Hotel and Northern Pacific ticket office. Earl Layman is not responsible for the unfortunate collapse of the Olympic's east wall on the night of March 22, 1972. However, he thinks he heard it creaking two nights earlier while attending a preservation meeting at the Brasserie Pittsbourg in the basement of the Pioneer Building.

Nor is Layman responsible for the missing center tower on the Pioneer Building, although he would have liked it put back when the Pioneer Place's centerpiece was recently renovated. That and many other district towers and cornices were precautionarily removed after the 1949 earthquake. Layman was not around in the early 1960s when the

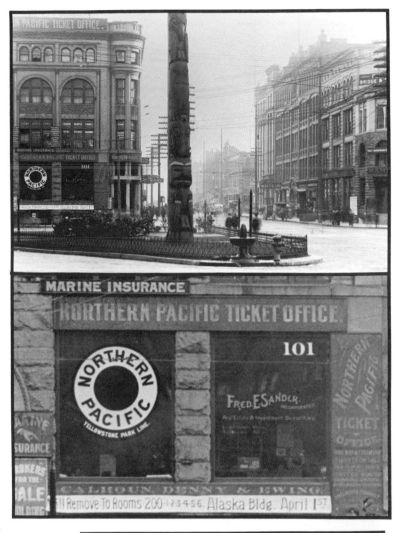

Seattle Hotel was razed for what is called the "sinking ship parking garage." This ugly scar in the side of Pioneer Square continues to have the ironic effect of making preservation of the remaining structures a cultural necessity.[1]

There have been improvements since 1970. The renovated Pergola is in its place. Layman stands on restored cobblestones before a decorative wrought-iron fence that is an effective duplicate of the original. And the sycamores continue to grow.

Layman credits three persons as primarily responsible for fighting the preservation wars of the 1960s: architects Ralph Anderson and Victor Steinbreuck, and gallery owner Richard White. Layman then pauses before he adds a fourth name, that of Bill Speidel. Speidel adds Times columnist John Reddin and the students of Cleveland High School.

Bill Speidel's place in Pioneer Square is actually under the sidewalks, and his time, before the fire of 1889. By his own confession, "I got the idea for an underground tour when I was drunk, but I had to sober up to get it passed. I had my last drink on November 4, 1964. The following winter students from Cleveland High came down every Saturday and cleared out truckloads of debris." Then with the money he saved by not buying Jim Beam, Speidel opened the tour on Know Your Seattle Day, May 31, 1965. Five-hundred people were waiting to go underground.

It was Times columnist John Reddin who in the late 1950s first reported that there was a "ghost town of subterranean shops below Pioneer Square . . . a city beneath a city." Reddin advised that regular access into what he called the "Yesler Way Catacombs" might result in a tourist boom.

Some time shortly before November 4, 1964, Bill Speidel agreed.[2]

33 Department Store Santa

Around Thanksgiving time 1907, seven-year-old Robert Roach decided he wanted a sled for Christmas. It had to be "one with red steel runners, not a homemade wooden one."

This was a requirement only Santa Claus would understand, so the boy persuaded his mother to take him to the Pioneer Square grand arrival of Garvey and Buchanan Company's department store Santa. And, indeed, somewhere in our historical scene, Robert in his winter coat and his mother in her best hat are lost in the holiday swarm that surrounds Santa, the reindeers Dancer and Prancer, and their faithful Eskimo attendant Kuzukatuk. The photograph was taken soon after the 10 a.m. prompt arrival of Santa on Saturday, November 30, 1907.

Today the 83-year-old Robert Roach still remembers that childhood adventure with the happy clarity that helps bring this Yuletide scene into focus. He recalls that he was a little concerned as he and his mother rode the Beacon Hill electric trolley into town along a barren 12th Avenue S. "I wanted snow because I thought Santa couldn't come

without it. We changed to a cable car at the James Street barn. Sitting inside so mother's hat wouldn't blow off, we clanked and bumped down to stop outside the Seattle Hotel (at the foot of James Street). There were usually a lot of men around Pioneer Square, but today there were women and children too. They were all waiting for something."

Robert's mother nudged him forward. "I wiggled and squeezed to the front just as a shout went up. Two strange animals pulled a funny buggy around a corner and stopped right in front of me. They had shaggy coats and horns that reached far out over their heads. I reached out to touch a reindeer, but he looked at me and I pulled back my hand. Santa waved and laughed, and a photographer yelled for everyone to look at the camera."

But as the photo reveals, most of them ignored the photographer's pleadings for a saleable crowd portrait and continued to gaze upon the "children's saint," Saint Nick. Soon after, Santa's "funny buggy," or what

the Times reporter called his "sleigh-of-state," started off on a long and winding parade through the shopper-packed streets of downtown Seattle.

Many of the children followed after, picking up the candy and tin horns Santa threw to the trailing entourage. But not Robert. "Mother stopped me." He never got the chance to ask about the sled.

The parade ended in front of Garvey and Buchanan's department store on the west side of Second Avenue near Seneca Street. Another crowd was waiting there for an audience with this roly-poly immortal who liked listening to the whispered desires of good little girls and boys.

But Messieurs Garvey and Buchanan were more interested in the parents. Although the biggest signs read "SANTA'S HEADQUARTERS" and "TOYS," the show windows below them were filled with the "MOST WONDERFUL SALE OF SUMPTUOUS NEW SILKS!" "The Store That Serves You Best" was betting on both silks and Santa.

The scene in front of Garvey and Buchanan's Department store.   courtesy, Museum of History and Industry

And reindeer too. On Sunday a full-page P.I. ad proclaimed, "A Bargain Event Positively Without Precedent in the Annals of Seattle Merchandising...the GREAT REFUND SALE—a 20% Cash Discount on Everything!" That was for the parents. For all "the little people" this ad also announced the "Dancer and Prancer Poetry Contest." The five dollar first prize would be awarded to the best three-verse poem including "Garvey Buchanan Co. Toyland" and "Dancer" and "Prancer" in each verse. The ad also was "sorry to announce that 'Dancer,' unfortunately, lost another horn Saturday, making him now entirely bereft of antlers."[1]

By 1911 Garvey and Buchanan were bereft of a store. Ultimately, cut-rate silks and department store Santas could not keep them in business. And yet they are remembered by Robert Roach as the store that brought Santa to Seattle twice in 1907, first on November 30 and then again on Christmas Eve. But, Roach's recollections ruefully conclude, "He didn't bring me a sled either time."

34 Denny's Knoll

In January of 1979 the Olympic Hotel was nominated for the National Register of Historic Places. We might have hoped that years earlier the same had happened for the old Territorial University which once stood in its place. The old school was surrounded with living memories as profoundly loving as those offered the Olympic by citizens successful in their efforts to save it from demolition. However, in 1907, the year of the university's removal, a booming spirit of progress was simply too insistent to be forestalled by meditative memories of school-days.[1]

This photographic image, clouded with the exhaust fumes of steam shovels and the dust of cave-ins, is of Fourth Avenue being cut through the site of that old school. The photographer is above University Street and his camera sights south across Fourth towards Seneca.[2] There in the center of the picture the gathering cloud half obscures what was the exact location of the old university. The building was 20 to 30 feet higher as the exposed cliff on the left reveals.

Atop the cliff is a sign reading "Metropolitan Building Co., Lessee of University Tract." That name "Metropolitan" was chosen to help attract eastern capitol to finance a project its local boosters advertised as showing a "business boldness amounting almost to romance...it will probably be the largest commercial development of its kind undertaken in any part of the world." And the signing of that lease in the late winter of 1907 turned into a very big deal indeed. Within five years the entire grass-covered tract was congested with buildings returning rents to Metropolitan and lease monies to the university.

The photograph was taken during the winter of 1907-08. For many years before, the only thing growing on this knoll—besides young minds—was the deep grass, maples, and firs that girdle the western slopes of Denny's Knoll in a greenbelt of inviting calm. From 1861, the year it was built, through the many decades of its dominance as the young community's most imposing landmark, the clapboards, cupola, and fluted columns of the old university shone with a hard white enamel.

When in the mid-1890s the regents moved the university to its present location, their image of the old acreage switched from one of academic sanctuary to the pragmatic stage of real estate. Successfully resisting a city plan to turn the knoll into a park, they dickered for a decade while the city doubled in size and commerce began to press in on the picket fence. Still, in 1907, when the deal with Metropolitan went through, the old university building was not destroyed. It was moved 100 yards or more to the northwest, near Fifth and Union, where it waited while its alumni, under the charismatic urgings of Professor Edmond Meany, tried to gather support to have the building either relocated to the new university site or somehow saved. They failed and had to settle for those fluted columns alone, which now stand at the present site of the "University of a Thousand Years."[3]

(Readers interested in studying the elaborate history of Denny's Knoll are advised to read *Denny's Knoll* by Neil O. Hines. This recent publication by the University of Washington Press is an excellent overview filled with fine detail.)

This 1878 view of Denny's Knoll looks from Denny Hill across Second Avenue and Pike Street.

The ground-breaking ceremonies for the new Y.W.C.A.

35 YWCA

In the spring of 1911 some Seattle women organized a five-day "whirlwind campaign" to raise money for a new Y.W.C.A.

The old one is evident in our historical view. Within the single story of this "cottage" at Fourth Avenue and Seneca Street, the women ran a service for single girls coming to the big city to look for work. They kept a watch out for them at the depots and so saved these "innocents from the raw and vulgar advances of uncouth and cowardly men."

Here the Y.W.C.A. daily served hundreds of nutritious and economical meals and each evening cleared the cafeteria for classes in culture and marketable skills. And sometimes there were parties or vespers. It was a resourceful albeit difficult arrangement. One reporter remarked, "it takes a vivid imagination to picture men putting up with such quarters...only women, and young energetic and resourceful women at that, would think they could do it at all."

On Tuesday May 9, 1911, these young women began to not put up with it. Organized into squads they marched into every business block selling their Y.W.C.A. pennants for whatever offering they could get, and wanting 400 thousand dollars. It was a winning strategy, for the "golden flow ran unabated all day." The P.I. reported that it was "so big that it can't be counted until noon" the next day. Then at Wednesday noon, the city's whistles and church bells announced together that the first 100 thousand had been surrendered to the women.

Later that day several hundred "working girls" responded with music of their own—one of the campaign's marching songs. Sung to the tune of "Marching through Georgia," it included these rousing lines. "Hurrah, Hurrah, we'll visit everyone/Hurrah, Hurrah tis work as well as fun/But we'll never quit the task/Until the goal is won/Till we raise 400 thousand."

Here we see the formation of the campaign's Grand Auto Parade. With emergency car loans from the Seattle Taxi Company and the Y.M.C.A. this procession eventually swelled to over 100 cars, and the drive's accumulated fund to more than 222,000 dollars. The P.I. editorialized that this quick success proved that "girls are worth saving, they are one-half and the better-half of the humanity of tomorrow."

Three years later, on May 25, 1914 the Y.W.C.A.'s new nine-story building opened for guided tours.

In May 1984 the Seattle Young Women's Christian Association celebrated its 90th year with the publishing of a pictorial history titled *Seattle Women: A Legacy of Community Development.*[1]

courtesy, Young Women's Christian Association

36 Denny Hall

On a bright Fourth of July 1894, a crowd of one thousand, protected under sun bonnets, bumbershoots, and tophats, gathered at the University of Washington's new campus for the ritual masonic cornerstone laying of the site's first permanent structure—Denny Hall. Combining provincial pride with the day's patriotism, the celebrants came by wagon, electric trolley, and special excursion train to listen to 13 speeches. They were also treated to a rendering of the Star Spangled Banner by Mrs. Fanni Ferguson of neighboring Latona. The Post-Intelligencer reported that she sang "in such sweet tones and such warmth of feeling as surrounded the patriotic fervor fitting to the day."

Within a year this cornerstone was extended into the four floors of Enumclaw sandstone, pressed brick, and terra cotta details rising like a French chateau above the bushes in our historical photograph. By September 1895 its 35 rooms and 20,000 feet of floor space were opened to a total student body of little more than 200.

At first called the Administration Building, the hall housed all six of the university's colleges in six laboratories, 10 classrooms, a library with 60 chairs, a museum, faculty rooms, professors' studies, a music room, student lounge (although the best lounging was done on the front steps) and a 700-seat lecture hall named Denny. This "Denny," of course, was the Arthur Armstrong Denny who was commonly called both "the father of the University" and "the father of Seattle." During the July ceremony, Denny gave his speech after the governor and the mayor.

Confirming his taciturn reputation, Denny began his speech reluctantly. "Were I to consult my own feelings I certainly would say nothing on this occasion;" but then in "deference to the wishes of the regents," he read a prepared text dryly detailing the Ter-

ritorial University's early history. However, in the decorum of that moment, Denny did not say one complaining word of how the territorial legislature, through the school's first forty years, had consistently faltered in supporting it. The combined provincial and patriotic elation of this occasion promised something better and for a time dissipated old resentments.

Arthur Denny's short address was then followed by 10 more. Enough of these were overwrought and, no doubt, many of the 1,000 celebrants were happy that they'd packed a picnic lunch.

It might have been a picnic that brought Carrie Coe, her camera and family to this site (possibly in 1895) to admire the new building and photograph it. The Coes were friends of both education—Coe School on Queen Anne Hill is named after Carrie's husband Dr. Frantz Coe—and the Denny family.[1]

On May 20, 1861 the cornerstone to Arthur

Denny's original Territorial University was laid. Inside it were a Bible and the Constitution. In 1894 this stone was extracted from its original site and, with Arthur Denny, put on the program for the July 4th celebration. Denny introduced it in the concluding line of his brief speech. "That stone with its contents, we today transfer to this new site to be here deposited, and here may it remain for all time only to be disturbed by some convulsion of nature."

In 1910 the Administration Building was officially renamed Denny Hall. Now 90 years after Arthur Denny's dedication no "convulsion of nature" has toppled it. Only once was its existence threatened. In 1954 one regent complained that "Denny's belfry stuck up like a sore thumb above the modern campus" and suggested the entire hall be razed. Happily, that was one modern urge which did not prevail.[2]

courtesy, Historical Photography Collection, University of Washington

37 Denny's Bell

You'll need a guide with special keys, two ladders, a catwalk, and trapdoor to reach the belfry of the University of Washington's Denny Hall. But the shaky climb reaches to a tree top panorama of the city. It also puts you face to face with Denny's Bell.

The bell was put here in 1895, the year Denny Hall was completed as the first building on the new campus. Denny's Bell was noted for the "quality and power of its tone," and with northerly winds it could be heard as far south as Renton.

In its original home on Denny's knoll, it rang through 34 years of classes, and signalled many other local excitements from fires to the Fourth of July, from its first belfry atop the Territorial University. But the first time it rang, in 1861, was from the vicinity of the Kingdome.

Strapped to a forward deck, Denny's Bell survived the hazardous voyage around Cape Horn, only to reach Elliott Bay in a dense fog. Here, its carrier, the bark Brontes, missed Yesler's wharf and ran aground on the tideflats south of King Street. Although temporarily stuck in the sand, lost in the fog, and out of sight of Seattle, the captain could still call to it. He used the bell's first penetrating clangs to get the town's attention, and was rescued.[1]

From the belltower atop Denny Hall practically everything has changed except the basic topography. The nearly vacant foreground of 1895 is now crowded with a budding landscape that reaches as high as the chimneys, now capped. The clearcut hills and peninsulas which overlap into the distance are now thoroughly dappled with trees, houses, and towers.

On the left of both panoramas and across Portage Bay is the north end of Capitol Hill. In the historical photograph, it is joined on the right by the Latona Bridge to the sparcely settled neighborhoods of Wallingford, Latona, and Brooklyn, now the University District. Seattle annexed these communities in 1891. The Latona Bridge, completed in 1892, was slightly west of the present University Bridge. It extended David Denny's electric trolley into a region all expected would soon be booming with a land rush. But the line reached its Ravenna terminus in 1893, just in time for the International Crash. The boom went bust and Arthur Denny's younger brother went bankrupt.[2]

But the new "Great State of Washington" went ahead with moving its university and its "destiny to build the necessary symbols of statehood." With the help of the depression it could build the older Denny's namesake hall well under its $150,000 budget.

Above the Latona Bridge is the southern point of Wallingford, now Gas Works Park. (In the contemporary photograph this is obscured by the Freeway Bridge.) Beyond that the long ridge of Queen Anne Hill extends to the left and then beyond and behind it rises the West Seattle peninsula. Vashon Island can be faintly seen in the cradle between them.

Denny's Bell rang the class hours until 1912 when the Blethen Chimes, a gift from the Times publisher, took up the tolling from a converted water tower. The old bell was reserved for ceremonial use.

When the Blethen Chimes burned to the ground in 1949, the Times reminded its readers that "the ancient bell is still in its graceful belfry and once a year only, with the gallantry of an old maestro, it sings out on homecoming day to reawaken slumbering traditions. On this day for many years Professor Meany pulled the rope."

Now that Meany is not around to pull for these traditions, Denny's Bell has been chained, and in its place four loudspeakers broadcast bell-like sounds on the hour. Like the old bell claps these taped sounds cross Portage Bay and bounce against Capitol Hill. They are even heard in Wallingford across the white noise of the freeway when there isn't any rush hour roar. They do not, however, reach Renton.

Below, the Princess Marguerite passing beneath the Freeway bridge, at site of old Latona bridge, above.

38 The 1882 View from Beacon Hill

Early in this century Thomas Prosch assembled and captioned three albums now preserved in the University of Washington's Historical Photography Collection. The Prosch collection is a reliable source for identifying the earliest pictorial record of Seattle.

Prosch's caption for today's panorama from Beacon Hill reads: "Seattle in 1882 from Dearborn Street and Twelfth Avenue South looking Northwest. Among the buildings are Stetson and Post Sawmill, Gas Works, County Courthouse, Catholic, Episcopal, and Methodist churches, Squire's Opera House, Post Building, and Yesler's Mill Co."

None of the buildings Prosch names are any of those homes in the foreground that sparsely inhabit the western slope of Beacon Hill. Nor has he descriptively located or cross-referenced with numbers his buildings. But in the early century many of Prosch's readers were still familiar with the churches, sawmills, and public buildings of 1882. It was then only 30 some years since the photograph was taken, and the fire of 1889, which destroyed almost everything in the heart of

Avenue and Jefferson Street and was the only major structure on Third Avenue destroyed by the 1889 fire. *(See feature 22.)*

To the right of Trinity Church is the county courthouse Prosch mentioned. Also new in 1882 this large white boxish structure with seven windows showing is at the corner of Third Avenue and Jefferson Street. Unlike the church, the courthouse survived the fire as jurors and witnesses reluctantly adjourned from a murder trial to spread wet blankets across the roof. In 1891 it became Seattle's city hall. *(See feature 23.)*

The slender pointed spire of the Methodist Church is just to the left of the courthouse. When it was first built in 1855 at Second Avenue and Columbia Street it was the town's first church. *(See feature 7.)*

Squire's Opera House is the dominant dark structure near the center of the photograph. Its location was on the east side of Commercial Street, the present First Avenue S., between Washington and Main Streets. In 1882 it was still the largest auditorium in town; however, its grandest night was already two years past. On October 11, 1880, President Rutherford B. Hayes spent a gregarious evening at an opera house reception shaking two thousand hands. *(See feature 8.)* Prosch recalls in another place, that "the town was brilliantly lit by bonfires...and thousands of candles in windows." However, in places it was somewhat obscured, for in 1880 the crown of Beacon Hill was still covered by virgin timber. *(See feature 11.)* By 1882 the hill's top had been clearcut; then the nightime panorama of the city showed the glow of some of the 30 gas lamps that sparsely lined the city's streets. (The gas company building can be seen in the crook of the bay.)

1882 was a boom year. In the November election, 1,274 votes were cast, the most in the territory and for the first time 60 more than in Walla Walla. New buildings with stone and iron facades were being planned, many of them modeled after the Post Building at Yesler and Post Street. Although Prosch lists it in his caption, the best view of both the Post Building and Prosch himself is in the smaller historical photograph printed here.[2] Prosch is the bearded figure standing at the base of the steps. In 1882 he was editor and part owner of the Post-Intelligencer, which had been formed the year before from a merging of his Daily Intelligencer with the Daily Post.

Prosch died on March 30, 1915 in an automobile wreck while crossing the Duwamish at Allentown. He was returning from a meeting of the Tacoma Historical Society.

this panorama, was still a vivid memory for even relative newcomers.

However, in 1984, more than a century since the photographer took his view from Beacon Hill, Prosch's captioned list of landmarks are as unfamiliar as the photographic scene that includes them. A century has eradicated the past as viewed from Beacon Hill in 1882, except for this panorama and the steady presence of the Magnolia peninsula in both the "now and then."

Identifying the buildings Prosch names will require of the reader a careful hide-and-seek. (For readers who want it, a drawn outline of this panorama that identifies the primary landmarks is included in the notes.)[1] The easiest to locate is the Stetson and Post sawmill. It is the daring intrusion onto the tideflats at the far left. Built at the present location of First Avenue S. between King and Weller Streets, in 1882 it was brand new. Dur-

ing the next year its crew of 117 men cut some 14 million feet of lumber.

The second accessible landmark is the Catholic Church, Our Lady of Good Help. *(See feature 30.)* It is the large white and most evidently church-like gothic structure on the right. Like the mill, it also was brand new in 1882 and replaced Father Prefontaine's first church at the same northeast corner of Third Avenue and Washington Street. The new church also came with a new pipe organ, the second in town.

The first pipe organ was installed in Trinity Episcopal Church in July of the same year. Visiting organist Samuel Gilbert, advertised as "formerly of Grace Church, New York," inaugurated it with a well-attended grand organ opening. Trinity Church is the white structure just to the right and a little above Our Lady of Good Help. Dedicated in 1871, it stood at the northwest corner of Third

Peterson Bros.
Photographers
Seattle W.T.

courtesy, Seattle Engineering Dept.

39 Pike Street Coal Bunkers

In 1876 an ambitious cataloger named B.L. Northup published the first Seattle city directory. Northup's census indicated that in the quarter century since its first settlement Seattle had grown to include 1,013 buildings and 3,700 residents.

Two of these were Norwegian immigrant brothers, Henry and Louis Peterson, who arrived that year to open a photographic studio on the second floor of the Intelligencer Building. Both the daily paper and the brothers were listed as on Front (now First Avenue) at the head (now the foot) of Cherry.[1]

The Peterson Brothers are remembered for a number of exceptional photographs they took of Seattle in the late 1870s. This scene of Elliott Bay is one of them and is typical both for its panoramic sweep and its clarity. It probably was taken from or very near the back porch of the Petersons' studio at the "head" of Cherry Street.

On the far right is the back shed addition to Schmieg's Brewery near Columbia Street. The framework in the immediate foreground (on which the Petersons have inscribed their name) is part of the ways of William Ham-

mond's shipyard, which was between Cherry and Columbia Streets.

Since any ideal view of Elliott Bay will include the Olympic Mountains, here they have been lightly retouched onto the scene's horizon in the original glass negative, which, very remarkably, still survives. In its own and familiar form, Magnolia Bluff enters from the right into the upper center of the photograph. Stranger is the forest on the far right which covers the western slope of Denny Hill.

The Peterson Brothers opened their studio in June 1876. This view was most certainly taken sometime between then and the following June 11, 1877. For, as the Olympia weekly newspaper, the Washington Standard, reported, on that "Sunday morning at about half past 8 o'clock, a remarkable mishap occurred at Seattle—the falling of the coal bunkers of the Seattle Coal and Transportation Co."

Those coal bunkers are the dark rectangular form seen behind the sidewheeler docked at the end of the Pike Street wharf (at the present location of the Seattle Aquarium.) In October 1875 this wharf was

improved to the grand dimensions we see in the Peterson Brothers' record. It was 70-feet high and more than 200 feet long, and expedited what throughout the middle and late 1870s was Seattle's principal industry, coal.

The Pike Street bunkers were the Elliott Bay end of a long and difficult trip which began at Coal Creek on the eastern side of Lake Washington and continued by steamer up the lake to Montlake, across the isthmus to Lake Union, down that lake to a narrow-gauge railroad that ran up the line of the present Westlake Boulevard and Pike Street, to finally terminate after 17 miles at the bunkers. The trip, although clumsy and expensive, was worth it.

The Seattle Coal & Transportation Co., incorporated in 1871, was the first fat infusion of outside capital into the labor-and-land-rich but cash-poor local economy. By 1875 the San Francisco owners were regularly running seven ships betwen their Pike Street wharf and coal-hungry California. The Seattle economy, which survived its first years in the early 1850s supplying pilings and rough lumber for a San Francisco that was then regularly burning down, was in the 1870s keeping the Bay area's fires burning with high-grade Seattle coal. In 1875, the Central Pacific Railroad alone contracted for 6,000 tons a month of the "black diamonds" out of the Newcastle mines.

Only ten minutes before those bunkers at the end of the pier collapsed, a coal car derailed on the steep incline (seen in the forest on the far right of the photograph) which followed the line where today the Pike Street Hill Climb ascends to the Public Market. Since the laborers all ganged up to right the spilled gondola, several men were saved from going down with the 3,000 tons of coal that dropped into the bay when the bunkers caved in. The loss to the company was reported at about $26,000 in coal and $10,000 in damage to the wharf. The company could afford it. The next day, Monday, June 12, 1877, its local representatives signed a contract with the Seattle & Walla Walla Railroad, which had just completed its narrow-gauge line to Renton, to extend that road another 6½ miles to Newcastle.

On January 29, 1878, the last coal car awkwardly unloaded its extraction into the company ships tied to the only partly patched up Pike Street wharf. One week later, February 5, the first coal-filled cars pulled out of Newcastle on their new route around the south end of Lake Washington, over the tideflats south of town and onto the Seattle & Walla Walla's new and improved King Street wharfs.

The Pike Street wharf was abandoned to the tides' corrosion and the insatiable appetites of the wood-eating teredos that had infested its pilings and would reduce them within three years to a line of stubby timbers barely visible at high tide.[2]

The Peterson Brothers' panorama is one of the few photographic records of that quickly vanishing Pike Street wharf. Their view also includes the best evidence of one of the more photographically familiar figures in the city's history, the Winward: the mastless ship anchored on the left in the midst of Yesler's logs.

In December 1875, the year the bunkers were built, the Winward ran aground in Useless Bay off Whidbey Island. James Colman, the man who eventually completed the Seattle & Walla Walla Railroad to Renton and Newcastle, purchased the wreck, towed, and anchored it offshore from his property at the foot of Marion Street, just west of the present site of his namesake Colman Building on First Avenue.

Today Colman's Winward is still "anchored" behind the Colman Building, but it no longer sways with the tides. It was covered

The Pike Street coal wharf after the bunkers had collapsed.

intact during the late 1880s filling-in of Railroad Avenue. Now it permanently jaywalks below Western Avenue between Marion and Columbia Streets. That is just below the center of our contemporary view which was photographed from the fifth floor of a parking garage on First Avenue, just north of the foot of Cherry Street.

A detail of the Pike Street coal bunkers.

40 Up Coal Creek

The civilized cover of lath and plaster was first applied to Seattle's walls in 1863. That year Doc Maynard returned from his futile farming at Alki Point to open, with his wife and nurse Catherine, Seattle's first hospital. That year also, the University of Washington officially opened; the city's first newspaper the Seattle Gazette began publishing; John Suffran opened his iron works; and Lyman Andrews stumbled into town carrying a sack of coal on his back.

Andrews first tripped over his exposed coal on a claim at Squak—today's Issaquah. Now he was rushing his sample to Suffran's foundry for a testing. It came to fire quickly and "burned exceedingly hot." It was "pronounced a superior article for almost any use or purpose." Immediately Andrews made plans to exploit his discovery by extracting and exporting it.

What Lyman Andrews did not discover, but soon would know, was that his coal field also ran west under the hills that separated him from Lake Washington. There, later in

that year, Edwin Richardson came upon those same seams as they resurfaced only three miles up a creek from the lakeshore. Today those hills are called Cougar Mountain, the stream, Coal Creek, and the coal site, Newcastle. Andrews' claim on the far side of the mountain was eclipsed for almost a quarter century by Richardson's claim, which, closer to ship and shore, was mined for a hundred years.

Now not all of the miners are departed from Newcastle. Milton Swanson still lives along Coal Creek and always has. "Some people," he said, "are like a rock with a flat side, they just stay there." In the "now," Milton Swanson stands only a stone's throw from the place of his birth. But the old home is gone, as is the entire town of Newcastle. Covering its place are slag heaps overgrown with alders.

In the historical scene, taken from very near the same location as the "now," we see Newcastle in its prime, as it was a century ago. It was to this community at that time

that Swanson's French Canadian grandfather Marcel Fournier migrated to work as a miner and raise a family.

Newcastle was first settled in the late 1860s by a pair of entrepreneurial protestant pastors, George Whitworth and Clarence Bagley. Overwhelmed by the expensive task of getting their coal to ships in Seattle, they soon sold out to a brawny group of San Francisco speculators. By 1872 California capital was financing the transport of Newcastle coal across Lake Washington and Lake Union on steamer-pulled scows, and along three narrow gauged tracks. This clumsy roundtrip required 10 handlings of the cars, and was abandoned in 1878, the year the Seattle and

Walla Walla Railroad's new all rail route was completed around the south end of Lake Washington to the new King Street coal wharfs. This was the system—mines, company town, railroad, and wharfs that Henry Villard's Oregon Improvement Co. bought in 1880, and for whom Marcel Fournier worked until 1894.

That year Milton Swanson's grandfather was killed in a cave-in. During his short and dangerous stay in the booming Newcastle, Fournier had lived through the mob expulsion of Chinese miners in 1885, the violent strikes of 1888 and 1891, which the company broke by importing black miners, and the financial crash of 1893. Fournier did not live

to witness another disaster —the 1894 burning, flooding, and abandonment of the main shaft.

In 1895 the Oregon Improvement Co. sold out to the Pacific Coal Co., which continued operating the mines until 1930 when a combination of petering resources, burning bunkers, competing oil, and a national depression closed the operation. The mining, however, was carried on by smaller independent truck miners like Baima and Rubattino. Milton Swanson worked 17 years for them.

Today Cougar Mountain is honeycombed by abandoned mineshafts and crossed by a network of nature trails which soon may be part of the Cougar Mountain Regional

Wildland Park.

Milton Swanson has both worked under this mountain and hiked over it. Now as president of the Newcastle Historical Society and as a strong supporter of the Wildland Park, Swanson invites you to enjoy the mountain's paths but also to watch out for its holes.

courtesy, William Mix

41 The Seattle Lake Shore and Eastern

On January 7, 1887 the Seattle City Council gave away a right-of-way 30 feet wide to the Seattle Lake Shore and Eastern Railroad. That marked the beginning of a waterfront that now pushes 500 man-made feet out beyond the original high tideline. In 1887 Elliott Bay still lapped at the timber cribbing that supported First Avenue.

For years this built land was called Railroad Avenue, and by 1900 there were sixteen rails along the waterfront—a switchman's nightmare. In the historical photograph we see its start: the 16,640-foot pile trestle to Smith Cove, which the local contractors Surber and Egan began building in the winter of 1887.

The view is to the north from near Seneca Street. The trestle makes its graceful turn near Union Street, where the waterfront still bends today. About three blocks behind the photographer was the railroad's first depot at Columbia Street. *(See feature 46.)*

The Seattle Lake Shore and Eastern—the S.L.S.&E. for short—was incorporated by names still connected to local landmarks: T.T. Minor (of the school); John Leary (of the Way); David Denny and George Kinnear (of the parks); and most actively by Thomas Burke and Daniel Gilman (of the bicycle trail that follows the line of the old S.L.S.&E. rail bed). Using eastern capital and English rails—the first shipful left Worthing on the English Channel in February—the company worked hard and fast and managed to give a couple hundred pioneers a Thanksgiving Day excursion ride over British steel all the way to Bothell.

The grand purpose of this railroad was, like its predecessor—the Seattle and Walla Walla Railroad of a decade earlier—to give Seattle its own direct transcontinental connection. Now the company lavishly advertised that it would make not one but two such connections: one of them east to Spokane Falls across "Seattle's own" Snoqualmie Pass and the other north for an international meeting with Canada's transcontinental, the Canadian Pacific.

These were the stated goals, but the target was Tacoma—the company town of that old irritant the Northern Pacific Railroad, which for 14 years had been trying to run Seattle off of Puget Sound by not regularly running its trains to it.

In the year 1887, free local mail delivery also was established; the 22-year-old performance center, Yesler Hall, was closed; Ballard was platted; one of the city's original settlers, William Bell, died at the age of 70; and Seattle's first building of pressed brick was constructed.

That brick building was not part of Bell's namesake Belltown: the frontier community in the upper right of the photograph, clinging to the western slope of Denny Hill. In 1887 this was North Seattle. The home with the tower was the residence and office of Dr. O.G. Root who said he put his practice there as a lighthouse of hope to the sick and suffering. Some of his patients complained that they suffered the more for having to climb the hill to get the medicine. The doctor's home was near the southeast corner of First and Lenora, and about 40 feet higher than that prominence has been since First Avenue north of Pine Street was regraded in 1899.[1]

In 1888 the Polk Directory estimated Seattle's population at 20,390; Tacoma's 13,355; Olympia's 2,408; and Port Townsend's 2,040. Despite the efforts of the Tacoma Land Company, Seattle was still the largest town in the territory and growing. Each week an average of 150 new residents moved in, and a few of them went on the S.L.S.&E.'s waterfront trestle to the new town of Ballard. The round trip suburban fair, begun in August of 1888, was a quarter.[2]

That year the S.L.S.&E. added 100 more miles to its line, reaching Snohomish to the north and Fall City to the east. Ultimately, it did connect with the Canadian Pacific near Sumas, but the Snoqualmie road to Spokane Falls never even made it to the pass. It didn't need to, for the Great Northern was soon coming the other way.[3]

However, the local excitement created by the building of Seattle's own railroad did finally reach Tacoma, with the desired effect that the Northern Pacific surrendered and soon began regular service to Seattle at Tacoma rates. Within a few more years the Northern Pacific also bought up the S.L.S.&E.

The Great Fire of 1889 wiped out the waterfront and this trestle as far north as near that curve at Union Street. Then the really serious pile-driving and land-filling began.

The "now" view of trolley tracks—what is left of the rails on Railroad Avenue—was actually photographed a little further "out to sea" than the scene of the old trestle. The line of the S.L.S.&E. was somewhat closer to today's Western Avenue.

courtesy, Michael Maslan

42 The Ravenna Neighborhood

Shortly after the Burke-Gilman Trail leaves the University of Washington campus and passes north below the 45th Street viaduct, it begins a gentle but steady curving to the east between the Ravenna neighborhood on the north and University Village on the south. Although this trail for cyclists and joggers can be vaguely seen in the center of the contemporary photograph, its origin as a railroad bed is very evident in the historical panorama. Both views look northeast from Ravenna Avenue near N.E. 50th Street.

The Seattle Lake Shore and Eastern Railroad (S.L.S.&E.) was first organized in 1885 by Judge Thomas Burke and entrepreneur Daniel Gilman (hence the trail) and a few eastern capitalists (hence the rails). It was intended to go north around Lake Washington and then east over "Seattle's own Snoqualmie Pass" to Spokane and a promoted hook-up with the transcontinental Union Pacific Railroad. By 1887 it got as far as Union Bay, where you see it here.

One of the S.L.S.&E.'s most pleased passengers was the local Reverend W.W. Beck, who besides his spiritual offerings, advertised himself as a "wholesale dealer in gold, silver, iron, coal, timber, granite, plat-ting properties, garden and fruit proper ties, stocks of all kinds, parks, and townsites." It was the last two, "parks and townsites," that the energetic Presbyterian pastor was thinking about in 1887 when he stepped off at the railroad's Union Bay Station—the white structure just right of center.

William Beck bought 300 acres and cleared much of it to stumps for his townsite; but 60 lush acres he kept and protected as a park. He named them both Ravenna. Beck's lightly settled Ravenna town runs through the center of the old panorama. The southeastern end of his park is evident on the far left. (Feature 69 treats Ravenna Park.) The photograph was taken some time in the early 1890s. The park was still furnished with a virgin forest of giant cedars and firs and would be until 1911 when Beck sold his park to the city.

By Thanksgiving 1887 the railroad reached Bothell, 20 miles out. Thomas Prosch, in his chronological history of Seattle, told how "all along the line the road's construction caused a tremendous stir . . . logging camps, mills, mines, and towns sprang into existence as if by magic." It fed not only mill workers but their families to the new towns of Ballard, Ross, Fremont, Latona, Brooklyn (now the University District), and Henry Yesler's namesake milltown on Union Bay, Yesler, now part of Laurelhurst. In 1888 Gilman's railroad reached the coal mines of Gilman (now Issaquah), and on July 4, 1889 the first of many packed and popular excursion trains left the Seattle waterfront for Snoqualmie Falls.

So W.W. Beck had the right idea: start a town by the railroad only 3½ miles from the city's center, promote an industry like the flour mill on the right of the panorama, preserve a park for communing with nature, and start a finishing school for girls.

The Seattle Female College is the churchly structure upper center in the panorama and is seen close up in the other historical view. "Business Manager" Beck's advertisement in the 1890 Polk City Directory asserted: "The school will be select, not reformatory. . . Parents and guardians desirous of securing the best advantages for their daughters and wards should correspond with the principal." The "townsiter" Beck confidently concluded that "this institution is located at Ravenna Park, as charming a suburb as any city ever had."

Five years later, in 1895, "President" Beck claimed in another Polk directory advertisement that his school was "the safest and best

place on the coast to educate your daughter...The school, non-sectarian but distinctly Christian, is located on the border of Ravenna Park, one of the most beautiful places on the American continent." 1895 was also the school's last year. Probably the lingering effect of the 1893 economic crash, the arrival in 1895 of the University of Washington onto its new and present campus nearby, and the failure of Beck's township to develop into anything like Ballard, Freemont, or Latona combined to force its closure. Seven years later, on April 1, 1902, an adventurous Burley family left their farm near Fullerton, Nebraska and headed west in a wagon. They reached Ravenna in the fall and rented the then vacant Female College for a temporary winter home. They kept their horses in the barn which, in the photograph, can be seen just above the passenger station.

In 1902 Leon Burley was ten years old. Now, more than three quarters of a century later, his "reading" of this Ravenna panorama is filled with loving memories. He played in the abandoned flour mill, fished for suckers and trout in Ravenna Creek which transects this view, delivered supplies by wheelbarrow to Roper's Grocery on 24th Street, the storefront just left of the tree trunk, and with Beck's boys explored their parents' park.

Burley also remembers attending in 1912 or 13 a youth Christian Endeavor meeting at the old Female College and hearing his future fiancee, Marie Phillips, and her friend, Fay Bayley, sing in duet "Saved by Grace." The meeting was interrupted by fire, and that night Reverend Beck's old school, saved by nothing, burned down.

Marie Phillips lived in the home which can be faintly seen half-way between the college and the left border of the photograph. It is still there and is the home of Marie's sister Constance Palmerlee, who is writing a history of the Ravenna neighborhood.

In our "now" view, the Palmerlee home, which was built in 1890, is hidden behind trees. Actually, those trees, that old house, and much else in the Ravenna neighborhood might have been filled with the R.H. Thomson Expressway had not Constance Palmerlee and many other neighborhood activists in the Ravenna Community Association victoriously fought the freeway fight of the 1960s.[1]

courtesy, Historical Photography Collection, University of Washington

43 'Magnificent Stupendous Snoqualmie Falls'

In 1855 the region's only newspaper was the weekly Pioneer Democrat, published in Olympia but read up and down the Sound. Under the headline, "Pleasure Excursion," the July 27 issue playfully reported:

"On Tuesday morning last a large party of ladies and gentlemen of Olympia took a departure in a first class canoe with the intention of paying a visit to the magnificent, stupendous Snoqualmie Falls. The party had a gay and propitious departure, but we fear the return of the voyagers before they have feasted their eyes on the grand and magnificent scenery of the spectacle of the falls of Snoqualmie."

A little less than one month later (or about the time one must now allow to reserve a table for breakfast at the Snoqualmie Falls Lodge), the Pioneer Democrat again reported "that pleasure party did not back out as we predicted. They bore the heat of many days and actually went to the falls. Last week they returned looking much improved in health."

Then the writer, perhaps wishing to transport his readers directly to the falls without the aid of a "first class canoe," continued:

"No falls are so high, there is no natural curiosity more lovely, more beautiful and more sublime in the United States. The Mammoth Cave is a wonder, the Natural Bridge, a prodigy, and Niagra Falls, a great natural curiosity, but Snoqualmie Falls surpasses them all.... Let anyone who doubts this, visit these falls and they will agree with us."

Most likely, the writer himself had never been there, for it required more muscle than poetic license to paddle and pole oneself up two rivers to get to the falls. But since the roar of reports of those few who had made it there before 1855 was some times as loud as the falls, the Pioneer Democrat felt safe in making its booming challenge.

Now for nearly 130 years nature lovers have been making it to the brink of the 270-foot falls for awe-inspired gazing and feeling the spray. They will also often eat breakfast, take snapshots, and, a little less than once a year, one of them will fall over the edge.

Natives, of course, already had been visiting the falls for centuries when in 1848 a few guides first led a surveyor named Washington Hall, and then two years later a second white adventurer named Samuel Hancock up the Snohomish and Snoqualmie Rivers to the falls. Hancock set up camp near the base of the cascades, and later recalled that "it was impossible to sleep soundly, the roar was deafening."

The next day, as he was preparing to leave, his "attention was attracted by the Indians to a rainbow that had just made its appearance about midway of the cataract, formed by the rising sun upon the water. It was one of the most beautiful sights I have ever beheld."

Hancock reported that the falls were "two trees high." Two years later, in 1852, one year after Seattle was settled, James Swan and

Floyd Jones took positions above the falls and ran a thread between them. They "found them to be 260 feet high, perpendicular." Swan's reminiscence concluded, "they were truly grand."

In 1889, the year the Seattle Lake Shore and Eastern Railroad first reached the falls, travel time from Seattle was reduced from a circuitous two days down the Sound and up the rivers by light-draft steamers, to an easy two-hour railroad trip directly from Seattle's waterfront. Now "one of the rare wonders of the West" was open for Sunday family excursions and bulky view cameras as well. (The first photograph of the falls was taken in 1866 by Seattle's first resident photographer. Sammis photo graphed the falls in his studio from a sketch. *See feature 7.*)

In 1890 the Northern Pacific photographer F. Jay Haynes took an unconventional picture of the brink of the falls. About ten years later, Seattle photographer A.C. Warner posed his family a few precarious feet from the edge of the opposite southern side of the gorge. Looking a little anxious and very vulnerable, Mrs. Warner restrains their youngest daughter, Alice.

The Warner photograph shows the Snoqualmie Falls Power Company plant upstream which first delivered current to Seattle on July 3, 1899. However, the Warner view does not show "Seattle Rock," the building-size boulder seen in part on the left of Haynes view. Despite protests from turn-of-the-century conservationists, the power company blasted the basalt boulder away, apparently to make easier the construction of their low level dam behind the falls.

"Seattle Rock" got its name from a story of how Chief Seattle invited a party of bellicose natives from east of Snoqualmie Pass to a peacemaking potlatch. However, instead of the traditional gifts, Seattle gave his guests, who were unfamiliar with the river, a ride over the falls. As planned, he jumped to the rock in time to save himself.

In this Harper's Weekly sketch of the falls, Seattle Rock is still intact.

There is neither any indication of how he got off the rock, nor any likelihood that the story is true. The remnant of his rock can be seen in the center of the "now" photograph.[1]

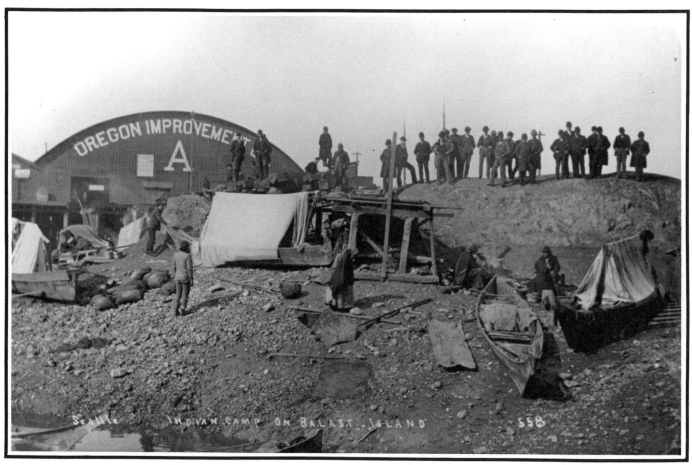

44 Ballast Island

On January 5, 1865 the Washington Territorial Legislature granted Seattle its first incorporation,[1] and the small town of about 3,000 residents responded by quickly electing a board of trustees. Then this council answered their citizens' urge for municipal order by giving them twelve laws.

The first was for taxation. There followed ordinances for promoting the public peace by prohibiting drunks, restraining swine, and setting a speed limit against reckless horse racing on the city's stumpy streets. However, the fifth ordinance was not so well-disposed.

Titled "The Removal of Indians," it read in part: "Be it ordained that no Indian or Indians shall be permitted to reside or locate their residence on any street, highway, lane, or alley or any vacant lot in the town of Seattle." For the Indians' hospitality and help in teaching the settlers the ancient techniques of nurturing the abundant life on Puget Sound, they were given reservations, smallpox, alcohol, blankets, a kind of Christian education for their segregated young, and the

"security" of the white man's laws.

In Seattle in 1865 this included that ordinance to keep them out of town.[2] Actually, the citizens both wanted the natives out of town and in it, and often both at the same time. For many years a kind of solution for this ambivalence was a rocky man-made peninsula called Ballast Island. Near the foot of Washington Street the natives set up camp in their canvas and mat-covered dugout canoes and bartered the price of clams and curios with customers and curious Indian-watchers. From here they also ventured into town to sell baskets and other artifacts on the street corners and meet employers offering odd jobs.

Ironically, this new native home was made from the hills of Australia, the Sandwich Islands (Hawaii), and in largest bulk, San Francisco. Ballast was the stabilizing dead weight junk of rocks and rubble that the many masted ships carried here and simply dumped in the bay. They then filled their empty holds with coal or lumber.

Sometime in the 1870s the captains were persuaded to unload this ballast in one place: along the southern side of the short wharf at the foot of Washington Street. The site was a good one for it was in between the city's two busiest piers, Yesler's wharf and the Oregon Improvement Company's King Street coal bunkers.[3]

Our historical scene of "Ballast Island" was photographed by Arthur Warner-sometime in the early 1890s. After the 1889 fire destroyed the entire waterfront south of Union Street, property owners usually rebuilt three or four times grander than before the destruction.

The Oregon Improvement Company filled the waterfront between its coal docks off King Street and Yesler's wharf with two large pier sheds it designated simply, "A" and "B." The area between these sheds and the business district along First Avenue S. was, as our picture reveals, neither entirely filled nor covered. Thus up until the mid-90s, it was still possible for native dugouts to make their way between the Oregon piers and up under the overhead quay to their Ballast Island.

During the winter of 1891 the Oregon Im-

The post-fire view north from the King Street coal wharf past docks A and B.

provement Company seeking to improve itself pressured local officials to remove the "some 40 clam-selling, garbage-raking remnants of a great people" who were then living on the island. The eviction was only temporary, for Ballast Island had its own necessities. This was especially true every fall when the island was the jumping-off spot for natives from as far north as upper British Columbia who gathered here to pick hops in the White and Snoqualmie River valleys.

In 1895 the Oregon Improvement Company went bankrupt and needed no longer worry about its image. By then the native encampment had also moved south toward Utah Avenue and Massachusetts Street. Then the ambiguous area between the waterfront and the wharves was at last filled in and Railroad Avenue was planked over Ballast Island.

courtesy, Dorothy Gibbert

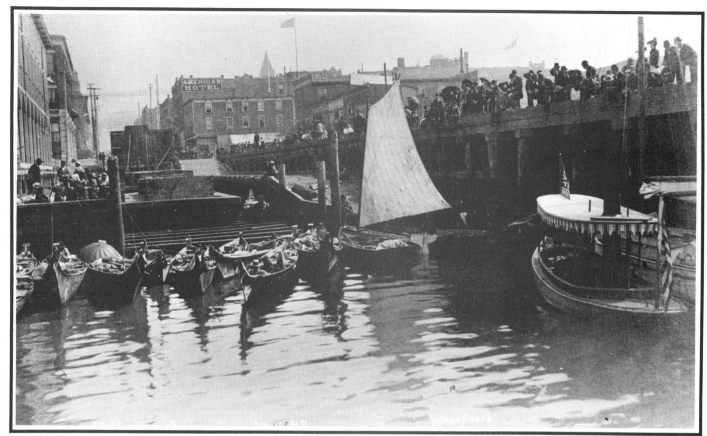

courtesy, Michael Maslan

45 Dugouts at the Foot of Washington Street

Today is Waterfront Day in Seattle. At Pier 55, the Virginia V will toot its steam whistle at one o'clock to begin the festivities, including row boat races, a parade of working boats offshore, and a casual procession of waterfront walkers on shore.

Many of the vessels in the slips between piers will be open for tours. And on the Virginia V, the last of Seattle's century-old Mosquito Fleet, there will be a photography exhibit of maritime Seattle. Today's historical photo is one in the show.

The view here looks east from the waterfront foot of Washington Street. The scene is from the early 1890s, but the occasion is not known. Why should the wooden quay on the right be topped with a row of gawkers? They are probably in line for that popular post-pioneer pastime, Indian watching.

Below them are a dozen dugout canoes. Behind them, and out of the picture to the other side of this pile trestle, is Ballast Island, then a frequent camping ground for natives on their way to hop picking in the fall or canoe races in the summer. (There are pro-

bably many more dugouts there and perhaps another line of sightseers.) Only on the left are the races mixing. Judging from the postures and the costumes (the natives are sitting and the "suits" are standing), it's possible that some bartering for curios or clams is transpiring there.

By the 1890s the native Americans were mass-producing the items of their ritual culture—masks, totems, baskets— for the consumption of the acquisitive whites. The Indians themselves often preferred the pro-

ducts of "civilized design and white manufacture" with one notable exception— the dugouts.

The enduring success of the cedar canoes was explained by Myron Eels, a missionary to the Puget Sound Natives. "The canoe is light, and one person often travels as fast in one with one paddle, as the white man does with two oars. He looks forward and sees where he is going...True, we think the boat is safer, but the Indian, accustomed to his canoe from infancy, meets with far less accidents than the white man."

Today at 2 p.m., folks will be racing backwards in rowboats with two oars here at the foot of Washington Street. There may be some accidents.[1]

TYPES OF SIWASH, OR PUGET SOUND INDIANS

The Basket Weaver   The Belles Pose for a Photograph
    Whaling Canoes: Large Buoys Used to Float the Dead Whale's Carcass   An Old Buck   An Indian Cemetery

A page from a turn-of-the-century Seattle tourbook.

courtesy, Tacoma Public Library

46 The Columbia Street Depot

Before it ever laid a mile of track, the Northern Pacific Railroad had to convince Congress to help it bring civilization to Puget Sound and the Pacific Northwest.

In its 1869 report to the Senate, the railroad used an ancient example: "No higher proof of the grandeur and wisdom of the Roman rule of the world need be sought than the wonderful system of arched roads that radiated from Rome." And the lesson, "in exact proportion to the abundance and excellence of highways are the communication of thought...the growth of comfort and the development and consolidation of the civilized state."

The government agreed and gave the railroad its own comfort with a land grant of 50 million acres. (This was an area just a bit smaller than the entire Washington Territory.) With this go-ahead, every primitive spot on Puget Sound stirred with commercial hope that it might be chosen as the railroad's end-of-the-line. In 1869 while the N.P. was surveying Snoqualmie Pass, a

building boom ensued in Seattle. Downtown lots jumped from $50 to $500 and one hotel changed its name to "The Western Terminus."

However, the proper model for a transcontinental's terminus was not a hotel but a Roman shrine. For a truly civilized citizen with a cultivated interest in the ceremony of train arrivals, it was not getting the railroad that was most important but having an unsparing station in which to wait upon real trains like the exotic Oriental Limited and the practical Puget Sound Express. But in 1869 the citizens of Seattle would have to wait a long and humble time for their classical temple in which to act out urbane railroad rituals.

In 1890 the Northern Pacific at last regularly unloaded here, but it did so at a little shack-like depot on the tidelands south of Pioneer Square. Two years later it moved into a second clapboard shed, the Columbia Street depot, seen on the right of the historical scene. And here it stayed until 1906 when it joined the Great Northern in the new

King Street Station. This was a modest copy of the Campanile in Venice's San Marco Square.[1]

This is another of F. Jay Haynes photographs which was recorded during the Northern Pacific photographer's visit here in the summer of 1890, or a year after the fire of 1889. Therefore, practically everything in this scene which looks east up Columbia Street is either brand new or still under construction.

For years Western Avenue was popularly called "Produce Row." Here on the photograph's left and to either side of that street are the warehouses of two of these wholesale grocers. In 1890 Western Avenue was still named West Street, and here through 1896 the namesake West Street House rented relatively cheap rooms above Produce Row.[2]

Just behind the hotel are the first two stories of the ornately arched Colman Building. It is the only structure in this scene which is still around; it was lavishly redone in 1904 into the seven still-standing elegant but archless floors.[3]

Above the Colman Building are the landmark towers of both the Methodist Episcopal Church at Third and Marion and the Central School at Sixth and Madison, and the unfinished brick bulk of the Haller Building at the northwest corner of Second and Columbia. Just to the right of the Haller is the southern wing of the wood-framed Rainier Hotel at Fifth Avenue. *(See feature 19.)*

The unfinished rear facade, right-center, with the ladder pointing to its top floor, is the post-fire home of Toklas and Singerman. This pioneer partnership was begun in 1874 and claimed a number of "local firsts" including: the city's first department store; the first store to have a telephone, in 1883; the first to use electric lighting, in 1886; and the first to run an illustrated ad, in 1887. *(See feature 8.)*

Next door is the City of Paris, a notions store. It gives a little class to the Northern Pacific's claim that from their dumpy depot one could buy "tickets to and from all parts of the world." In 1890, the time of our photograph, this depot still belonged to the Seattle Lake Shore and Eastern Railroad. However, in 1892 the S.L.S.&E. was purchased by the Northern Pacific, and the N.P. moved in. When the first transcontinental Great Northern arrived a year later in June of 1893, it unloaded at its own modest terminus only one block north at Marion Street.

Briefly, in 1899 this city thought it might at last have its depot-palace. Then the Northern Pacific proposed to fill up the waterfront with an 800-foot freight shed running from University Street to Madison Street and a $500,000 passenger depot arching the block south from Madison to Marion. The competing Great Northern's president, James J. Hill, warned that this cutting off of the city from its waterfront amounted to "commercial suicide."[4]

However, the crowning objection to these grand plans came from old Judge Orange Jacobs who complained, "in the future if I should desire to go to the waterfront to catch a tomcod I might be charged more for passing over private property than the fish would be worth." The city coucil agreed, and within a year the Great Northern and the Northern Pacific were sharing the little depot at Columbia Street and making plans to bore a tunnel under the city to the King Street depot, that Venetian temple on the tideflats where Amtrak still calls.

Haynes 1890 view south down Railroad Avenue from Madison Street.

courtesy, Bill Greer

47 'Longest Tunnel'

In the late spring of 1893 every Seattle school child knew two things very well—summer vacation was coming soon and so was the Great Northern.

Some of their parents had waited a quarter century for this "second coming" of a transcontinental railroad to Puget Sound. The first, of course, was the neglectful Northern Pacific which ten years earlier came only as far as Tacoma. But when the first Great Northern passenger train did arrive in June of '93, it was an imperfect and unbecoming coming, for there was no grand platform for the attendant inaugural pomp.

The actual end-of-the-line was a shabby little depot at the foot of Marion Street—a clapboard which might have set well in Odessa or Ephrata but not here at the terminus of the Puget Sound Express, "the shortest route to and from anywhere east of Fargo." Here in 1893 there was no marble stage for the always exciting railroading

drama of "getting there on time." Nor would there be for 13 years more.

The "empire builder" himself, James Jerome Hill, had an oft-quoted response for all these depot anxieties, that was as homely as the old station itself: "he is a wise farmer who develops his farm before he builds a palace on it." And for those who had been off the farm too long, the Great Northern's founder explained the moral. "It is more important to Seattle to have goods delivered to it cheaply than to have a fancy depot."

What J.J. Hill did want in 1893 was to move all his trains, freight, and passengers alike freely up and down the waterfront, and eventually to the sheds and side tracks he was planning to build out over the tideflats south of Jackson and King Streets.

So in April of 1893 Hill asked the city council for a franchise to do just that. One month later R.H. Thomson, the city engineer, advised the council to reject Hill's

request. The almost obvious reason was that such unconstrained train traffic would strangle the waterfront. Soon J.J. Hill, with Judge Thomas Burke the intermediary, met privately with Thomson and asked, "Do you know what we ought to do?"

The city engineer answered, "I believe I do...cut a tunnel under the city."

And the builder baron replied, "It will take considerable time but I will build as you want." And he did, ten years later.

By 1901 Hill was in control of both the Great Northern and the Northern Pacific. In May of 1903 the two railroads, splitting the cost, began to split the earth under Seattle beginning at the spot we see in both the "now" and "then"—the tunnel's north portal at Virginia Street.

When it was built it was the highest, 25.8 feet, and widest, 30 feet, tunnel in the world. The hole was bored from two ends, which when they met a year and a half later were off by only one-eighth inch at the ceiling and one-fourth at the walls. The entire tube was lined with concrete varying between 3½ and 4½ feet thick.

The 1,000 men who did the work cut

The York Hotel at First and Pike.

through the remains of a prehistoric forest under Fourth and Marion, were periodically flooded by fresh springs, and occasionally stalled by litigation from property owners overhead who felt and feared the boring below them.

The tunnel's deepest elevation is at Fourth and Spring, 110 feet beneath the street grade. There the passing trains still disturb the lower stacks of the city's public library.

The largest casualty of the excavation was the 12-year-old York Hotel at the northwest corner of First Avenue and Pike Street, (the building seen on the left horizon of the historical photograph.) It was razed in November of 1904 and partly replaced by the Pike Place street platting which shapes the contemporary market.[1]

On January 1, 1905 J. J. Hill began to build his marble palace at the southern end of the completed tunnel. The Union Depot opened in May 1906 without fanfare to a Burlington train which was 12 hours late. The train's last mile out of Kansas City was through the 5,141.5-foot long tunnel under Seattle, which the still-told local joke claims is "the longest in the world, running all the way from Virginia to Washington" (streets).[2]

The Tunnel's southern entrance.

courtesy, Washington State Historical Society

48 Smith: The Man and the Cove

Here is photograph number 6577 of the some 30,000 negatives included in the Asahel Curtis collection.

Asahel was the younger brother of the celebrated Edward Curtis whose romantic posed photographs of American natives will currently cost you hundreds of dollars each. However, number 6577 cost me only a little more than four dollars paid to the Washington Historical Society, and it is easily one of the most popular images in the history of local photography.

Asahel's photograph, actually, has its own variety of staged romance. Besides its pleasing composition, this scene resonates with a local industrial drama which in 1905, the year the younger Curtis recorded this view from Queen Anne Hill, was staged here on Smith's Cove.

In the foreground is the Oriental Limited rushing its passengers from St. Paul and all points west over the last few miles of trestle into Seattle. In a few months it will be trailing its white ribbon of steam under Seattle while passing through the Great Northern's new tunnel. And soon it will exhale its last transcontinental gasps alongside the new King Street Station, which in 1905 is still under construction. *(See features 46 and 47.)*

Beyond are the Great Northern docks and between them the largest steamers in the world, the railroad's Minnesota and Dakota. They are being prepared for their trans-Pacific routine of delivering raw cotton to the orient and returning with raw silk.

The director for this industrial drama was James Jerome Hill, the Great Northern's "empire builder." Years before, Hill discovered that "one acre of Washington timber will furnish as many carloads of freight as 120 years of wheat from a Dakota farm." So when the first Great Northern freight train rolled into Seattle in 1893, Hill was anxious to turn it right around and head east with carloads of lumber. This was actually a radical departure from the old notion that railroads to the West were built to carry people and cargo in that direction and then return east almost empty.

In 1905 J.J. Hill was moving his show onto the biggest stage. Acting like Atlas, Hill developed his double docks at Smith Cove to be the shoulders upon which the world would turn. Having moved the country around, Hill was here attempting to revolutionize international trade.

For 300 years most trade with the orient had passed India and Africa. Now with the encouragement of Great Northern steam on both land and sea, the empire builder taught some of it to follow the shorter great circle route past Alaska. Here the perishable silk was unloaded from the jumbo steamers Minnesota and Dakota and sent rushing east on trains that had priority over all other service including mail, passenger, and that mainstay, lumber.

In 1853 Dr. Henry A. Smith built a log cabin at his namesake cove. Smith's arrival was less mighty than the Minnesota's but he

stayed longer. For 63 years, Smith was easily one of the most remarkable characters on Puget Sound. Most of that time he spent at Smith Cove. Today he is best remembered as an ethnologist and linquist who translated Chief Seattle's prophetic treaty speech.

But Smith was also a surgeon who successfully used hypnotism as anesthesia, a psychotherapist who encouraged dream analysis for solving personal problems, a poet who published in Sunset Magazine under the pen name Paul Garland, a botanist who grafted the area's first fruit trees, and a universally-loved gentleman farmer of whom one of his seven daughters, Ione, wrote: "Papa had a passionate love for the beauties of nature, was kind to all the farm animals and they, in turn, seemed to understand and love him."

Smith was King County's first school superintendent and a very rare statesman who seemed to inspire absolutely no resentment. As a territorial legislator for several terms, he still "never sought office, never asked for a vote and was never defeated in an election."

When the 22-year-old Smith first arrived at Smith Cove, the highest tides filled potholes for sun-warmed swimming farther north than today's Galer Street. When he died here at his Interbay home in 1915 at the age of 85, it was from a chill caught while setting out tomato plants in his garden. At that time the tideflats of Smith Cove were being filled in by the cove's new owner, the Port of Seattle. The consequences were the half-mile long piers 90 and 91 which were the longest earth-

[1]Henry A. Smith

filled piers in the world.

The lucrative silk trade which J. J. Hill had originally channeled through Smith Cove was severely torn in 1940 by a filament made from coal with characteristics of strength and elasticity called nylon. Two years later Smith Cove itself was separated from the Port of

Seattle by the Navy for a condemnation fee of 3 million dollars. The Port bought it back in the mid-'70s for about 15 million and added another four million in improvements, including Smith Cove Park.[1] There in the spring of 1978 a plaque was placed honoring the very remarkable Dr. Henry A. Smith.

49 'The Greatest Naval Parade Ever'

"It was night. Ten thousand people stood in the white light of the electric age, waiting. For hours they stood patiently, tirelessly. They stood there to give an ovation to an uncrowned king: the king of the American people."

However, before "it was night," it was a day which "nature knowing was stupendous had with magnanimous hospitality" covered with a 'clear blue sky as a triumphant arch for this distinguished guest to march under."

These reporter's rhapsodies are but fragments from the many pages of the May 23, 1903 Sunday Times covering the comings and goings of Teddy Roosevelt's weekend visit to "the only city on the Sound." T.R. came on the 23rd, left on it and returned again that night. On both occasions this "New Yorker, westerner, cowboy and soldier, author and statesman," who was "in every line of effort the embodiment of power and energy and in every achievement, unique and picturesque," was for all these timeless qualities, still late.

On a Western tour whose schedule had been prescribed weeks earlier in the White House, old "Rough and Ready" was due at 1 o'clock in the afternoon to step off the steamer Spokane at the foot of University Street. But at that hour, what is still probably the "greatest naval parade in the history of Puget Sound" was out of sight waiting for T.R. to escape Tacoma's embrace and finally pass through the waiting flotilla behind Alki Point to lead the grand procession into Elliott Bay.

Here packed for blocks to either side of Arlington Dock, "the largest crowd in the history of the state" waited in "a blaze of bunting, a forest of flags, a mystic tangle of red, white, and blue." It waited nervously like "a gigantic caldron bubbling over with Seattle Spirit, and all in honor of one of the grandest men the world has ever known." Who was still late.

The congested crowd scene was photographed well before T.R.'s 1 o'clock missed appointment. By the time Roosevelt at last tipped his hat on the gangplank, all the roofs and windows in this scene along Railroad Avenue were packed.

In the foreground of the second historical photo, the presidential steamer Spokane is rushing in. In its wake is part of this "greatest naval parade in the history of Puget Sound."

A close count reveals nearly 30 steam-powered ships in this scene, and according to newspaper reports there are many more still behind the curtain of Duwamish Head.[1]

Pop Wagner's band welcomed the flotilla but it was only part of a general cacophony for "as the Spokane was coming in, every whistle in town began its screaming tribute...every heart beat with excitement...the very air seemed to resound with cheers and greetings for 'our President'." The general roar continued as T.R. crossed the gangplank, tipped his hat, and with his famous toothy smile met the simple greeting of Mayor Tom Humes.

Then his "eyes fell upon the long line of

Phillipine veterans standing at attention nearby. With utmost grace, Roosevelt stepped forward a few feet, removed his hat, and saluted the boys in brown." With this "the great throng of people grew strangely silent. Even the ripple of the waves as they lapped against the piling could be heard by those who stood upon the dock." Then the Times reporter allowed "there was just the shadow of a tear at the eye of the president."

This silent sentimental pause was broken by continual roaring when T.R. boarded his carriage and, accompanied by phalanxes of city police, national guardsmen, secret service agents, and 15 other buggies, was led by Wagner's band through a serpentine route of city streets to the old university grounds (the present site of the Four Seasons Olympic Hotel).[2]

There, before a swaying and crushing crowd of 50,000, T.R. interrupted his shortened speech twice to plead to the few in front who could hear him: "Stand just as quiet as possible. Do not sway. Just stand as quiet as possible. I will only keep you a few minutes."

And he did, and so made up time enough to be back on schedule for his late-afternoon excursion to Everett. But delivering the lengthy speech there that was meant for here, the time stretched out again.

Thus, when he returned to Arlington Dock, "it was night. Ten thousand people stood in the white light of the electric age—waiting."

The
Roosevelt
parade.

[3]Roosevelt spent that night as the first guest of the Washington Hotel atop Denny Hill. As this cartoon reveals there were some anxieties about how to get him there. *(See feature 50.)*

KEEP OFF THE GRASS

T.R.

Emjen

THE PRESIDENT WILL OCCUPY A SUITE AT THE DENNY alias WASHINGTON.

courtesy, Historical Photography Collection, University of Washington

courtesy, Bill Greer

courtesy, Historical Photography Collection, University of Washington

50 The Hotel on Denny Hill

For 16 years from 1890 to 1906, the Denny Hotel dominated the Seattle cityscape. From where it topped the front hump of Denny Hill, this hotel easily surpassed all hucksters' attempts to exaggerate its glories. From this "largest and best equipt hotel in the Pacific Northwest," one could have "one of the most beautiful views that can be found anywhere in the United States."

For years Arthur Denny had reserved this six-acre double block atop his original donation claim for a state capitol. He called it "Capitol Hill." However, in 1888 he was convinced by fellow patriarchs like Thomas Burke to abandon these political dreams for another stately speculation.

As the local historian Thomas Prosch described it only a few years later: "It was thought that if a large, showy, modern house were built upon an eligible, commanding site, with spacious grounds and grand view, properly managed and with the money-making idea of secondary consideration, that tourists from all parts of the country would be attracted to it, and that the town would be greatly benefited thereby."

Denny agreed that his most eligible hill would be the first asset of the Denny Hotel Company. And the plans were indeed lavish, inspired by something more like civic pride than a quick profit. The 200,000 locally subscribed dollars were for a hostelry with 100 more rooms than the competitive Tacoma's prestigious Tacoma Hotel.[1]

The beginning of construction on the Denny was announced in the March 20th issue of the Weekly Intelligencer, only two-and-a-half months before the Great Fire of June 1889 would wipe out most of Seattle's hotels. Ten years and ten days later, the March 30, 1899 issue of the P.I. still vainly promised that "within six weeks from today the building which bears the honored name of the pioneer founder of Seattle, will be completed to the original plans and ready for occupancy." It actually would not open to its first guest, Teddy Roosevelt, for another four years. What happened?

The cost of building the Denny Hotel had more than doubled when that notorious international crash of 1893 stopped the work and put all parties in the courts. While this litigation dragged on toward the twentieth century, the city was running wild with a population and building boom that by 1900 would completely surround Denny's vacant hotel and make it the centerpiece of over 500 structures that covered his namesake hill.

But for more than a decade only a solitary watchman lived in this nearly completed "castle" whose looming presence above the city must have seemed haunted on moonlit nights.

There had been no "quick profits" with the Denny. Yet, after the developer James A. Moore took it over in 1903, spent over $100,000 repairing and appointing it, and renamed it the Washington, it became a paying hotel every day. (It is not recorded whether T.R., its first patron, paid for this inaugural slumber.)

Moore set competitive rates with the "hotels downtown by the depots," attracted special events and conventions to its larger halls, and proclaimed the clumsy but effective line, "a trip to Seattle without a stop at the Washington is no kind of a trip to brag of at all!"

But even before the spring day in 1903, when the Washington Hotel opened to its impressed guests, the regrade rhetoric was preparing for the "great work" of both closing the hotel and dropping the hill into the sea. Only when Moore was at last convinced that a "New Washington" highrise (today's Josephinum) on lowland could make more than this grand hotel on the hill, did he surrender to the city engineers and their engineering urge to flatten North Seattle into today's Denny Regrade district.

Mr. and Mrs. Moore hosted the Old Washington's last hurrah on Monday night May 7, 1906. The lobby and grand ballroom were draped with scotch broom, Easter lilies, ferns, palms, rhododendrons, roses, and carnations. Red tulips shaded the lights. Mrs. Moore was draped in cream silk, lace, and diamonds. Many more of the distinguished

courtesy, Old Seattle Paperworks

guests wore black jetted lace, white chiffon and taffeta, yellow satin, and lots more diamonds.

Both one of the party guests and one of the hotel's original investors, Judge Thomas Burke, had earlier on this the hotel's last day announced to the press: "It is a matter of the greatest regret that the Washington Hotel is to be taken down, and what used to be known as the Denny Hill is to be leveled...From a commercial point of view and certainly from an aesthetic one, it would have been much better to have saved Denny Hill by carrying Third Avenue under it, [with the proposed tunnel] thus obtaining the desired result while preserving the natural beauty that means so much to any city...If the city could have acquired the hotel, the site would have been ideal for a park, or even for an art gallery."

All of this might sound familiar.[2]

·HOTEL·DENNY·

courtesy, Old Seattle Paperworks

Plymouth Church and Denny Hotel in the distance—before the regrade.　　　　　*courtesy, Seattle Public Library*

51 'The Largest Brick Church'

The year is 1906.[1] In the distance the half-razed hulk of the old Washington Hotel looks down on a Third Avenue scarred with regrading.

The parishioners of Plymouth Congregational Church—their tower commands the center of the photograph above—have decided that it is time to relocate. They have been approached by a developer with a proposal to construct an office building in place of their church at the northwest corner of Third Avenue and University Street.

The city is booming. The speculator offers the congregation $350,000, or $100,000 more than will be needed to build a new sanctuary on First Hill. The congregation decides to sell and records that the profits beyond costs shall be used "for the upbuilding of Christ's Kingdom under Congregational auspices."

In 1906, the city's population of 150,000 is more than three times what it was 15 years earlier when the foundation was laid for this, "the largest brick church in town."

In 1891l, Third Avenue was a neighborhood street sided by large leafy trees, residences with wide lawns, small businesses, and churches. From the back of Plymouth an unpaved path led up Denny's Knoll through high grass and fir trees to the front steps of the University of Washington, at what is now the northeast corner of Fourth and Seneca.

But in 1906 this pastoral scene is being leveled—a full story at both Seneca and Spring—and "improved" for the urbane ambitions of commerce.

The street is a mess, and only one year later so will be the economy. The national panic will destroy the developer, and the congregation will be left holding its "old church" until 1911 when it will again be sold—this time to Alexander Pantages for a theater and a nice profit. And by 1911 not only will the old hotel on Denny Hill be long gone, so will the hill as far east as Fifth Avenue. The resulting grade on Third from James to Denny will be as it is today: smooth, unobstructing, and unassuming.

Plymouth Church after the regrade and in its last days.

52 Second and Bell: Remnant of a Lost Neighborhood

There is one shared feature between this "now" and "then;" the apartment building with the three bay windows on the left. The decorative cresting on the gables is gone, and the original clapboard has been covered with the imitation-brick asbestos siding known as "war brick;" but it is the same old apartment at 2222 Second Avenue.

Both views look south across Second's intersection with Bell Street. The older scene is a rare record of the pre-regrade Denny Hill neighborhood. This is the northwest corner of Denny Hill at a quiet moment sometime in 1901, 2, or 3. Up until 1900 cable cars to and from Queen Anne Hill ran up and down the middle of this street; in 1901 the tracks were removed. In 1903 work on removing the hill itself was begun. By 1906 this part of Second

Avenue was lowered to the grade it still settles at today.

I first glimpsed this scene in the summer of 1978 while flipping through a stack of old prints at the Old Seattle Paperworks in the Pike Place Market. This one was not captioned, and although I was, by then, familiar with the historical outline of Seattle's hills, this topography was strange to me. The mystery grew uncanny and my pulse quickened when I half suspected and half hoped that this might be an intimate detail of Denny Hill in its twilight or the last moments before its destruction.

A magnified search of the old print revealed that the street sign on the power pole left of center read "Bell St." Then my in-

quisitive researcher's intuition carried me to the contemporary corner. There this three-gabled remnant of the old neighborhood pleased me immensely by surviving.

But its neighborhood of modest homes, boarding houses, and apartments had been regraded in both elevation and character. Now the apartment sits not on a hill but atop the Hawaiian Tavern and a Thai restaurant, the Rama House. Up the block is a Greek restaurant run by Nick[1] and next door a Mexican cafe with a proprietor named Mama. The cosmopolitan character of this side of the street is completed in the center of the block with a new wave chic restaurant and boutique combination named Soho after London's arty neighborhood.[2]

Second Ave. after the regrade, looking south from Bell St. with the Moore Theatre and the New Washington Hotel in the distance.

courtesy, Katharine Sparger

53 The Ups and Downs of Second and Virginia

In the spring of 1903 City Engineer Reginald H. Thomson and James A. Moore, land developer, met to decide the fate of a city intersection: Second and Virginia.

Thomson, who was described by the Times as "a man of iron will and bulldog tenacity," and Moore, who was called "a man whose energy, force, and capital pushed Seattle 20 years ahead as a city of importance," could not agree. Thomson wanted the regrading to cut into that corner and Moore didn't. In this meeting of wills, something had to give. At first it was Thomson.

More than 40 years later when the city engineer wrote his memoirs titled *That Man Thomson,* he still remembered and regretted James Moore, their meeting, and what he was prevented from doing to the corner at Second and Virginia.

"I picked on Second Avenue as a street that should be regraded fully and thoroughly, from Yesler Way to Denny Way...A great hotel had been built on the summit of a ridge which cut across the city from First Avenue to Fifth Avenue....This left Virginia Street a low spot between two peaks. People said it was like a saddle on a two-humped camel. I felt that Virginia Street should be cut down to a level about 20 feet lower than it then stood. Unfortunately, the Washington Hotel Co. had passed into the hands of Mr. James A. Moore, and he positively refused to sign any release of damages to permit any cut to be made which would reduce the grade."

What Thomson got instead is what we have today: the highest point in the regrade, an intersection from which all streets descend. In 1903 it was the low point on Denny Hill, but still an elevation Moore could profitably live with.

In the spring of 1903 Moore was preoccupied with his new acquisition, the "great hotel" Washington atop the front hump of Thomson's camel. In May the entire city was distracted with its grand opening to the first guest, Teddy Roosevelt. What the president enjoyed is what the Moore Investment Company advertised as "the Grand Hotel of the West situated in the midst of six acres of beautiful grounds which, with the broad driveways, green lawns, and a profusion of roses and carnations, makes the location an ideal one."

The only way to direct a carriage to those broad driveways was around that corner at Second and Virginia. It was an around about ride, but well worth taking, for once reaching those flower bedecked grounds, one could enjoy "with one sweep of the eye mountains, lakes, sound, and harbor together with an

J.A. Moore's grand plan for an enlarged Denny Hotel joined to the Moore Theatre.

courtesy, Historical Photography Collection, University of Washington

unequalled bird's-eye view of the entire city of Seattle," the advertising continued.

This was a prospect that Moore, "the man who handled millions as an ordinary man handled dollars," wished to preserve, and so he handed Thomson a rare defeat by insisting that the grade at Second and Virginia be kept a comfortable one for delivery wagons, hotel hacks, and sightseers in carriages.

In 1903 Moore also had his own plans for that intersection. A weekly tabloid, The Commonwealth, ran an artist's rendition of his vision and reported, that "Jas. A. Moore, the well known and progressive up builder of Seattle, will shortly build an elegant theater

[which] has been a subject of general conversation in Seattle the past few weeks. The grounds of the Washington Hotel will be at the same sight as the roof of the new building. An immense roof garden will be a feature of the block. The theater itself will be the most artistic and beautiful to be found in the West."

The artist's rendering shows a much enlarged Washington Hotel and an even grade from Stewart Street to Virginia Street, instead of the hill's forward hump. In 1903 the hump reached to near the present fifth floor of the Josephinum—the building at the far right of the "now" image. The sketch also shows the intersection at Virginia at the same grade "then" as it is "now" or 20 feet higher

than what Thomson so dearly wanted. *(See notes for sketch.)*

However, in 1906 Thomson got the whole hill when Moore suddenly decided to surrender his grand Old Washington Hotel, then only three years open, and go modern with a New Washington (later the Josephinum) at Second Avenue and Stewart Street. By 1911 Thomson would have Denny Hill eliminated as far east as Fifth Avenue, but that intersection at Second and Virginia would stay the same: the highest point in the regrade which was once the lowest point on the hill.[1]

When his theater opened in 1907, James Moore, the man who had "given" Seattle whole neighborhoods, hotels, and business blocks, received a standing ovation. It was said of Moore that "the magic of his name identified with any enterprise is sufficient promise of its development and prosperity." But it was not sufficient to save his own fortune from a bad speculation in iron smelters. In 1914 he moved to Florida where he tried again be become a man of large affairs by starting a town named Moorehaven. This time the Midas touch of the Moore name fell literally flat by an act of God: a hurricane wiped out his town.

When Moore died in 1929 in San Francisco's Palace Hotel, he was probably still making plans in high relief. In Seattle there was little left to remember him by than that Moore name lightly embossed above the entrance to his theater. It is still there at the "top" of Denny Regrade, reminding us of the ups and downs not only of our landscape but also of our plans.

Looking Northeast from Second and Blanchard with Queen Anne Hill (and High School) in the distance.

54 Close Encounters on The Regrade

Of the millions of photographs that are partial records of Seattle's history only a very few are ever published or exhibited. And of these there are a core of images which both reveal some side of our past and stir the imagination. These are the 'classics' of local cityscape, and this is certainly one of them.

But what is it and where is the "city" in this cityscape? This scene looks less like a photograph of Seattle than like a surreal painting in which the artist has collaged a melodramatic sky and a few cut-outs of tilting houses onto a lunar landscape. With this photograph, if you ask "what is it?" you get answers instead to "what is it like?" A few I have heard are "an archeological dig in southern Utah"; "landing platforms for close encounters," or more simply "World War Two." But as almost every citizen will either know or strongly suspect, this is not the work of bombs or aliens but of steam-shovels, water hoses, and engineers, some of whom only seem somewhat extraterrestial.

These are a few of the parts of Denny Hill that still stood as dirt monoliths called "spikes" when Asahel Curtis recorded this panorama early in 1910. But which parts? The photograph was taken from the north side of Bell Street and a few feet east of the alley between Third and Fourth Avenues. The view is toward the south and across the line of Fourth which today runs from the lower left hand corner of the photograph to just left of the butte in the center distance.

Immediately beneath the scene's exact center is the spurting nozzle to one of the large hoses that wore the hill away. These streams were only temporarily diverted from those spikes or buttes which were also called "spite mounds" and "monuments to the anti-regraders." The resisting butte in the immediate right foreground is just across Bell Street. The building at the picture's far right, half hidden by the spike, is the still-standing Calhoun Apartments at Second and Virginia.

It would require a hook-and-ladder to photograph the "now" image from Curtis' original position. Instead, I have taken it from the roof of the Adams Apartments at Third and Bell. This is less than half a block to the west, and from here one can see those Calhoun Apartments on the far right. Otherwise they would be hidden by the Cornelius Hotel.

This adjusted view also shows the contemporary "spike" of dark glass one block away at Fourth and Blanchard. The original hill reached its highest point there, or about 110 feet above the street grade today. Thus, if Denny Hill is ever put back, the dirt will reach to the eighth floor of the 24-floor Fourth and Blanchard Building.

The "lesser" historical image was taken from Second and Blanchard. From there we get a glimpse of the ridge from which Curtis took his photograph. It can be seen just above the roof of the apartment, left of the scene's center and just below the old Denny

courtesy, Lawton Gowey

School, the building with the tower at Fifth and Battery. (The then-new Queen Anne High School is seen in the distance atop its Queen Anne perch. That hill was high enough to save it from the "forces of regrade."[1])

This view from Second Avenue is dated June 27, 1910. There have been a few changes. Most evident, the "tilting house" on the left of Curtis' image has been skidded down to the south side of the butte, here right center and in Curtis' photograph in the right foreground.

The billboard along Second reads "Diamond Tires, Users Know." Already in 1910 these "users" also knew that the automobile was turning the primary rationalization for leveling the hill—that it was too steep for horses to climb or get around—into an example of antiquated horse sense.[2]

courtesy, Historical Photography Collection, University of Washington

55 The Cliff Along Fifth Avenue

This is not view property. Although the house on the hill provides its owner with a first-rate prospect, within a few years the hill, the house, and the view will all be gone. The reflecting pond with its grassy banks is little more than a temporary puddle in the middle of Fifth Avenue.

The photograph reveals what some residents still remember. For nearly 20 years from 1911 (about the time the picture was taken) to 1929, a cliff bordered the east side of Fifth Avenue from Lenora Street almost to Denny Way. The view here is from Lenora north. That bluff marked the last line of defense against the temporarily stalled "forces of regrade."

In those intervening years this unnaturally carved cliff grew its own habitat of grasses and scrub bushes tentatively clinging to the clay and glacial gravel. On the far left of the photograph the belltower of Denny School at Battery Street is barely visible. Many of its graduates still recall how much fun was had roaming the hill, digging foxholes in its side, and rolling through its grasses. It was neither too dangerous nor too safe.

But for the adults in charge of the serious business of progress, the cliff was a temporary scar dividing the flat efficiency of the Denny Regrade to the west from the funky confusion of what remained of Denny Hill: a rough landscape between Fifth and Westlake and north almost to Lake Union.

The Hill's original regrading began in 1898 at First Avenue. A cut was made from Pike to Denny Way—at its deepest only 17 feet. Eventually, the leveling continued but with much deeper incisions, up to 107 feet at Fourth and Blanchard, until it reached Fifth Avenue in 1911. And there it stopped, but on-

ly after taking the west wing of Denny School. However, it did continue to threaten the families that lived on what was left of the hill with years of domestic uncertainty.

In 1929 the waiting was over. Local headlines read: "Take One Last Look at Old Denny Hill"; "Sentiment Is Loser As City Tears Down Old Homes"; "No One Bids for Old Denny School"; and "Shovels Massed for Attack."

The Seattle Times reported that "you might call Denny Hill Seattle's Old Quarter. Its unpaved streets, its unpainted weather-beaten houses, its absence of traffic, its general air of somnolence all seem to say 'we're waiting. Waiting for what? Who knows? Just Waiting.'" It is a section of homes of working people...citizens with a quaint fondness for their little 'free city' like an island in the roaring sea of the downtown business district . . . Here are quiet and peace, homely joys and picturesque beauty. No wonder some of these folk seem to regret that civic progress won't let them alone. Yes the day's of Old Denny Hill, the rebel, are numbered!''

The second photograph of the bluff *(see notes)* was taken in 1929 from Battery looking south down Fifth Avenue. In less than two years, those attacking shovels would gouge away the rest of Denny Hill and deliver it via conveyor belts along Fifth—seen in the photograph—and out Battery to Elliott Bay.

On the last day of digging, December 12, 1930, the Times reported: "In realization of Seattle's dream of years, the removal of surplus earth from the historic Denny Hill, where many of the city's people were born and went to school, was completed today. . . . Mayor Frank Edwards removed the last shovel-full while crowds of city officials, workmen, and former residents cheered.''

"At last the way was opened for giant new buildings, for the forward sweep of the central business district northward on level grades into territory which only a few months ago barred progress with a lofty barricade of clay banks, ill-kept, run-down residences. . . . Early this afternoon four of the huge power shovels were toiling close together for the last bit of earth that is to be taken. With this done, the removal of 4,354,625 cubic yards of surplus has been accomplished.''

This was also a lot of suplus talk for 1929, the beginning of the last regrade, was also the start of the Great Depression. There would be no "giant new buildings.'' All that would "sweep northward'' would be a slow invasion of one and two-story ware houses and at least two ironies.

The first irony is that the original regrading of Denny Hill began in 1898 to make it easier on the horses. What we got eventually were a lot of parking lots.

The second twist was noted by Times columnist John Hinterberger. Now that those "giant new buildings'' are suddenly appearing and obscuring each other's viewing corridors, "what the Denny Regrade really needs is Denny Hill. But is it possible to regrade?''

The "now'' photograph of Fifth Avenue also looks north from Lenora Street. The monorail has taken the place of the conveyor belt. The picture was taken during the summer of 1981 when the entire city seemed to be "regraded'' with dancing cowboys and cowgirls here for a national square-dancing convention.

The "Old Quarter."

Denny School before the regrade on Fifth Ave., took its western wing.

56 The Jackson Street Regrade

You have to sign a release to climb to the top of the King Street Station's clock tower. A steel stairway ascends through room after empty room until you reach the larger chamber with the four clockworks. Next, a somewhat shaky spiral staircase leads up to the catwalk beneath the tower's pyramidal roof. There, 240 feet above the railway tracks, you can enjoy a 360-degree, unobstructed view that is rarely seen. Hardly anyone ever takes the time or gets permission to make this aerobic climb.[1]

Both of the "now' and "then" panoramas were photographed from the east side of the tower looking down upon the International District. The older view was taken sometime between 1905 when the tower was completed and 1907 when work began on the Jackson Street regrade.

The difference between the "now" and "then" is almost total. The hill has been cut away as deep as 85 feet, and the neighborhood, originally part of pioneer Doc Maynard's claim, has been entirely made

over. Only one structure from the "before" remains in the "after."

In the 55 years between 1876, when First Avenue was smoothed out between Yesler Way and Pike Street, and 1930, when the last of Denny Hill was removed, more than 50 million tons of Seattle earth were scraped and shifted about in the city's more than 60 regrade projects. Of these, after Denny Hill, the Jackson Regrade was the largest.[2]

Even from as high as the campanile's catwalk, the grade change below is obvious. King Street which runs up the center of both views from Fifth Avenue is now a gentle incline. In 1907 the two-block grade between Sixth, Maynard, and Seventh Avenues was a cliff too steep for a street. The steepest grade along Jackson Street on the left was reduced from 15 to 5 percent.

The regrade's promoters referred to Jackson Street as "the Pike Street of the South." Their stated purpose for the project was to make the Rainier Valley as accessible as Capitol Hill was by way of Pike Street.

Jackson's deepest cut was 85 feet at Ninth Avenue. In the contemporary view that would be on top of the Interstate-5 freeway. Then it was just to the left of the rooftop of Holy Names Academy, the dominant structure whose gothic spire pierces the center horizon of the historical scene.

Holy Names was built along the east side of Seventh Avenue in 1884. Six years later, South School, the dark profile on the right horizon, was put up at Twelfth and Weller. Both of these landmarks were razed by the regrade.

That one structure that was not removed was the Japanese Baptist Church. This recently renovated four-story clapboard still stands at the northwest corner of Jackson and Maynard. In our "now" view, its imitation war-brick exterior is the dark structure which rises directly across Jackson Street from the much larger Bush Hotel.

In the historical view the Baptist Church is the three-story gabled building located across Jackson Street from the large vacant lot just

During the regrade.   *courtesy, Seattle Public Library*

left of the photograph's center. The actual work of lowering and so preserving this church "fell upon" one L.B. Gullett who advertised himself as an "experienced house mover"; he used a picture of the Japanese Baptist Church to prove it.[3]

Actually, this church was one of the few spiritual institutions in a neighborhood of flophouses for single immigrant men and establishments with names like "The Dreamland Cabaret," "Miss Emma's New Stars," "The Gaity," and "The Red Light." On November 1, 1909 the politicians and promoters who thought this kind of neighborhood expendable gathered on the regrade to celebrate its conclusion. They envisioned a new neighborhood of modern construction. Fortunately, we got the International District instead.

Today there are several ways to see this still cosmopolitan International District. One is on Ed and Betty Burke's Chinatown tour. Another is from the top of the King Street Station tower.

57 Filling the Tidelands

"Probably no one with a business eye has viewed the tidelands which stretch across the head of Elliott Bay without being struck by the vast possibilities that lie undeveloped therein. Upon this new land could spring up a myriad of lumber and shingle mills, warehouses, elevators, and industrial establishments of many kinds whose smokestacks would rival the firs on the neighboring hills."

What the editor of the weekly newspaper Argus envisioned in 1894, a Webster and Stevens photographer recorded only 20 years later in 1914. But what the editor actually saw was far different than what he imagined. Then at almost any tide, except the very lowest, Elliott Bay lapped against the sides of Beacon Hill. South of town, it was a sheet of saltwater, only sporadically traversed by a few roads high on pilings, including First and Fourth Avenues. *(See feature 16.)*

Twenty years later, as shown by our historic picture, there was already vast evidence of "progress." Our 1914 view shows only a small part of the nearly 2,000 acres of reclaimed tide lands. The most evident landmark in both the early and contemporary photos is the bright building on the far right. Earlier it was the Sylvester Brothers Wholesale Grocers which was still elevated on pilings; in the "now" photo, slightly darker in color and owned by the Squire Shop, it is just below the center of the Kingdome.

Above the center of the older scene, the dark bulk of the Seattle Construction and Dry Dock Company's pier shed protrudes into the bay. It was here that 10 years earlier the Moran Brothers built their battleship *Nebraska*, and Skinner and Eddy set records in ship construction to meet World War I demands.

In the foreground of both views, Airport Way South makes its oblique way along the foot of Beacon Hill. However, what in 1914 was the often smelly site of Armour Packing Company is today the roaring mass of I-5. Also here are the unfinished wings of the freeway's foresaken hookup with the never-built R.H. Thomson Expressway.

A few of the still-standing warehouses along First Avenue South can be made out just this side of the shipyards. Today all of the historical waterfront uses of these reclaimed tidelands are one continuous sprawl of cranes and containers.

In the thirties a combination of waterway dredgings and sluiced fill from Beacon Hill and the Jackson and Dearborn Street regrades had managed to push back the sea. During these years a few made their fortunes following the popular real estate slogan that they "Get the tideland habit, it will make you money while you sleep."[1]

Pipe Line on Tide Flats May 1896

Looking back at Beacon Hill across the tidelands in 1896, the year systematic reclamation of the flats began.

courtesy, Historical Photography Collection, University of Washington

58 Frank Osgood's Horse Cars

Throughout 1884 the Seattle Post-Intelligencer ran a daily listing of local news notes called "Brevities." The column for Saturday, September 20 said: "A new moon has made its appearance. The roads are in fine condition for driving...hop pickers are needed in Puyallup...the supper by Methodist ladies netted a nice little handful of money for the Battery Street Methodist Episcopal Church." But more newsworthy events were transpiring way out on Belltown's Battery Street.

The Seattle Street Railway's three-mile line terminated at Battery's intersection with Front Street (now First Avenue). This first streetcar system in Washington Territory got its inaugural run that weekend in 1884. The next day's Brevities reported, "the cars were placed on the railway for the first time yesterday and several trips were made over the line. Each car is drawn by a span of horses. The track was found to be all right, but it was necessary to make one or two changes at the sharp curves to prevent the cars from running off. The opening of the road proved a gala day for the average small boy who followed the cars from one end of town to the other."

It was also a gala day for Frank Osgood, David Denny, George Kinnear, and Addie Burns. A year earlier Osgood had come west from Boston with a pocketful of eastern capital and a letter of introduction to local super-booster Judge Thomas Burke. The judge advised Osgood to build the streetcar system, and pioneers David Denny and George Kinnear sold him the franchise they'd won a year earlier from the city council. Both Denny and Kinnear owned large parcels of real estate north of town and looked forward to the rewards that ease of transport, sales, and settlers would bring them.

Addie Burns lived with her husband Captain Francis Burns in their home on the northwest corner of Second Avenue and Pike Street, the house on the left of the "then" image. From her sitting room Addie Burns could look down on one of those sharp curves the horse line negotiated as it turned west on Pike Street from Second Avenue and continued on to Front Street. There it took a right angle turn north for the final leg out to Battery Street. From their side windows along Second Avenue, Addie and Francis Burns could witness all the action in and about the horse barn across the street and just off-camera to the right. It was here that the line's 20 horses and their hay were kept. So it was here that the four "bobtail" cars stopped to attach the one or two extra horses needed, depending upon the load, to make the line's last and steepest ascent over the western shoulder of Denny Hill. (Fifteen years passed before First Avenue was regraded to its present elevations.)

The return trip from Belltown included an exhilarating descent down that same First Avenue hill. More than once the entire loose assemblage of cars, horses, and passengers derailed at the Pike Street turn and careened off down First Avenue.

In our 1884 photograph, car No. 3 poses with its span of horses, driver, and some boys alongside. Although a slow conveyance, the service was still a clean one for the hay on the car floors was consistently less sticky than the usually muddy and dung-strewn streets.

The line began on Main Street a little west of First Avenue South. At Occidental Avenue it turned north to Yesler Way. This was the city's commercial center and in 1883-84 the scene of a building boom that featured the community's first multi-storied masonry structures. After a one block ride east on Yesler Way, the line turned north up Second Avenue until it reached this corner at Pike Street, where it turned west and continued on its trip to Belltown.

Another branch went east on Pike Street to Eighth Avenue and then to Stewart Street. A short time later both branches were extended—the Belltown leg out to Mercer Street, completely across David Denny's claim and to the southern edge of Kinnear's Queen Anne property. The Stewart branch was lengthened to Lake Union. There Osgood's company built a pleasure grounds with walks, swings, bathing beach, dance hall, and a wharf to transfer passengers from the steamer ride out to the new mill town of Fremont.

Probably, the most mileage Seattle got out of Osgood's transportation system was not in the trip to Lake Union, but in the city's persistent race with Tacoma for commmercial and cultural primacy on Puget Sound. The rivalry was at its hottest in 1884. Tacoma, which advertised itself as "The City of Destiny," had the Northern Pacific Railroad. Or rather, the Northern Pacific had Tacoma. It was largely a company town.

Seattle, calling itself the "Queen City of the Sound," was the center of steamer service. It was also run by a gang of relatively independent entrepreneurs—Burke, Denny, and Kinnear included. Acting under the self-righteous spirit of city survival, they promoted such a variety of Seattle-based services and Seattle-made products that many of the flood of opportunity bound immigrants, that followed the 1883 completion of the Northern Pacific's transcontinental at Tacoma, jumped a steamer and continued on to Seattle. Here, where the opportunities were more diverse, their chances for success were often better.

Of course, this flood of opportunists included a trickle of eastern capitalists. This smaller stream with the silver lining included restless Frank Osgood who fit in well. By 1886 he was dissatisfied with the expensive routine of feeding 20 horses and 10 men and decided to investigate other sources of horse power. By the spring of 1889 the Burnses were no longer watching the changing of horses from their side windows. On March 30, 1889 the first car of the first electric line west of the Mississippi made its inaugural run

The horse car at Mill Street (now Yesler Way) and Occidental at the beginning of its inaugural run.

on the same rails that guided the discarded horses. The only passenger, in addition to the officers and employees of the company, was the captain's wife, Addie Burns.

A tragic but ironic postlude to this civic enterprise soon followed in 1893. That year

David Denny bought the electric line, and that year David Denny lost it and all else to the great International Crash. The original pioneer, who patiently worked and waited decades for the city to reach his claim, was finally driven from it by the rails that crossed it.

59 Promise and Depression in Belltown

In 1883 the transcontinental Northern Pacific Railroad at last reached Portland and Puget Sound. Seattle and the rest of the Northwest was yearning for this invasion.

Arthur Denny and William Bell, two of the Midwestern farmers who years earlier had come to this wilderness to start a city, waited with subdivided real estate for the coming tide of settlers. Only 32 years after they landed at Alki Point, their city of close to 7,000 residents was the largest in the territory, and their contiguous claims were next in line for serious development.

The border between their claims ran diagonally across Denny Hill. A view from the top looked south over Denny's land toward the center of town and, turning around, one looked north toward Belltown. Here, in November 1883, William Bell completed his namesake hotel: a four-story landmark with a showy mansard roof and central tower.

It was the 66-year-old pioneer's last promotion. Within the year, Bell's depressing symptoms of fits and confusion confined him to his home two doors south of his hotel. There, on Wednesday, September 6, 1887, he died of what then was called "softening of

the brain." Bell's only son, Austin, then living in California, rushed home to his father's funeral and a Belltown inheritance that appeared much as it does in the historical photograph.

This 1887 (or perhaps 1888) panorama looks north from near Second Avenue and Blanchard Street—that's Blanchard at the lower right. William Bell's hotel is the centerpiece of both this picture and the neighborhood, and his home is the house with the white picket fence and the cheery white smoke escaping from its chimney.

The corner of Front (now First Avenue) and Bell Streets is seen with a posing pedestrian center left. Front Street is lined with a few frontier facades and down its center runs the railway for the horse-drawn trolley, which in 1884 began its somewhat leisurely 17-block service between Battery and Mill (now Yesler Way) Streets.

Belltown was first a forest into which William carved a small clearing for a garden and log cabin. There, January 9, 1854, Austin Americus Bell was born. When the 1856 native attack on Seattle destroyed the Bell home, William moved the family to California. At David Denny's urging, he ten-

tatively returned in the early 1860s to subdivide his claim, but not until the early '70s did William Bell come home to stay.

In 1875 the family moved back to Belltown and into the home with the picket fence. One year later, as a member of the city council, Bell voted with the majority for Seattle's first public works ordinance, which provided for the regrading of Front Street from Mill to Pike Streets. When a boardwalk was added for the additional six blocks out to Belltown, this long and relatively unmuddy walk became Seattle's favorite Sunday and sunset promenade.

For the decade preceding his father's death, Austin Bell spent most of his time in California. Returning in 1887, he and his wife Eva moved into their home at Second and Blanchard (just right of our scene). Now Austin began to act like a promoter, and by 1889 when he moved his offices to 2222 Front Street (just left of our scene), he had more than doubled his inheritance to an estimated quarter million.

On the afternoon of April 23 of that year he took a nephew for a buggy ride through the streets of Belltown. Stopping on Front Street, between his father's old home and

courtesy, William Mix

namesake hotel (then renamed the Bellevue House), he enthusiastically outlined with dancing hands the five-story heights to which his own planned monumental brick building would soon reach.

That night Austin Bell slept fitfully but arose at 8 o'clock to a "hearty breakfast." At 9:30 he walked one block to his office, locked the door and, after writing an endearing but shaky note to his wife, shot himself through the head. He was dead at 35, the same age his father was when he first carved the clearing in the forest that later became Belltown.

Among the crowd of hundreds that gathered outside the office was Arthur Denny who recalled for reporters the history of both William and Austin Bell. He indicated "that the symptoms of his father's disease also had begun to manifest themselves in Austin. This he fully recognized himself and the fact played on his mind so that he finally killed himself."

Eva Bell completed Austin's decorative five-story brick monument and fittingly named and dated it, "Austin A. Bell, 1889." However, the rebuilding of Seattle's center after the Great Fire of that year thoroughly diverted attention away from Belltown and

Bell's new building, which even before the 1893 international money crash was popularly called 'Bell's folly.''

After this, a series of reversals, including the early-century Denny Hill Regrade, the election failure of the 1912 Bogue Plan which included a proposed new civic center in Belltown, prohibition, and the Great Depression all conspired to keep Belltown more or less chronically depressed.

Today the neighborhood is inflating with highrises all much taller than five stories, but none of them monumental. However, now one also can choose a window seat in the Belltown Cafe, order an Austin A. Bell salad, and gaze across First Avenue to the depressingly empty but still grandly standing red brick Austin Americus Bell Building.

The Bell Hotel and the Austin A. Bell buildings side-by-side.

60 David Denny's Claim

By far the most popular Seattle view today is south from Denny Park on Queen Anne Hill's West Highland Drive. The city from there gathers its skyline around the Space Needle as if directed by a postcard designer.

One hundred years ago the most popular view for photographing or sketching the city was from Denny Hill. However, in the "then" image, Denny Hill—in the middle distance—is itself a prominent part of the view. The year is about 1895 and the photographer, named LaRoche, is on Queen Anne at Second Avenue and Prospect Street, or only one block south of our contemporary scene from Highland. The Denny Hotel, just left of center, sits atop Denny Hill, and to its left is Denny School at the northeast corner of Fifth and Battery. Immediately this side of the school is Denny Way. It traverses the entire width of the photograph and marks the southern border of David Denny's claim. His 320 acres extended from Elliott Bay to Lake Union and included part of today's Seattle Center.[1]

In the immediate foreground of LaRoche's view is a windmill, its blades facing the bay. Just a little distance above the

mill is the steeple of the Second Presbyterian Church. That is the southwest corner of Third and Harrison, or what is today the grassy rise between the International Flag Plaza and the northwest corner of the Center House. One block north of there, David Denny built a cabin in 1857. This was one year after the Indian war when it was considered safe for settlers to leave Seattle's palisades and return to their claims.

David and Louisa Denny's family farm on the other side of Denny Hill for years after provided a healthy portion of the produce for Seattle. The land with its natural meadows and willowy marshes, bordering the fresh waters of Lake Union, and its abundance of wild duck and other game was, for the humans at least, almost like Eden.

Before white settlement, Native Americans had used this meadow as a gathering spot for the ritual of gifts, the potlatch. And many years later the Denny daughter, Emily Inez, recollected her childhood experience of the "gift" of this land in her book, *Blazing the Way.* "Traditions did not trouble us; the Indians were generally friendly, the bears were only black ones and ran

away from us as fast as their furry legs would carry them; the panthers did not care to eat us up, we felt assured while there was plenty of venison to be had by stalking, and on a journey we rode safely, either on the pommel of Father's saddle or behind Mother's, clinging like small kittens or cockleburrs," she wrote.

David and Louisa Denny were generous with their land, giving parts of it to the community and friends for parks, schools, churches, and a children's home. *(See feature 63.)*

When Seattle finally began to reach them in the late 1880s, they sold portions for profit. With this, David built Louisa a mansion at what today is the southeast corner of Mercer Street and Queen Anne Avenue, a street which they, ever sober, had named Temperance. That mansion is the gothic structure with the tower and wide surrounding lawn at the far right of our view.[2]

At the time LaRoche photographed it, most likely David and Louisa no longer lived there nor owned it or any part of their claim. They lost everything in the international financial crash of 1893. Finally, they moved to a bit of land at Licton Springs near Green Lake. Years earlier they had given it to their daughter Emily.

In 1900 the Denny swale was used as a government corral for mules either returning from the Spanish-American War or waiting

shipment to the Philippines insurrection.[3] In 1903, the year David died, a baseball park was built on the site. For years thereafter the cleared land between Harrison and Mercer was filled with entertainment, and at the time of Louisa's death in 1916, the chances were good that either a circus was performing or carnival sideshow exhibiting in her garden.

In 1928 the Civic Auditorium, later remodeled into the Opera House, was opened along Mercer, as was the Ice Arena. In 1939 the National Guard Armory, the present Center House, was completed. Throughout most of the '50s the Armory was used as a popular spot for bobby-sox hops. In 1962, when part of the world gathered here for a Fair with the "forward look," there was no looking back to the Denny family farm.

The next time you visit Seattle Center you may take time to relax in the grass just north of the International Fountain. You will be resting in David and Louisa's garden. There you may remember the potlatch and imagine that all around you natives are exchanging gifts.

The circus at Seattle Center, Queen Anne Hill beyond.

Queen Ann Hill
Counterbalance.
Looking North from Mercer St.
on Queen Ann. Av.

courtesy, Lawton Gowey

61 The Queen Anne Counterbalance

In the late morning of Saturday, September 27, 1902, while Seattle's Mayor Tom Humes was stepping off the Lake Washington steamer Kirkland onto the Leschi dock, the photographer Asahel Curtis was recording this view from a perch a little ways south of Queen Anne Avenue's intersection with Mercer Street.

The afternoon Seattle Times' front page headline read: "MAYOR HUMES LOST FOR A DAY AND TWO NIGHTS IN THE TALL TIMBER TO THE NORTH OF SQUAK [now Sammamish] SLOUGH." Back in the city, the politician quickly found himself again and proclaimed, "You can say that the Mayor is very much alive and that he will still continue to be mayor of the town." Humes had been lost on a hunting trip. What Curtis shot was what many still call the Queen Anne Counterbalance.[1]

At one time Seattle had four cablecar lines. Three of these, the Yesler Way, James Street, and Madison Street lines kept clanging up First Hill until 1939-40. But the fourth, the Front Street cable line, gave up most of its underground mechanics for overhead elec-

tricity in the late 1890s. The one part of cable it could not abandon was that under the most precipitous part of its franchise, the lightheaded 20% incline up Temperance Street (now Queen Anne Avenue).

Since cablecars were particularly good at climbing hills, the Seattle Electric Company used them here in tandem with the new electric cars. They also elaborately modified the simple cable design into the counterbalance by linking the streetcars via the cable with an underground truck that ran on narrow gauge tracks through a tunnel. While the subterranean "streetcar" weighed 16 tons, the passenger cars above were a heavier 18 to 24 tons. Thus, while the truck went down hill it helped pull the street car uphill. And, working the other way, the electric streetcar's descent was restrained by the counterweight's ascent.

The progress both ways was slow—about 8 miles per hour— but still steady enough to stay in service for over 40 years.[2]

Curtis' shot of the 1902 counterbalance is a record of its last muddy months. Within a

year work began on surfacing this entire messy stretch with a hard and decorative layer of granite curbs, vitrified brick gutters, asphalt outerlanes, and centers of sandstone blocks which neatly framed the by then two counterbalance tracks.[3]

In this view only the original righthand track is in place; however, the rough dirt scar that runs up the western side of the street to the top of the hill marks the work-in-progress on the second tunnel.

Although the streetcars were attached to the counterweighted cable at the base of the hill, the two tunnels continued another half block south towards Mercer Street. This stretch was filled with a cushion of sawdust and timbers to soften the blow of any runaway counterweights.

On the evening of March 5, 1937, the Seattle Municipal Railway staged a counterbalance contest between a streetcar and a trackless trolley. For the latter, a power line had been temporarily installed beside the tracks. "Scores of citizens thronged the start

The lower Queen Anne landmark (Kinnear Mansion, top and half of it, bottom. (The Kinnear home is also showing in the upper-right-hand corner of the "then" photo.)

and finish line for the counterbalance race." The streetcar was given a headstart halfway up the hill, and the trackless trolley was loaded to capacity with 92 dignitaries. A flag was waved and they were off.

The next day's Times reported that "the modern trackless coach embarrassed the Queen Anne streetcar last night making the 2,150-foot hill in less than half the time required by the streetcar." With four stops the loaded trolley could make the full run in a minute and a half. Over the same distance the counterweighted streetcar required three minutes and five seconds, or time enough to boil an egg.[4]

Regular trackless coach service began on September 2, 1940. The tracks and two streetcars were kept for winter service, in case of ice or snow, until they were removed in 1943. "Now" practically everything else in the "then" is gone except for what was always hidden, those two counterbalance tunnels that still run up, down, and under Queen Anne Avenue.

62 Mansion upon a Proper Hill

Seattle is an overlapping system of ridges that have been conventionally called hills with names like Capitol, First, Yesler, and Profanity.

All of these named are continuous parts of the same ridge which runs down the center of the city like a backbone. Indeed, Beacon Hill was also continuous with this dorsal divide until the city's engineers performed an early century "lumbar operation" on it with the Jackson Street regrade and Dearborn cut. *(See feature 56.)*

But Queen Anne Hill is different. Seattle's "miniature mountain" is cleaned by winds, girdled by greenbelts, and topped by towers and mansions. When one pauses on any nearby ridge—like Capitol "ridge"—and looks across at it, this picturesque 446-foot pile of glacial till can become the city's

Acropolis and the abandoned high school on top its Parthenon.[1]

Perhaps it was something like this sublime impression that inspired Colonel Alden J. Blethen in 1901 to move his family into their new classical colonial home on Queen Anne Hill's West Highland Drive. That year Colonel Blethen also prepared to move the Seattle Times, a newspaper he bought and brought out of bankruptcy five years earlier, north to the corner of Second Avenue and Union Street.

Alden J. Blethen, who was described by another Queen Anne resident, Clarence Bagley, in his three-volume *History of Seattle*, as a man who "kept his mind, as it were, on the pulse of the public," believed in this "natural northerly expansion" of his new hometown and so moved both his residence

and business in that direction. His paper expanded in all directions from four to twenty pages, while the circulation quickly doubled and then doubled again.

Thus, the Blethen's could afford their unobstructed full "marine view property" on the south side of Highland Drive, while just across the street a baker, Dennis Duffy, and his family enjoyed property with only "marine glimpses" to either side of the Blethen mansion.

The Blethen is on the right side of the historical photograph. The scene looks east down Highland Drive and we can get a glimpse of the Duffy's front steps and windows on the far left. It is from there that the frontal view of Blethen's property (see the notes) was photographed, probably by the older of the two Duffy boys, Edward, who in

1902 graduated from the University of Washington with letters in four sports and an aptitude for engineering and photography. (Many more of Ed Duffy's scenes of early-century life along West Highland Drive are included in Lane and Murray Morgan's *Seattle, A Pictorial History*.)

It was also at this time, about 1903, that Gilbert, the younger Duffy son, began to regularly glimpse across Highland at Florence, one of the two Blethen daughters, who for 10 more years would regularly glimpse back.

These two sides of West Highland Drive represent roughly two generations of architectural taste. On the Blethen's side, the lots were larger, and the Stimsons, Kerrys, and Clives built real mansions there with libraries, ballrooms, and separate servants quarters. On the Duffy side of the street, the houses were more modest in construction and conservative in design. It was from homes styled like some of these that the Hill got its name.

In the late 1880s when pioneer Thomas Mercer's north Seattle wilderness first opened to steady settlement, the hill's lower southern slope was soon dappled with houses some of which were built in the then-popular Queen Anne style with towers, tall chimneys, fish scale shingles, circular bays, and irregular roof lines.

Throughout the 1890s a cable car climbed Queen Anne Avenue as far as Highland Drive. And so, the houses climbed the hill. In 1900 when the cable was replaced by a counterbalance, a new electric trolley spread settlement across the top of the hill. These "hill people," Alden Blethen included, returned home on their common carrier each evening. When the counterbalance paused at the brink of the hill for the Times publisher and his neighbors to step off, they were met by a gas-lit Highland Drive which Blethen personally paid to have ignited each night.

The colonel and his neighbors set such an elegant example that by 1906 the entire hill began to lobby the city for a ring of boulevards and drives to crown its top. Queen Anne Boulevard was completed in 1916 and West Highland Drive, of course, is still part of it.

Three years earlier, on the night of Thursday, September 11, 1913, Colonel Blethen and his wife Rose received 700 guests to celebrate the marriage of their daughter Florence to Gilbert Duffy, who that night ended a decade of gazing at each other across West Highland Drive.

The Duffy home on Highland.

The Blethen mansion as seen from the Duffy's.   courtesy, Gerald Johnson

63 Seattle's First Charity

Seattle's oldest charity is now one hundred. On April 3, 1884, fifteen of the city's "leading ladies"—Sarah Yesler, Babette Gatzert, Mercie Boone, and Mary Leary included—gathered in the large living room of the Leary mansion at Second and Madison. There they pledged themselves to "the systematic benevolent work of aiding and assisting the poor and destitute regardless of creed, nationality, or color." Incorporating as the Ladies Relief Society, these women activists gave birth to "one of Seattle's biggest families," nurtured now for a century in the Seattle Children's Home.[1]

From the beginning the "quality of their mercy" focused on "orphans and friendless children," those little Nels and Oliver Twists who had seemingly stepped out of Charles Dicken's novels and onto the back streets of Seattle. 1884 was a depression year, and Seattle, then recently the largest town in the territory, had its depressing and even desperate parts. The women's charity was needed.

Within a month, the group's membership grew to more than 100. The women divided the city into districts and themselves into visiting committees responsible for searching out the "needs of the poor within their districts' boundaries." What they uncovered were new accounts of that old story of the runaway father and the distraught mother.

The Society needed a home, and in August of 1886 the first Seattle Children's Home was opened to 30 children. The home's site, donated by Louisa and David Denny, was at what is now another children's gamboling ground, Seattle Center's Fun Forest.[2]

Pictured here is the charity's second home and its first at the present location on Queen Anne Hill. "Here," the Town Crier reported in 1912, "45 children, either orphans or fatherless are cared for...under the gentle guidance of Mrs. Anna Dow Urie and two assistants...700 loaves of bread a month and a jolly old janitor who never lets the furnace die down."

This was a kind of family, and the religious Mrs. Urie never had any doubt as to its head. She said, "I have never taught creeds in the home, but all these children have been told of God, and His love, and that He will be a father to them when earthly fathers forsake, as they so often do."

Now in its fourth home and 100 years since its founding, this "family" enters its second century with the support of Society volunteers, donations, and the United Way. A professional staff of childcare specialists now adds its earthly skills to Mrs. Urie's heavenly variety of "kindly custodial care to orphans and friendless children."[3]

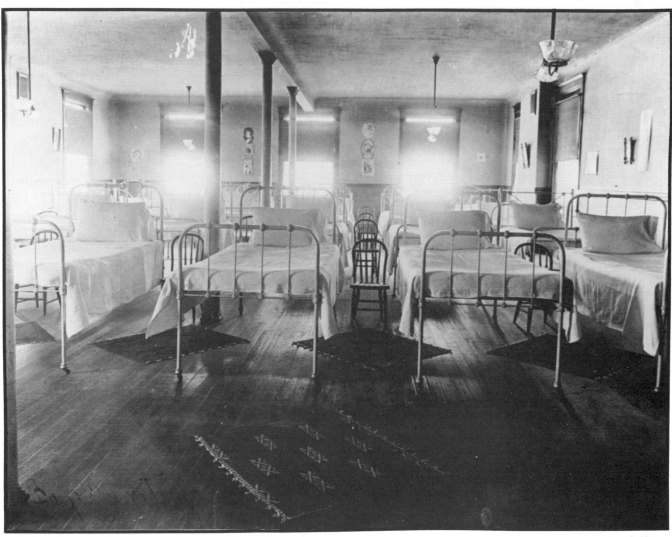

courtesy, Seattle Children's Home

Looking north on the pile trestle with Fremont in the distance.   courtesy, Historical Photography Collection, University of Washington

64 The Electric Bridge to Fremont

Around 10:30 on the evening of October 24, 1890, the John Craig family, then living on the north shore of Lake Union, was "terrorized by the hideous gestures of a death-like image in the form of a woman whirling a glimmering torch." The Post-Intelligencer reported this disturbing story under the headline, "A Ghost That Haunts the Shores of Lake Union."

In the same column of news, "From around Lake Union," the paper noted in a single understated sentence an event whose effects would be regularly felt for many days and nights long after the Craig family spook had returned for good or evil into the shadows along the lake. The P.I. reported that, "The electric cars have taken all the patronage from the boats on Lake Union."

Those were the streetcars which were then first running across the two miles of pile bridge that supported tracks and trolley poles along the western shore of the lake. The boats, which had departed for work on Lake Washington the day before, were the small steamers "Latona" and "City of Latona." For nearly two years they had been round-tripping the lake carrying freight and

passengers to and from the settlements of Fremont, Brooklyn (now the University District), Edgewater, and Latona.

It was between Edgewater and Latona (in today's Wallingford) that the Craig family lived and their ghost appeared. However, this spirit was "probably corporeal." The P.I. reported that "although he cannot account for it, John Craig believes it to be the work of someone trying to scare him into selling his property for less than it is worth." Such was the excitement of real estate about the shores of Lake Union in 1890.

The historical view of the electric trolley atop the pile trestle to Fremont is also "about" real estate. It is one of two dozen promotional views prepared by the photographer Frank La Roche for a bound report titled, "A Prospectus of the Lake Union Improvement Company."[1] This firm was only one of the many inspired enterprises which sprang from a born promoter named Luther H. Griffith. Most of Griffith's schemes had to do either with real estate or with getting to it.

Griffith was described by pioneer historian

Clarence Bagley as a "promoter of Seattle, whose sagacity is keen, whose vision is broad and whose efforts are practical and resultant." A friend said simply that he wished he could "shut Griff up in a room and pay him 50,000 a year to produce nothing but ideas."

The town of Fremont, its name (Griffith had come to Washington in 1883 from Fremont, Nebraska), its lumber mill, and this "electric bridge" to Fremont were all "resultant" Griffith ideas. It was he who in 1888 had won from a sceptical city council the franchise for Seattle's (and every spot west of the Mississippi as well) first electric railway. And it was he who in 1890 was again victorious in a city council sanctioned race between his electric system and the competing cable cars to get the first line out to Fremont and to his real estate.

When Griffith rode his inaugural electric ride to the north shores of Lake Union, he was still a "boy wonder" in his 20s. In the decade of public enterprise which followed his move to Seattle, he also helped start the Seattle National Bank, the Seattle Theater, the first electric plant in Blaine, the first elec-

tric interurban to Tacoma, and the California Colonization Company. Then in 1896, he was off to Guatemala to build its first electric railway, and soon back in Seattle starting his Seattle Transfer Company.

When the miners began rushing to the Yukon in the late 1890s, Griffith responded with his Boston and Alaska Transportation Company. Later he promoted the Westlake Market, (it was claimed that washing vegetables was his innovation), the Jackson Street regrade, and the Pacific Coast Highway. In 1915 while Bagley was writing his *History of Seattle* and praising him, Griffith was taking subscriptions for a proposed tunnel running under the city from the recently completed Smith Tower to Leschi Park. Untypically, nothing came of this, his "four minute ride to Lake Washington."

By 1917 the Lake Washington Ship Canal was formally opened and "always working" Luther Griffith's Lake Union began working full time too. When Griffith died of a heart attack in 1925, his wooden viaduct to Fremont had long since been filled in by Westlake Avenue, as you see it "now."

courtesy, Bill Greer

65 Lake Union's Swimming Hole

For most of its natural life, Lake Union harbored a little cove at its southwest corner, at the base of Queen Anne Hill. Where today there are small businesses selling washing machines, signs, and emergency animal care, there was once a natural wading pool. Since the water near the tules along the shore was shallow, it was quick to warm up and safe for tikes with parental guidance.

The sister and brother knee-deep in these waters lived nearby on Denny Hill. Their amateur photographer father took their picture, and although about 300 of his glass negatives have recently resurfaced, his name has not. But among his surviving photographs many are autobiographical. They tell us about his affections, first for his family and then for his city.

One of these uncovered but uncaptioned scenes shows his little girl and boy celebrating the 1902 Seattle Elks Carnival.[1] In that setting and in this, the children appear to be the same age. So we may conclude that here is the look of things at the southwest corner of Lake Union in the summer of 1902.

And we are further tempted to speculate about this scene's precise occasion. It may be a little past noon of July 19, when the mercury reached 94.3 degrees, then the highest temperature ever recorded since the establishment of the local weather bureau. But with such heat, there would probably be many more waders in the scene. (Or were they jumping into Puget Sound?)

On the horizon is the ridge line of Capitol Hill, and in the middle distance the Brace and Hergert lumber mill which was founded here 20 years earlier by David Denny.

The pile trestle this side of the mill is Westlake Avenue N. It separates the shallow cove from the rest of the lake. In 1937 David Denny's grand-niece, Sophie Frye Bass, remembered it in her book, *Pigtail Days in Old Seattle.*

"Westlake North—at one time called Rollin—from Roy Street to Fremont was built along the shore over Lake Union on piles covered with heavy wooden planks...Gradually it was filled in underneath with earth....Little house boats are now tied along the lake shore and Fremont does not seem so many miles away as it did in the early days....As I look back the changes seem to have come quickly. It is as though I suddenly awakened to find I live in a city, a civilization about me, forests receding, beauty spots gone, and where I had picked lady-slippers, trilliums, and Johnny-jump-ups, there is hard pavement."

And to where many of the wild flowers have gone, so have some of the swimming holes.

courtesy, Bill Greer

66 Tampering with Lake Union

Both the historical and contemporary views look east over Lake Union towards the distant incline of Capitol Hill's northern face, and both scenes were photographed from Fremont bridges—although from different ones.

Both views are also transected by bridges, one high and the other low. And both of these bridges were called "Stone Way." This was the original name for the Aurora Bridge in its planning stages, and the only name for the long timber trestle that cuts across the top of the historical photograph. It gently rises to a pony truss whose narrow span is wide enough for the passage of logs and small boats.

To the picture's right side and the bridge's southern, or Westlake end, the moving blur of a double-ended streetcar is heading north towards Fremont or south towards town—we cannot tell which. This odd long bridge that once interrupted the northwest corner of Lake Union has something to do with the wing dams, flood gate, log pool, and

eroding land that fill the fore ground of the historical photograph. The dam was designed to speed the building of the Lake Washington Ship Canal. It was temporary.

This is the third and last of the Fremont dams. The first, with gates, was constructed in 1888 by a millman named Burlingame who worked at the Fremont lumber mill, just north of the dam. This obstruction was partially eroded in the winter of 1899 when some angry farmers from the Green River Valley dynamited the small canal between Lakes Washington and Union, hoping to lower the former and save their farms from the effect of the lake's high spring water backing up its tributaries and flooding its drains. The immediate effect, however, was to suddenly raise the level of Lake Union by more than two feet until it spilled over Burlingame's dam and just missed flooding Fremont.

In 1903 the dam did go, lowering the lake by two feet. The Army Corps of Engineers built a new one, but this one gave out in 1914,

spilling logs into the bay, wiping out the center of the Fremont Bridge, and setting houseboats askew on the exposed lake shores.[1]

The dam in our historical photograph is the Corp's second and Fremont's last. It was built in 1914 to replace the washout. In two years the ship canal was completed—the small lock was opened in July of 1916—and the waters of the canal were as high as those of the lake. Which means, of course, no more dam. The Stone Way Bridge, however, stayed put for yet another year.

The Seattle Electric Company, which ran the street cars, and the city split the bridge's building costs and first opened it to traffic on May 31, 1911. It took the place of an old Fremont bridge which was razed to allow the Army Corps a freer hand to work on their canal.

The Stone Way Bridge performed its short-lived service up until June 15, 1917. The next day the P.I. reported that the city "acting on orders from the War Department" was tear-

The Fremont bascule bridge soon after its completion.

Looking across the Westlake Viaduct and the Stone Way Bridge towards Wallingford.

ing out the Stone Way Bridge. It added that the Traction Company "acting on its right to be fully compensated" was trying to stop them. Traction Company president Leonard had waved in front of the city council a franchise which gave him the right to run his street cars across Stone Way Bridge until 1934.

Leonard's objections were strictly rhetorical: a ploy to relieve his company of paying a share in the construction of the then brandnew Fremont bascule bridge—the one we still cross.

The Lake Washington Ship Canal was formally dedicated July 4, 1917. Seattle's longhoped-for "inland fresh water sea" was opened to battleships. Of course, this fleet of wide-beamed dreadnoughts never came, but the Stone Way Bridge with its slender span still had to go.

And so did the Puget Sound Traction, Light, and Power Company, a new name for those who ran the streetcars. 1919 was the first year of municipal ownership.

67 The Aurora Bridge: Sunrise and Sunset

The long squabble that recently preluded the final design of the West Seattle Bridge was a repeat of the public noise that more than half-a-century ago accompanied the planning and construction of the city's first big span, the George Washington Memorial Bridge.

Of course, no one calls it that today. Rather, it's Aurora, after the Roman goddess of the dawn. On some mornings the name fits for this long span lets communters glance east to the sun rise that greets them from behind the Cascades. But the actual origin of its popular name involves a story more human than divine. Before the high bridge connected neighborhoods, it would set neighbor against neighbor, city against state, and street against street.

The bridge might have been called Whitman, Linden, or Albion. All had their supporters. But it was first called Stone Way Bridge because the high span was originally visualized as reaching from Dexter Avenue to Stone Way North. Stone Way was the name that Bertha Landes, the city's only woman mayor, took with her to Olympia in 1926 in an attempt to get the high bridge built with state money. She asked for a million and a half and returned with nothing.

Many of the legislators were typically resentful toward their state's biggest city. The state's governor, Roland Hartley, who was then fighting a recall, was against anything that would cost the state money. This included parks, libraries, and schools. The recall move was sparked after Hartley fired the University of Washington's president Henry Suzzallo for, among other things, building an "extravagant" library. (The high profile of the cathedral-like Suzzallo Library can be seen on the left horizon of the historical photograph. It is a bit left of the power pole.)

The governor also disliked paved roads which he referred to as "hard surface joy rides."

Bertha Landes promoted the bridge as a necessary link in the Pacific Coast Highway, which was then being built. Many of the legislators and their wives finally agreed to board a convoy of big busses for a state patrol-led visit to the proposed bridge site. There, they were promised they would witness first-hand the "unspeakable condition of the traffic on the inadequate Fremont Bridge."

Whether by accident or design, the city's timing was perfect. The Fremont Bridge was tied up for 20 minutes by what the Times reported as "an energetic tug escorting a pile driver. Including the caravan from Olympia there were more than 500 autos and 30 street-cars in the jam south of the bridge." Somewhat impressed, the solons responded

with $50,000 for a feasibility study.

This money was also fuel for a long public battle over where to locate the bridge and how to pay for it.

On April 21, 1928 the State Highway Department indicated a preference for either Aurora or Whitman Avenues. The Wallingford Commercial Club responded with a May 2nd mass meeting under the banner, "A Stone Way Bridge on Stone Way." At 10 a.m. a caravan of 100 cars carrying "Stone Way" banners, 10,000 protesting signatures, and their own engineering reports left for Olympia and an audience with Governor Hartley.

The politician responded with what the disapproving Seattle Times described as "a raid on the State Highway Department."

There were many more mass meetings, caravans, and high level audiences, but Hartley's sympathies for the Stone Way supporters was a demogogic bluff. Once safely reelected in the fall of 1928, he dropped his Stone Way sympathies and meddling with the highway commission. Within days the commission unanimously chose the Aurora site. Stone Way advocates first threatened injunctions, and then dreamt of building a subway under Lake Union.

After many more months of fussing over bridge funding, design, and land condemnation along Aurora, on June 1, 1931 (or only nine days after the historical view was taken) the Times headlined "Steel Will Meet Steel on Aurora Structure Today."

The bridge was dedicated on February 22, 1932, the bicentennial of Washington's birthday. A douglas fir was used for a ribbon, and on one end of the six-foot saw was Governor Hartley. Across from him was a representative from Canada; while between them a man from Mexico oiled the saw. Immediately after the log fell to two pieces "from both sides of the bridge, throngs poured forth surging towards each other over Lake Union."[1]

After it was determined that there were 30 other bridges in the country dedicated to Washington, the official name was quickly forgotten along with most of the squabbling that accompanied the "dawn" of its construction.

What might be called the sunset history of the bridge of dawn began on January 30, 1934 when William Reith, a clothing salesman who was despondent over his wife's health, jumped head first from the railing. Thereafter, the Aurora Bridge was often in the news as a popular platform for suicide. As of May 1983 out of 263 recorded attempts, there have been an estimated 150 successes who according to local dark humorists have all "gone down in history."

This view of a jam at the southern end of the Fremont Bridge is not as huge as the solons', but it makes the point. Indeed, the photo was probably taken to make it. Throughout the mid-1920s the Seattle Engineering Department's photographers kept a record of the mess at the Fremont Bridge.

68 Woodland Park:
From Country Estate to African Savanna

Ninety years and a few feet separate this "now" and "then." Both views look south over upper Woodland Park from the park's center.

The historical scene was photographed from an upper story of the old Woodland Hotel, now long gone, and the contemporary scene from the concrete roof of the bear grotto.

This radical change in the landscape contrasts two different visions of nature—although both were developed by Englishmen. The older scene is arranged with the manicured formality of the English country estate, while across the center of the contemporary view sprawls an African savanna.

The English garden was the dream retreat of Guy Phinney, a Nova Scotian of English descent, who arrived here in 1881, broke and alone. After 10 years of successfully dealing real estate, Phinney moved his family into his park.

The "wild kingdom" is the sensitive design of zoo architect David Hancocks. After a Greyhound tour of America, this English-

man adopted Seattle as his home in 1975. Within a year he was named director of the Woodland Park Zoo. The African savanna is the grandest example of his visionary intent to transform the zoo from a prison for animals to a natural habitat where they can act like themselves.[1]

Guy Carleton Phinney was described by a contemporary as the "best exemplification of push and enterprise." Standing six-foot-three and weighing 275 pounds, Phinney was in shape for pushing. Guy Phinney, all of him, stands just to the right of the raised rock flower bed at the left. He is probably admiring his handiwork which includes at the grounds' central axis a fountain set atop a rockery with "1891" decoratively embossed in stones. This was the year the actress Sara Bernhardt visited the park, and, probably also, the year this picture was taken.

It was the pioneers' common desire, and in some cases obsession, to civilize the dense and unkempt condition of the northwest forest into rational examples of the land-

scaper's art. Phinney has kept a few traces of the old forest and contrasted them with features which were conventional for a country garden. These include the small trellised garden pavilion that spans the path right of center, and the parterre or geometric garden above the fountain in the center of the scene.

Faintly visible just to the left of the four tall fir trees is the white conical roof that tops the estate's garden conservatory. It sits at the present site of the rose garden. A glimpse of the marble arch entrance to the old Woodland Park is visible between the third and fourth of the tall firs. To the right of this, the gatekeeper's cottage is behind the strand of smaller firs. It was the Phinney's temporary home, while they made plans for their mansion.[2]

Not shown here are the park's dance pavilion, its racetrack for bicycles, a hunting lodge, boathouse, and pumphouse along the shores of Green Lake, a church, and the Woodland Hotel from which the photographer took his picture.

The Phinney family opened their park to the public with a few posted conditions. No guns, liquor, or dogs could go in and no flowers were to be taken out. The animals, including the deer, beaver, skunks, and Bosco the bear were not to be molested.

In 1893 while preparing to build his mansion, Guy Phinney died. So did the economy. His widow was left with the difficult task of keeping the park open and maintained during the depressed years that followed.

In 1899 the Seattle City Council, overriding loud citizen objections and the mayor's veto, bought Phinney's Woodland Park along his namesake ridge. Seattle entered the twentieth century with its own English country estate and one small zoo.

By now this zoo has been changed into a habitat increasingly sensitive to "animal rights." Today through the center of our scene one can often see zebras, giraffes, springboxes, Egyptian geese, and patas monkeys gamboling about a savanna amazingly like their African home.

An early version of the Woodland Park Zoo.

69 Ravenna Park

The first written promotion for Puget Sound is from the journal of its English discoverer, Captain George Vancouver. "I could not believe," he exclaimed in 1792, "that an uncultivated country had ever been discovered exhibiting so rich a picture... the abundant fertility that unassisted nature puts forth, require only to be enriched by the industry of man... to render it the most lovely country that can be imagined."

A half-century later the first rush of white settlement on the Sound was concerned more with conquering the dark forest than in cooperating with the captain's "unassisted nature." The settlers' idea of communing with nature was usually to take an axe or gun to it. Towns like Seattle were built on cleared land as fortresses against the dark profusion of unpruned nature, wild animals, and unpacified natives. The heroes of this "lovely country" were men like Henry Yesler who had the capital and persistence to build steam sawmills to subdue it.

However, most of these settlers also knew in their hearts, and many of them by heart, the lines of the then popular American nature poet William Cullen Bryant: "To him, who in the love of nature holds/Communion with her visible forms, she speaks/A various language..."

When in the 1880s Seattle first began to resemble a city, its citizens started to long for those natural excitements the poet Bryant envisioned might relieve them from the synthetic city with its successes and stresses. Bryant's nature speaks to the sublime and the serene: sentiments that played as little a part in seizing a frontier as in building a city. The settlers' old frontier fortress against nature was now an urbane enclave beside it.

One of Seattle's best natural retreats into the sublime and serene was found in a ravine north of town. The 1890 Seattle Illustrated declared: "Nowhere in this country or in Europe can one find a retreat of this size which so harmoniously combines the rugged and the picturesque [or the sublime] with the quiet, peaceful, and lovely [or the serene]. The whole effect is startling... as if nature had specially exerted itself to make this a park."

Actually, it was nature and Mr. and Mrs. William W. Beck. (See feature 42.)

Once a stream flowed out of Green Lake, wandered through picturesque meadows along what is now Ravenna Boulevard, cascaded through a ravine, and at last entered Union Bay where today the University of Washington's landfill parking lot covers a few acres east of 25th Avenue N.E. In 1887 the Becks bought the ravine and nurtured it into a park.

They named it Ravenna after the Italian town which sits beside an ancient forest, and which was also the last home of the exiled Dante and for two years the asylum for the restless Lord Byron who there probably proved his prescription, "there is pleasure in the pathless wood."

The "Big Stick" Roosevelt.

The Becks were a cultivated couple and fond of reading romantic poetry including Byron and Bryant. In their park there were plenty of paths along with fountains, mineral springs, water falls, dressing rooms, a music pavilion, and a gate with a 25-cent admission. In 1902, 10,000 paid the two bits. They saw how the Becks had followed Captain Vancouver's advice of enriching "unassisted nature" with their own industry.

Ravenna Park's most sublime attractions were its giant trees which the Becks, like Adam and Eve, had the privilege of naming. One of them, an ancient fir, they called Adam. Another they named Paderewsky, after the Polish pianist who was a friend of Mrs. Beck. Two giants that crowded one another were puckishly titled Mark Matthews and Hi Gill after the local pastor and future mayor who were usually fighting. The tallest fir, which at almost 400 feet was about two-thirds the height of the Space Needle, they named Robert E. Lee. And what Mrs. Beck humorously referred to as the "big stick," a giant with the largest girth, was named Roosevelt after the president who actually visited the park and whispered his sublime approval.

The Becks' natural utopia was indeed sublime and was always being compared to heaven. The writer for the Fine Arts Journal of Chicago gasped: "I am in no mood for speech. I pause spellbound...and lift my head in adoration and reverence to Ravenna Park, Seattle, the jewel of Puget Sea and baptize it "an artist's paradise.""

In an even more worshipful vein a writer for the Pacific Baptist exclaimed: "Ravenna is the unique thing in Seattle. Over it all, like an invisible dove with outstretched quivering wings, seems to brood holiness."

Tax-conscious U.S. Senator John L. Wilson said more prosaically: "Ravenna Park is the most valuable piece of property in Seattle."

The Becks sold Ravenna Park to the city in 1911 for a condemnation fee of $122,000. Eighteen years later Clarence Bagley in his History of King County described Ravenna Park as a "dark, damp, dismal hole in the ground for which the city paid an outrageous price." What happened to Eden?

In 1911 much of the serenity left with the babbling Ravenna Creek which the city diverted into its then new north trunk sewer line. Now Ravenna Creek passes 145 feet below the park not through it.

The sublime left with Paderewsky, Robert E. Lee, and Roosevelt. Soon, and for no uncovered nor convincing reason, those "structures for which time is the only architect" were axed. One researcher, William Arnold of the Seattle P.I., speculates that the felling was done for cordwood for the park department director's private sale.

My first association with Ravenna was with the hole, not the park. On November 11, 1957, 200 feet of Ravenna Boulevard collapsed 60 feet into a washout caused by a leak in the north trunk sewer. As a tourist from Spokane, I was taken to the edge of the hole. Behind us were signs restricting access to the park. There, once again, Ravenna Creek was babbling with more than the normal runoff from the 40 small springs on the sides of the ravine. Now the brook was carrying a three-foot-wide swath of raw sewage into Union Bay.

Today, the springs, subsoil drainage, and rain's runoff still feed a little brook in the bottom of the Ravenna ravine, and the scene is again serene. But in the place of Mark Matthews, Robert E. Lee, and Teddy Roosevelt is a tennis court.

70 Greenlake Way

In the late 1970s Don Sherwood, then a Seattle Park Department employee, organized his department's historical records. The results of this ambitious project are packed into four 5-foot cabinets in City Hall's Municipal Library. The Green Lake folder is the Sherwood Collection's thickest file, and the original photographic print for this historical subject is from it.[1]

Many of the homes in the older view are still around in the new. Because most are now hidden behind trees, I used the overlapping rooflines of the houses across the lake to locate the original photographer's shooting site.

Wallingford's Home of the Good Shepherd is faintly evident right of center and through the limbs of the almost leafless tree which is above and to the left of the touring car. Of course, this car and its riders are not touring but posing. There is no one in the front seat because the driver of the car is probably the photographer.

"1911" is lightly penciled on the back of the original print. The year is probably correct and the shedding tree suggests it is fall. It is certainly not spring. If it were, then this planked viaduct would be over Green Lake, not beside it; those two dark boathouses in the scene's center would be floating on the lake rather than leaning toward it,[2] and there would be no sandy peninsula intruding into this the southern end of the lake. 1911 was the year Green Lake was lowered seven feet.

The lake was lowered at the recommendation of the Olmsted brothers, those famous landscapers who designed much of Seattle's park system. Although the city owned the lake, only a narrow strip of squeezed land lay between the water and the privately owned streetcar line that nearly circled the lakeshore.

In 1908 the Olmsteds proposed that by lowering and thus shrinking Green Lake, it would become "a lake within a park." They asked for four feet, and three years later the park department obliged and went three feet more.

The lake's lowering created a park; however, it also provoked decades of "swimmer's itch," recurring attacks of anacharis cana densis (a lake weed with a political-sounding name) and clouds of algae. This small lake made smaller did not drain itself well, and so was forced to outfall into the city's sewers. The irritating "greening of Green Lake" followed with three-quarters-of-a-century of emergency studies, chlorinations, dredgings, and lake closings. Swimmers are still scratching.

The 1908 Olmsted report also recommended that a "pleasure drive run south along the shore of Woodland Park by easy curves." The pile bridge pictured here was the city's first response. The city council approved its plans on March 8, 1909. The plans (and the photograph in part) show three rows of pilings supporting a roadway of $4'' \times 12''$ planks, sided by three-foot railings made from $4'' \times 4''$ posts and $2'' \times 6''$ top and side rails.

Once stranded with the lake's lowering, this picturesque pile bridge's future was insecure. On October 14, 1914, the city council approved another "plan of improvement" for West Green Lake Way. Within a year the bridge was gone and a paved boulevard followed the grade and line of the Green Lake Way seen in the "now" photo.

1891 sketch of Green Lake from Woodland Park. Phinney's boat house is on the right.

16636
W&S

courtesy, Old Seattle Paperworks

71 Gas Works

In the spring of 1910 itinerate aviator Charles Hamilton made Seattle's first heavier-than-air flight. He lifted his bi-wing up from an improvised runway at Meadows Race Track and moments later crashed it into Meadows Lake, submerged but only slightly scratched. Although it may seem so, this high altitude 1910 look over the Lake Union Gas Works was not photographed in flight, but rather shot from the firm earth of Queen Anne Hill.[1]

This image number 16636 is one of an estimated 40,000 Webster and Stevens' negatives which are a recent addition to the Museum of History and Industry. The glass plate's large five-by-seven inch size reveals in fine detail this North Seattle scene which in 1910 was entering only its fourth decade of development.

In the early 1880s most of this setting was still covered with a virgin forest which was only then beginning to provide a steady diet for the first sawmills on the lake shores. Here, in 1910, on the horizon a stand of that primeval forest still lines the distant ridge that is now the Hawthorne Hills and View Ridge neighborhood.

The university campus is to the foreground of that wilderness tract. A darker line of second growth timber mixes with those sturdier buildings which remained after the temporary structures of the campus' 1909 Alaska Yukon and Pacific Exposition had been torn down. The last bit of skeletal framing of the AYP's Federal Building is evident just to the right of the old Meany Auditorium, the largest and brightest structure seen in this view of the campus. *(See features 27, 28, 29.)*

To the left of the auditorium is Parrington Hall. Behind it show the towers of Denny Hall which when it was dedicated in 1895 was the first structure on this then new campus. Both are still in use. *(See features 36, 37.)*

Just this side of the campus is—or was—the community of Brooklyn. Platted in the early 1890s, it was approached by the old Latona Bridge seen in the center of the photograph. Its wooden span reached from Capitol Hill's north end to Latona, then a quick-stop station for the Seattle Lake Shore and Eastern Railway. Brooklyn became the University District when the school moved to its new campus, and the little town of Latona eventually blended into Wallingford.

In the foreground Wallingford itself blends into the north end of Lake Union. Here in 1907 the Seattle Gas Company began urging homemakers to "cook with gas." The firm generated it here from the high-temperature cooking of coal. For a 30-mile radius this was the hub of its underground service.

However, an unrelenting disservice regularly escaped this gas plant in the form of soot and showering sparks which fell over Wallingford usually three shifts a day until 1937. Then the company switched from coal to oil and the pollution let up some. It ceased in 1956 when natural gas was first piped in from the southwest. Then the old gas works shut down and became a company parking lot. In 1962 the city agreed to purchase this peninsula from the gas company. Many years earlier this woodland promontory was a popular picnic stop for pioneers sailing about the then wild Lake Union. In 1962 this wilderness park was a 20 acre "layer cake of hydrocarbon contaminates...a slough of lampblack and oily wastes." And it was covered with the "totemic industrial artifacts of a pre-electronic age," which is to say, those black towers.

In 1970 the city hired local landscape architect Richard Haag to prepare a park master plan. With atypical understatement, the usually exhuberant Haag concluded that "the site resists becoming a conventional park."[2] Then to the delight of some and disgust of others, the visionary Haag proposed that many of those towers be saved and recycled as monumental free-standing sculpture.

Originally the work of these towers was to generate oxygen gas and separate tar. Now Haag's vision generated a local controversy that separated citizens between those who thought his proposal a "macabre joke" and those who saw in these towers an "iron stonehenge" or "a hanging garden of metal" or the best example of Marshal McLuhan's celebrated epigram, "Yesterday's technology is today's art."

Ever since Gasworks Park opened in September 1975 Haag's soft green setting for those hard black towers has been generating international awards and a profusion of non-polluting multi-colored kites.[3]

courtesy, Lawton Gowey

72 Ballard Avenue

This stretch of Ballard Avenue between 20th and 22nd Avenues N.W. was once the busiest part of Ballard. The commercial axis was poled by the towers of the Junction Block Building in the foreground at 20th and the Ballard City Hall in the scene's distant center.

The Junction Building's battlements were loosened by and removed after the earthquake of 1949. The Ballard City Hall's conical tower was slightly weakened by another "act of God" in the quake of 1965. However, within a year this entire monument to Ballard's early municipal culture was razed by an act of man in one of those too typical sacrifices to the post-war mania for progress and urban renewal that was regrettably still very active in 1965.[1]

Our historical scene was photographed in 1908, or one year after Ballard citizens concluded their long annexation fight and decided, as critics called it, to "submerge into Seattle." In a 1907 Post-Intelligencer story

headlined "What Ballard Brings to the City," the town's culture was represented as supported by "eighteen churches, three banks, seventeen shingle mills, three sawmills, three iron foundries...three machine shops, three shipyards...a mattress factory, the largest pipe factory on the coast, and about 300 wholesale and retail merchants and shopkeepers."

The same P.I. page included a story of how Ballard's lame duck Mayor Peck had fired two policemen for aiding in an escape from prosecution a bartender at the Monte Carlo Saloon and a fifteen-year-old girl of uncertain profession. The charge was for "running a disorderly house."

There were a lot of "disorderly houses" among Ballard's some 300 non-manufacturing merchants. They served the thousands of men working in this "Shingle Capitol of the World." It was said that Ballard was "the district with 22 mills and 22 saloons." (Sometimes 22 churches were added and

many of these were located on 22nd Avenue.)

Most of Ballard's saloons were here on Ballard Avenue. Indeed, somewhere in Ripley's "Believe It or Not" there is a brief description of this early-century Ballard Avenue strip as "four blocks with 27 saloons." (The number is approximate.) Many of them had slot machines, free lunches, private boxes, and rooms upstairs.

Ballard began in the mid-1880s as Farmdale, but its agrarian promise was soon upset. In 1888 its "big three" developers—Thomas Burke (of the bike trail), John Leary (of the Way), and William Rankin Ballard—platted their preserve into a boomtown they called Gilman Park. Within a year there were saw and steel mills and nearly 2,000 residents who incorporated a town and elected to call it Ballard.

By the end of the decade this "city of smokestacks" was building its grand city hall and promoting itself as a "metropolis in Lilliput, with every feature and luxury of a ci-

ty of the first class." At the time of its annexation it was the second largest town in King County and the seventh largest in the state.

The fight for annexation nearly split the town in half. Those arguing against appealed to civic pride, and those for to the need for better water. The latter's cause was helped considerably when a dead horse was found in the Ballard Reservoir a few days before the election.

On May 29, 1907, or one day before Ballard town officials surrendered their books and furniture to their Seattle counter parts, the anti-annexation forces wrapped their city hall in a mourning mantle of black crepe. Meanwhile Ballard's elated real estate agents were busy promoting a name change to Northwest Seattle. What did change were the street names: Broadway to Market, Main Street to 15th Avenue N.W. and Division to 8th Avenue N.W. But Ballard and Ballard Avenue stayed Ballard.

Fishermans Wharf dedication, 1914.

73 Ballard Skyline

When the long bridge to Ballard was completed in 1917, the community was already 30 years old. The walk across the bridge gave one a long look at the monuments of Ballard: those giant scrap-burning cylinders which rose like cathedral cupolas or capitol domes above the "shingle capitol of the world."

The most immense of these—the giant on the "then" picture's left—towered above the largest cedar mill in the world. Like a volcano this stack sent out its eruptions sometimes far from the source. It was not uncommon for Ballard residents north of N.W. 65th Street to be sprinkled with the Seattle Cedar Mill's unconsumed particles while homes in between would escape the shower. The Seattle Cedar Mill did not specialize in shingles but did it all—siding, gutters, studs, and all of it cedar. Its long rows of air-drying cedar boards were themselves many stories high. The cedar smell was subtle but effective. Some claimed that unsuspecting moths flew into Ballard only on windless days and then fled with the first whiff.

The Seattle Cedar Mill was working from 1901 to 1958 when it made a spectacular fire. The draft was of such force that it flung cedar planks across the railroad tracks and into Ballard.[1]

A Ballard smell and setting of a different sort is in the foreground: the mingled aroma of drying nets, halibut, salt, sardines, tar, salmon, and oil. This Salmon Bay site was purchased by the Port of Seattle in 1912. Two years later Fisherman's Terminal was dedicated, and by the late 1940s it was handling more than 1,000 boats. (This made it much larger than San Francisco's Fisherman's Wharf—unless you count the tourists. Now, of course, many of those boats are for sale.)

The first approaches to the Ballard bascule (teeter-totter) bridge were wooden and on hot days had to be protected from the burning embers escaping from Ballard's dozen saw-mills. Not until 1940 was the wood replaced with concrete and steel. This included the steel steps from which the contemporary photo was taken.[2]

courtesy, Lawton Gowey

courtesy, Inga Nelson Stangvik

courtesy, Michael Maslan

74 A Different Duwamish

It is probably no longer possible to precisely date this historical landscape. The original print comes from a collection of a dozen images. All the others are of popular Seattle landmarks around the year 1890. Staying close to home and the 11 other photographs, we may surmise that this pastoral setting is somewhere along the banks of the Duwamish River at about that time.[1]

But which part of the river? In 1890 the Duwamish was a different stream than it is today. From its origin, where the Black and White Rivers joined, to its estuary on Elliott Bay, the Duwamish covered eight miles in a serpentine course that meandered at least twice that distance. Then the river twisted through 16 S-curves; today only six and one-half remain. More than half of its wavy course has been straightened and widened into the Port of Seattle's Duwamish Waterway.

Here we can rediscover the old river. These are the first two curves the Duwamish River makes north of its origin at a place the natives called Mox-La-Push meaning "two mouths." We call it the Black River Junction. The view is to the south.

Just left of the scene's center is the junction's old railroad depot, and directly above and to its left is the bridge across the Black River. The bridge was built in 1883 as part of a line that connected Seattle with the Northern Pacific Railroad near where Auburn is today. For years this short connection was called the "Orphan Road" because either no trains or only one a day crossed it. (Throughout the mid-to-late 1880s the Northern Pacific's land and marketing interests lay in its Tacoma terminus, and both the railroad and the town preferred to make connections with competing Seattle clumsy.)

In the left foreground is a railroad oddity: a track with three rails. This is the original 1876 grade of the narrow gauge Seattle and Walla Walla Railroad which turned east at Black River to the coal mines around Renton and Newcastle. In 1883 a third rail at standard gauge was added to bring the Northern Pacific's Orphan Road in from the Black River Junction to Seattle.

To the right of center is the Foster farm. When Joseph Foster first set his claim here in 1853, Mox-La-Push was a forest. Foster was one of King County's most extraordinary pioneers. He was the first to pole logs to Henry Yesler's new steam sawmill, and as a trained tailor Foster was the first local to commercially cut and sew a suit of clothes. As a member for 11 consecutive terms in the territorial legislature, he introduced bills that resulted in the first road across the Snoqualmie Pass and located the university in

The Duwamish River near South Park, early century.   courtesy, Historical Photography Collection, University of Washington

Seattle. He was also a steady advocate for women's suffrage.

"Uncle Joe" Foster was still living here in 1909 when his claim was incorporated into the town of Tukwila. He died here two years later at the age of 85.

Since 1925 his farm has been a playground pruned by golfers at the namesake Foster Golf Course. This recreational use has preserved this last strip of greenbelt that runs between south Seattle's industry and South Park Plaza's blacktop. Indeed, parts of this green Tukwila gap are so overgrown that it was impossible to penetrate the jungle of alders and blackberries to get a contemporary photo to jibe with the historical view. For the "now" view, I moved a few hundred feet east and up to a precipitous landfill atop Beacon Hill. Below, the river is now hidden within the greenbelt. And it may stay so.

courtesy, Old Seattle Paperworks

75 Catholic Hill

Some 13,000 years ago when the ice age crept back north it left a Duwamish River Valley shaped like an hourglass with its slender waist centered near the present city of Tukwila. Here outcroppings of sandstone and harder stuff resisted the erosion of the melting flood and left a scattered field of sedimentary mounds. The most northerly of these Duwamish buttes is in South Park, that small community at the southern city limits.

In 1892 the Brothers of Our Lady of Lourdes were called all the way from the cultivated lowlands around Ostaaker, Belgium to do missionary work in the wild West around Seattle. Here atop this South Park mound, the skilled artisans among them built the quarters we see filling this historical scene.

The dominant structure in the foreground had a chapel, dormitory, and library. In the back to the right of the photograph, a second building included a kitchen and refectory. Behind the chapel, to the left, a third building had classrooms, a studyhall, and playrooms. Beginning in 1893, 40 day scholars and 18 boarders enrolled in this school for boys atop what from then on would be called "Catholic Hill."

The brothers landscaped their eight acres with rows of poplars, cedars, maples, and well-wrought hedges. Their gardens were blessed with oversized vegetables and an orchard bloomed with trees bearing apples, peaches, pears, cherries, plums, walnuts, and prunes. The last sublime touch to the Eden-like scene was the Grotto of Our Lady of Lourdes of the West which the brothers built as a close replica of their Lady's namesake shrine in France.

But not everything was heavenly on Catholic Hill.

In 1906 Brother Fulgentius in an appeal to the Catholic hierarchy described the school as a "house of disorder and confusion" and complained that "the money interests were more appreciated than the welfare of the place." After the brothers' regular obligatory contribution was sent off to their Superior General in Belgium, there was little left for the school. The buildings deteriorated along with the brothers' morale. Twice the school was closed for reasons of health. Brothers left and so did the boys. In 1914 Brother Theophilus wrote to Seattle Bishop O'Dea pleading, "We want to go back. We see the hopelessness of continuing." And in the summer of 1919 they left for good.

In that same year the Jergen family moved in. In the "now" photograph Richard Jergen stands on the site of the chapel and points to the location of the old refectory where his family spent the winter of 1919-20. They lived there, temporarily at the invitation of Father Francis who was the first Franciscan priest to pastor the parish of Our Lady of Lourdes. Richard Jergen and his brother Louis still live on the hill in their own home. They remember intimately the hill's entire history, both sacred and secular, since those other brothers left.

The deteriorating chapel was soon razed; the refectory was lowered to its basement level only; and the classroom building was remodeled as the new sanctuary for the Our Lady of Lourdes Parish Church. The grotto flourished and into the 1960s was the site for the annual pilgrimage of the May Feast of Mary procession. The hill stayed Catholic.

Before the Duwamish Valley was covered with gravel from the hills, this rich river land was checkered with truck farms. Many were owned by Italians. It was this community around Catholic Hill which in the 1930s celebrated annually the feast of St. Anthony. This June celebration was introduced at sunrise with the neighborhood-awakening explosions of cherry bombs and torpedoes. The Sunday activities included a procession to the grotto, accompanied by a 30-piece band, afternoon games, an ethnic pot luck, theater by the Grotto Players (of which Richard Jergen was one), Italian folkdancing, and was consumated in the evening by a lavish fireworks display.

The fireworks were stopped during WW II. At that time it was often necessary to answer to a "Halt!" on one's way to Mass. Then the old refectory basement was the barracks for soldiers who kept watch over the ammo-dump, anti-aircraft guns, and one barrage-balloon that covered the hill. Just below and across the river was the object of their concern, the new but entirely unoccupied camouflage neighborhood created atop the Boeing B-17 plant.[1]

The parish and grotto shrine were both bulldozed in 1970. Today the unsettled hill is surrounded by a straightened Duwamish River to the east, industry to the south, a freeway to the west, the Sea-Tac flight pattern overhead, and the single-family residences of South Park to the north.

courtesy, Old Seattle Paperworks

76 The Allentown Covered Bridge

This view of King County Engineer's bridge number 57C was photographed on September 14, 1951 by Albert Farrow, a retired Burlington Northern engineer. That makes it the youngest old photograph in this book. Of course, it doesn't seem so recent because its subjects, the old steam engine and the covered bridge, emit an aura of nostalgia.

Bridge 57C was built in 1921. Its engineering department name did not stir the imagination so its popular name became the Allentown Covered Bridge. On most maps it has yet another name, the Steel Hill Bridge; and the new concrete overpass is still called that on maps that have not been corrected (which are most of them). Its official new name is the Archie Codiga Bridge.

Codiga, a Swiss-Italian immigrant farmer, started a dairy farm here in 1908. Today his son and grandson continue to farm here, although they do not milk the cows but rather fatten the cattle. The Codiga barn can be seen on the far left of the "now" scene.

The old bridge was a 125-foot long link between the Duwamish Valley's old Tacoma Highway and Beacon Hill's Sunset Highway (later called the Dunlap Canyon Road and still later Empire Way) to Renton. It crossed the mainline tracks of the Northern Pacific, Union Pacific, and Pacific Coast Railway's southern entrance to Seattle.

The new bridge is seven times as long as the old and also much higher, spanning not only the tracks but Interstate 5 as well. It is here that the freeway makes its long sweeping curve toward the west and the Tukwila and airport exits. Here I-5 spans these mainline tracks and the Duwamish River and casts its shadow through the center of our contemporary photograph.

The three railroads shared the construction costs of the covered bridge. The roof protected not only the planking but also the motorists. During the 1920s as many as 200 trains a day passed beneath this span, and all of them, except for the runs on the electrically powered Milwaukee Road, were pulled by steam engines spouting soot and cinders.

That is why Warren Wing moved to Allentown in 1952 when the covered bridge was still being showered with the smoke and steam from locomotives passing below. Wing stands in the foreground of the "now" photo and points in the direction of both the old covered bridge and his Allentown home. He is the author of *A Northwest Rail Pictorial* and this historical view is one of the book's

200 plus railroading scenes. Wing is one of a special type called "rail fans." He's always hanging around tracks, and many of his waking thoughts, and a few of his dreams as well, are directed toward trains.

The Allentown Covered Bridge caught fire on May 30, 1958. By the time the volunteer fire department could respond to this Memorial Day emergency, the last public covered bridge in King County was a mass of flames.

For the ten bridgeless years that followed, the Codiga clan no longer needed to call their

kids into the farmhouse at a little before 4 p.m. It was then that the rush of Boeing workers started their weekday shortcutting across the old bridge to Renton. The 16-foot wide roadway beneath the canopy had given it the deserved reputation as the most accident-prone bridge in King County. The Memorial Day fire was its last accident.

On July 10, 1967 to a live orchestral rendition of the "Bridge over the River Kwai," a blessing from Father Palmasani and a ribbon cutting, the new bridge was opened and dedicated to Archie Codiga. And on Monday the Boeing rush resumed.

77 At the Leschi End of the Cable Line

A few Seattle neighborhoods have been blessed with their own historians whose love for their community has lured them into researching its past. Leschi has Wade Vaughn.

Vaughn's *Seattle-Leschi Diary* includes the record of his community's first big speculator's boom in 1888 when the cable line from downtown to Leschi was completed. In the "now" photograph Vaughn sits atop a roof of a Leschi home and points to the place of the old powerhouse and eastern terminus of that line.

For half-a-century pleasure-seekers, eastside commuters, and Leschi residents were transported over this three-mile roller coaster ride out Yesler Way from Pioneer Square. The final section was a thrilling 200-foot plus descent down an exposed ramp to the powerhouse. Passengers would disembark and walk the few remaining feet to the waterfront on a second ramp—the one pictured in the old panorama.

New passengers, perhaps returning from a steam excursion to the wilderness of Mercer Island, would step aboard and ride the cable south to Jackson Street where it would climb the hill on yet another precipitous ramp and return, via Jackson, to the city's center.

On a late winter sunny mid-day in 1890, the now celebrated photographer F. Jay Haynes made that round trip. Positioning his tripod some feet to the east of the powerhouse and sighting down the short ramp to the coal dock, Haynes recorded what is probably the earliest existing panorama of the Leschi waterfront. The coal from the barge at the ramp's end eventually would generate the steam that powered the cable that drove the line.

Also at ramp's end is the almost completed hotel which eventually was the home of the Lake Washington Restaurant, seen in the photo at right, believed to have been taken around the turn of the century.

Vaughn learned that the woman second from the right is Mrs. Benson, sister of the original owner and mother of Helmer Benson who eventually bought the restaurant from his uncle and made these identifications. The man on the far left is Carl Neuss, who landscaped and planted Leschi Park.

Vaughn's book also quotes the late L.P.

West, who worked as a conductor on the Yesler Way cable line after World War I. West remembered: "The hotel had a large room below street level for dancing. It served sandwiches to occupants of the hotel rooms, which were only occupied for an hour or so."

Although these accommodations probably were more often used by commuters who missed the last ferry to Medina, the other more risque room-letting surely took place, for Leschi was a hot spot for romping, mixing, and romantic recreation. And for everyone, families included, there was the park and lake front promenade where the strumming of banjos and small guitars accompanied the informal parade of picnickers in their Sunday best. There were all kinds of boats for hire and excursions on the steamer Fortuna.

There was a zoo with sea lions and a panther, and a magnificent casino for vaudeville and the city's largest dance hall. Leschi could get crowded—40,000 were counted for the 1908 Fourth of July celebration. The last returning cable cars often were packed with somewhat tipsy revelers.

Leschi got its name from a different sort of "whooping it up." Long before the cable cars and white invasion, there was an Indian trail that crossed the same route from the Lake to Sound. It was here that a few hundred natives gathered in January 1856 to plan and proceed with their attack on the small town of Seattle.

There are conflicting reports about whether or not the Nisqually native and farmer, Leschi, was one of that attacking band's leaders. Vaughn believes he was. At any rate, Leschi was later executed as a "bad Indian" who resisted white dominance. By 1891 the old white ambivalence toward Leschi had subsided. The rebel was sufficiently romanticized that Frederick J. Grant, the president of the cable company, dedicated the park to him. Grant did not thereby intend to encourage the return of natives but the suburban settlement of Whites who were then beginning to feel sentimental about the Indians.

In 1909 the city bought Leschi Park. In 1913 the first auto ferry, the Leschi, started regular service to the eastside. The floating bridge retired that. In 1946 the city attempted to sell off the Leschi waterfront and part of the park. That was stopped by citizen protest.

Wade Vaughn's book was motivated, in part, by a neighborhood protest. The *Seattle-Leschi Diary* was distributed by the Leschi Improvement Council as a fund-raising device for protecting and promoting the quality of life in that community. In 1982, the year the book was published, the targeted threat was the noise and pollution expected from a second I-90 bridge.

Vaughn's first chapter is titled, "Who Are We?" He answers, "Seattle is sandwiched between two north-south glacier scraped bodies of water, Puget Sound and Lake Washington. Leschi is the relish." And Wade Vaughn is part of that garnish.

courtesy, Lawton Gowey

courtesy, Columbia City Historical Society

78 Rainier Valley's Electric Railway

In the fall of 1884 Frank Osgood with the help of four horsecars, 20 steady horses, and three eager capitalists, opened Seattle's first street railway on three miles of track. Four years later he was ready to trade his horses for electricity. *(See feature 48)*

Adding a few more capitalists and convincing the city council to grant him a franchise over the objections of those common-sensical citizens who argued that since lightning traveled in a jagged route, so would these "lightning-propelled" streetcars, Osgood was ready to give his miracle its first full public test. On March 31, 1889 the first car crowded with hand-picked courageous riders ran effortlessly past the incredulous witnesses who lined Second Avenue.[1]

Osgood's Seattle Electric Railway was the first "wired" common carrier on the Pacific Coast. Its heroic bending of these "eccentric, shocking, and mysterious forces of nature" encouraged other developers to speculate about the penetration of the surrounding wilderness with electricity, transforming it into suburbia.

One of these opportunists was J.K. Ed-miston, a square-jawed banker from Walla Walla. The wild land he desired to subjugate with his own electric trolley was Rainier Valley, and principally the 40 acres he would clear and call Columbia City. In 1890 the valley was sparsely settled by a few pioneers separated by swamps and virgin forests. When Edmiston's Rainier Avenue Electric Railway pushed its way south, the settlers happily donated land for its right-of-way. The bogs and small streams were forded with an extensive system of viaducts that supported the tracks through their three lowland miles before the slow rise to Edmiston's cleared 40-acre townsite.

Here the Columbia Home Company sold its first lot on April 4, 1891. The ads promised "elegant lots with rich soil and free wood at $300, with 10 dollars down and a dollar a week." One of the buyers on that spring day was Will Brown. Today his grandson Buzz Anderson still runs the family furniture store, Grayson & Brown, seen in our contemporary photograph.

The four covered cars on Edmiston's electric railway couldn't handle the land rush so

two flatcars with benches were added. The cars carried banners reading "Watch Columbia Grow!" And it did. The company claimed that "the liberality of its terms far excels any offered elsewhere in or near Seattle." Their very sweet deal also provided that "should a purchaser die before the 300 weeks has elapsed, his contract would be marked 'paid in full.' "

With this kind of insurance, one year later the company boasted that "from 40 to 50 residences of inviting appearance have been erected besides several store buildings. By then Columbia City had a school with 75 students, two churches, a gravitation water system, post office, park, and half-hour service to Seattle on the Rainier Avenue Electric Railway.

One of the first conductors on King County's longest interurban was Fred Bond. Bond strikes a casual pose at the far right in the historical photograph. The scene was photographed in 1891 looking east across the mainline and Columbia City's passing track. By 1893 Fred Bond was on the Columbia City town council but his boss J.K. Edmiston was

The Rainier-Renton line along the western shore of Lake Washington

bankrupt and out of town. It was reported that he had left to "some spot on the earth's surface kept secret from all former acquaintances."

By 1895 that original electrical wizard Frank Osgood was in control of the Rainier line but not of its patrons. Osgood had a monopoly service to the booming valley but, while his profits and rates rose, the service fell and the condition of the cars deteriorated to the airy circumstances where umbrellas were required inside the cars as well as out. The riders organized petitions, public meetings, and even fare boycotts. Once when these grievances were to be aired before the Seattle City Council, Osgood shut down the line for the three hours before the evening meeting and forced his unhappy riders to either miss the meeting or walk to town and be late.

Osgood got out of his line just before the national financial crash of 1907. However, Rainier Valley didn't get rid the line or its poor service until 30 years later when the last car was switched off in the Columbia City car barn on the morning of January 1, 1937.[2]

79 Morningside

Rising from the center of our contemporary photograph is the twisted stateliness of what is probably the largest madrona in the Puget Sound area. Standing in the narrow path in front of the tree is Harold V. Smith. The tree is about 650 years old. Smith is only 93.

In the historical scene the same Harold Smith poses in the center of a different path which leads to that same ancient madrona. To the other side of Bingo, the family St. Bernard, is the young boy's Aunt Cora and behind the three-year-old is his mother Mary.

Mary Dibble Smith was one of the first graduates of Smith College. In 1888 she left a career teaching Latin and Greek to join her husband in a Seattle he promised her was cosmopolitan.

In 1885 Everett Smith, then a recent graduate of Yale Law School, came here to start a career and prepare a home. He wrote to his questioning fiancee Mary, "Cosmopolitan? I should say so. Walk down Front Street any day and you meet Chinese, Indians, Irish, Negroes, Italians, Germans, Jews, French, English, and Americans from every state. I never saw such a great small metropolis." Mary came and helped her husband help the city grow up. Here, in 1893 she relaxes at Morningside, the Smith home, with her sister and son.

The Smiths called their new home Morningside because from here one looked east over Lake Washington and past the wilderness of Mercer Island to the rising sun. From this clearing, the eye could sweep the long way north from Mount Rainier to Mount Baker. And to the evening side, the sun set behind a high hill which, in 1893, was still topped by a virgin forest. Through this dark woodland ran a path, today's Holly Street, which in half a mile reached Rainier Valley and a clearing with a trolley track.

In 1890 as a young attorney Everett Smith had helped build that suburban trolley by arranging right-of-ways and subsidies from landowners, of whom he was one, along the way. The Smith family were passengers on the trolley's March 1, 1891 inaugural trip.

Morningside was the five waterfront acres of 40 that Everett Smith platted in 1890 as Brighton Beach. A year earlier the Smiths bought this charmed land from a John Wilson who 20 years earlier accepted it as payment in lieu of $1,500 he'd loaned Asa Mercer (of the island).[1]

Apparently, the Wilsons were pleased enough with this repayment in land for they built a home here and stayed 20 years. When the Smiths took the Wilson place, they added a greenhouse, boathouse, barn, and a dog compound to restrain the chicken-chasing Bingo. Their landscaping included rows of elms (some of which still stand), a surrounding hedge and a grand treehouse nestled in the crooks of the madrona's twisting branches. Here Harold slept his summer nights, and here on an upper deck which could safely entertain 25, the Smiths were hosts for many happy occasions, including the Plymouth Congregational Church's annual summer picnic.

Everett Smith was the type of progressive Christian who nurtured this young city's parks, schools, and charities. He gave his form of cultured compassion to the Childrens Home Society, the Seattle School Board, the local council of Boy Scouts, Goodwill, and the Seattle Y.M.C.A. For many years he was the superior court judge in charge of juvenile cases, and when he died in 1933, the Times remembered him as "one of the kindliest men that ever presided over a King County court."

In 1919, after raising three sons and a neighborhood, the Smith family left Morningside and Brighton Beach. The eldest son, Harold still returns every year to explore what are now the grounds behind the old Martha Washington school for girls.[2]

The Seattle Park Board plans to give the Smith's old Morningside site an official park name. For many commemorative reasons, historical and philanthropic, Everett Smith Park would seem to be a fine cosmopolitan choice.

courtesy, Harold Smith

The Leschi steaming across Lake Washington

80 Meydenbauer Bay: The Bellevue Landing

In 1914 Bellevue was still a remote suburb of a few hundred berry and dairy farmers pitched between a front porch facing Lake Washington's Meydenbauer Bay and a back lawn of second growth forest. These farmers and loggers were also real estate agents. Trying to encourage a springtime flood of cross-lake migration, they published early that year a 14-page pamphlet filled with appealing pictures and well-nurtured hyperbole.

It reads in part: "Bellevue is a thriving, prosperous suburb of Seattle...lying directly across from Leschi Park. There is plenty of pure air and an abundance of the purest water (but no saloons). It is far enough away from the whirl of the city, yet near enough to be easily accessible; a truly ideal place for a home."

The pamphlet was timed to promote the first auto-ferry service to Belleve—a 15-minute ride on the then brand new Leschi ferry. When filled to its capacity of 400 passengers and "40 teams of autos," the Leschi could carry a good portion of Bellevue to Seattle.

In the quiet scene of the Leschi at its Meydenbauer landing, only one auto, half a team, and seven passengers wait for the gate to open for boarding. The day is sunny, and judging from the shadows, it is mid-afternoon. The fact that the Leschi's flag is at half mast is explained by the date the photographer, James Lee, inscribed at the bottom of his negative, 5-30-l4. It was Memorial Day.

At the very moment of this tranquil tableau, the Seattle Times was pressing its Decoration Day edition. The front page declared, "Glorious weather, a cloudless sky with a beneficent sun, nearly 150,000 citizens, 4,000 uniformed men...silken flags flashing, hundreds of automobiles garlanded in the Stars and Stripes—all these united to make Memorial Day epochal in the city's annals."

The Leschi resting dockside in this scene has probably just brought back a lot of Bellevue folks from what the evening Times headlined as the "Greatest Parade in City's History." Thus, this settled scene is most likely the quiet after the storm, or as it often is with ferries, the quiet between storms.

The Leschi stopped calling at Meydenbauer Bay in 1921 when it was determined that Bellevue commuters would rather enjoy

Construction on the floating bridge.

a second cup of coffee after breakfast and then rush off in their Packards to catch the ferry at Medina, the other eastside dock.

In 1939 King County agreed with Chicago bond buyers to eliminate the competitive Leschi-Medina run when their investment, the floating bridge, was completed. Thus, in 1940 the ferry Leschi was moved to the last remaining ferry service on the lake that ran between Madison Park and Kirkland.

Later in the '40s when tolls were lifted from the bridge, this northern route could not compete, and the Leschi made its last lake run on August 31, 1950. (Today, it's still afloat in Alaska as a fish-processing plant.)

Excited by this new toll-free ride to its front door, Bellevue in 1947 published a new pamphlet: "It's easy to see why Bellevue's population is increasing rapidly. No one could live in an area more filled with the good things its takes to develop a happy, healthy, well-adjusted life." Soon Bellevue would no longer be "far enough away from the whirl of the city."

18661

81   The Olmsted's Curves

The spring of 1909 bloomed upon a city busy getting beautiful for its first world's fair. The Seattle Park Department did its part by congratulating itself with an illustrated publication detailing its impressive plans and achievements. The introductory text concluded: "Seattle, though a young city, today stands foremost of the cities on the Pacific Coast in the matter of parks. . .and with the development of its system as outlined by the Olmsted Bros., it will take rank with the leading cities of the United States."

This historical scene shows off one of these Olmsted improvements; this part of the Lake Washington Boulevard was in 1909 the Olmsteds' most recent addition. The way its switchbacks imaginatively followed the natural contours of the Colman Park gulley was a landscaping design that characterized the Olmstead style, and so the entire "Plan for Seattle Parks, Playgrounds, and Parkways."

In 1856 when the few frontier Seattle citizens were huddled in a blockhouse behind palisades waiting for the natives to attack, the civilized city of New York purchased another old blockhouse, one left over from the War of 1812, and 840 acres that surrounded it. The city then commissioned a young landscape architect Frederick Law Olmsted to turn into a park. When the Olmsted brothers, Frederick's sons, came to Seattle in 1903 to fashion their plan for these parks and parkways, it was with a name which had for nearly half-a-century been synonymous with large scale innovative planning. It started with their father's and New York's Central Park.

Colman Park was only 16 acres, but it was just one setting in the crown of parks which was to, and still does, ring Seattle. All parks, of course, have their politics. The Olmsted plan to encircle the city was designed, in part, to pacify a bursting and boisterous city full of "unsympathetic strangers." The senior Olmsted had written that "parks tend to weaken the dangerous inclinations" by favorably directing 'the confined condition of young men in knots, rudely obstructing the sidewalks" to a "ground to which people may easily go after their day's work is done to stroll for an hour, seeing, hearing, and feeling nothing of the bustle and jar of the streets."

The pioneer solution to this urban anxiety was to simply walk into the country which was always nearby. But when cities got big enough for park boards, they were ready to bring the country into the city.

In 1884 when David Denny donated his namesake park to the city, Seattle's first park was still too close to the surrounding wilderness for anyone to give an idle moment's thought to planning an entire city about greenbelts and sylvan recreations. However, the local building and planning boom which followed the fire of 1889 brought landscape architect E.O. Schwagerl here in 1892 to propose some systematic park plans.

Then the city was letting off its steam at three commercial "amusement gardens": Madison, Madrona, and Leschi Parks. They lured the restless masses with their own often mad array of concerts, casinos, vaudeville, ball games, beer halls, steamer cruises, boat rentals, caged animals, swimming beaches, and real estate deals. All three parks were on

Another view on the Boulevard.   *courtesy, Municipal Library*

Lake Washington and at the end of their own cable or electric trolley lines. Schwagerl's plan called for connecting them with a landscaped parkway built along the lake's waterfront. These were the first plans for what later became the Olmsteds' Lake Washington Boulevard.

However, in 1893 while the Olmsteds were in Chicago enjoying their latest planning triumph, the "Great White City" of the World's Fair Columbian Exposition, Schwargerl was still in Seattle bemoaning that nothing was being done with his plans. And nothing much would be until the Olmsted brothers arrived for the rescue in 1903.

The Olmsted plan recommended that the entire "Rainier landslide" ridge from Mt. Baker north to Denny-Blaine be purchased by the city and topped by a "crestdrive" fronted by magnificent tax-rich homes. The city declined, but agreed to the plan's prescriptions for a parkway. By 1909 this practically completed Lake Washington Boulevard meandered all the way from the recently acquired Seward Park north to the Alaska Yukon and Pacific Expo grounds on the university campus. They too were designed by the Olmsteds.

Work during the 1937 dredging and landfill across Westmore Slough.

82 Wetmore Slough

On the 12th of July in 1916, the residents along the shores of Lake Washington watched the lake begin its retreat. For three months and nine days it withdrew, quickening the current through Sammamish Slough at its north end, draining the Black River dry at its south end, and spilling 8.8 feet off its top through the Montlake cut into Lake Union before its final escape into Puget Sound. On October 21 it stopped, 21 feet above the Sound's mean low tide, where, give or take a seasonal foot or two, it still wavers today.

One of the more telling effects of the lake's artificial lowering is revealed in this comparison of Wetmore Slough's "now" and "then." During those 100 days in the summer of 1916, it sank into a Wetmore swale. These two scenes were photographed from within a few feet of each other. However, the contemporary record was purposefully widened to show the lake's new level at its receded shoreline.

It is the same Lakewood ridge that runs across the middle of both settings, but a different Lake Washington Boulevard that bends around the ridge's northern face. On the "now's" left is Stan Sayers Park (with hydroplane pits attached, here unseen), and on its right the Genesee Playfield.

The pile trestle bridge over Wetmore Slough was constructed in 1912 to extend Lake Washington Blvd. to Seward Park. The historical photograph was shot a short time after that. The bridge was 26 feet wide, and its 760-foot length rose steadily from both ends towards the middle where an open span allowed small boats to explore the inner recesses of the slough.

When the lake was high (and its uncontrolled level could rise or fall five feet in a few weeks) and the winter rains flooded Rainier Valley, it was possible to row all the way to Columbia City. Indeed, that suburb once imagined that a dredged Wetmore Slough would make it a "seaport to the world." Such dreams withdrew with the waters of 1916.

Lake Washington's nine-foot lowering left this bridge high but not dry. The slough was soon transformed into a natural swale and grew in its ooze a new ecology of toads and cattails. This wallow slowly drained beneath the bridge and the bridge began to rot.

In 1924 the bridge was described as "very dangerous," and a park department report

recommended closing it. It was patched up instead. By 1929 another park department report indicated that "several cars have gone over this bridge" (over its *sides* was meant.) And on September 9, 1930 a Lakewood resident and neighborhood developer named Dodge complained to the park board that "the planks have been laid so insecurely that passing vehicles cause them to rebound, making a report like volleys from artillery and causing my wife who is ill to lose much sleep at night.

Mrs. Dodge and the neighborhood continued to sleep fitfully until 1937 when, at last, with the help of cheap W.P.A. depression-time labor and 40,000 feet of dredged lake bottom, the bridge was replaced with landfill. Some of the bog caught behind it continued to drain through a culvert beneath the

boulevard, but most of it slowly and simply leached its way into the lake.

In 1945 the city engineering department started using the slough for what is prettily called a "sanitary fill." This dump was Wetmore Slough's third historical habitat. For two decades the citizens along its sides dodged the dust, mud, rats, and seagulls, memorized the smells of a city's garbage, and pressured for the large park their neighborhood forebears had envisioned in 1917 when this bog was first uncovered behind the bridge. Today, these acres are Genesee Playfield, a green expanse of sod that is still settling. Beneath the grass, the compressed garbage churns and on occasion sends up a jet of methane gas. And beneath the boulevard the cut-off pilings of the old bridge over Wetmore Slough are still rotting.

83 The Montlake Cuts

No strip of regional real estate has engineered more dreams of empire than the isthmus that used to separate Lake Union from Lake Washington. From the beginning of white settlement, it inspired local boosters to imagine the cornucopia of raw materials that would come spilling out of Lake Washington right to the back door of Seattle once a cut could be made through that ribbon of land.

The line of the first cut can be faintly seen in our turn-of-the-century panorama from the north end of Capitol Hill. It diagonally transects the center of the photograph. The Lake Washington side ingress is just right of the four small and two tall trees. Built in 1883 by Chinese labor hired by local promoters David Denny, Thomas Burke, and others, it was designed for scooting logs from the big lake into the millpond of Portage Bay and eventually on to the mills on Lake Union, David Denny's included. *(See feature 64, 65.)*

Our view continues east across that dividing land, part of today's Montlake neighborhood, to Lake Washington's Union Bay, which was then considerably larger than today. Just beyond rises the largely denuded Laurelhurst peninsula, and in the distance Kirkland can be seen across the lake.

Although this setting has its pastoral touches, the signs of development are everywhere. Not seen, but just to the left of the photograph, is the town of Yesler. There, in the late 1880s, near the present site of University Village, pioneer Henry Yesler put up a namesake mill. Most of the clearcut Laurelhurst was probably stripped by Yesler's saws and shipped out on the Seattle Lake Shore and Eastern Railroad. By 1887 Thomas Burke's railroad had reached both Ravenna and Yesler at the north end of Union Bay. Today, on the railroad's old bed is the Burke-Gilman trail. *(See features 41, 42.)*

The lakes were first joined by name only on July 4, 1854. Most of Seattle had gathered to celebrate Independence Day on Thomas Mercer's claim at the southern end of a lake the Indians called "little water." Mercer proposed that the "big water" to the east be named "Washington," and that the little lake on whose refreshing shores they were gathered be called "Union." Someday, Mercer proclaimed, it would surely be the connection for an even greater union between that big lake and Puget Sound. The locals agreed, and from that moment on there was a steady agitation to consummate that union.

The first person to actually try it was Harvey Pike. Harvey followed his father John Henry Pike to town in 1861. The elder

The 1916 flooding of the Montlake Cut with the waters of Lake Union's Portage Bay. The north end of Capitol Hill is on the horizon.

Pike was employed to help design and build the then new territorial university. *(See feature 34.)* His son was given the job of painting it and his wage was a deed to part of that isthmus in present-day Montlake.

Harvey Pike actually tried to split his land in two with simple pick, shovel, and wheelbarrow. This, in the way of tools, was only a little more than Moses used to divide the Red Sea. But Harvey Pike had none of the divine aid, or in his case, federal subsidy, and so he had to give it up.[1] The subsidy didn't come until 1910 when a Rivers and Harbors Act passed by Congress included $2,750,000 for the construction of locks down at Shilshole, as long as King County

agreed to finance and build the canal. Which it did.

When the channel between the two lakes was opened in 1916, the greatest change was not the opening of a hinterland of opportunity and exploitation to military and industrial steamers, but the lowering of Lake Washington by nine feet and the exposing of thousands of acres of fresh bottom land. When the contemporary canal from salt water to fresh was completed in 1917 its Montlake cut was a few hundred feet north of Harvey Pike's strip of opportunity. Its primary traffic was, and still is, pleasure craft.

84 Receeding Union Bay

The 20th-century shrinking of Lake Washington's Union Bay is the most striking change evident in this photographic comparison of "now" and "then." However, discovering a more precise "where" and "when" for both of them required a little hunting. I went to Christine Barrett and Howard Giske for help.

The first time the older view was published was probably in Barrett's *A History of Laurelhurst.* She wrote this fine piece of neighborhood research in 1981 for the Laurelhurst Community Club. (That is the Laurelhurst peninsula stretching across the center of both our "now" and "then.") Like

this printing, the photo in her book was struck from the same original photograph preserved in the University of Washington's Historical Photography Collection. However, that vintage print gives us neither any date nor description of the photographer's precise position. Christine Barrett, who knows Laurelhurst history better than anyone, prudently hedged on the date with an approximate "circa 1897."

This took me to Howard Giske; for what Barrett did not have access to in 1981, Giske does today— the 45,000 negatives of the Webster and Stevens Collection which was recently acquired by the Museum of History

and Industry (MOHAI for short). The historical view has the Webster and Stevens number 3003 marked in its lower left hand corner. With this lead, Giske, who is head of MOHAI's photographic services, made a short search of the negative collection and discovered that the original 8 × 10 inch glass plate with that number was both there and intact.

Howard Giske also determined that number 3003 was but one of 197 consecutive negatives that the commercial photographers made of the then largely wild University of Washington campus. However, while Webster and Stevens were usually fastidious about their focus and exposure, they were rather lackadaisical about keeping records. [1] None of the 197 negatives were either captioned or dated.

This inspired the conscientious Giske to search further to either side of the University series. It took him back 533 negatives from number 3003 to number 2470 which was happily dated April 11, 1903. Next he went forward 99 negatives to number 3012 whose subject luckily included a wall calender showing the page leaf for May 1905. Giske was ready to conclude that our number 3003 was photographed from somewhere along the undeveloped eastern border of the University campus in the early spring, say April of 1905. We agree, the young foliage in the historical photo looks springlike, but we quickly ask "where is it precisely?"

The answer is soon in coming, for another of those 197 univer sity negatives reveals that the same fir trees that serrate the foreground of our number 3003 stand just to the east of what in 1905 was the girl's dormitory and is today the home of ROTC. Thus we conclude our "then" photograph was taken from the top floor of Clark Hall; our "now" is not, however. For the contemporary comparison we needed to move about 100 yards east to a balcony on McMahon Hall. This coed dormitory partially hides the now much narrower view of Union Bay available from Clark Hall.

The year 1905 is well within the vivid memory of many. They will remember, as the historical photo shows in part, how Union Bay extended far north of its present shores to cover not only the university's extensive parking lots south of N.E. 45th Street, but

The serrated line of firs on the right, in front of Clark Hall, correspond with those in the "then" photo.

also all of what since 1956 has been the University Village Shopping Center.

In 1906 a real estate triumvirate of McLaughlin, Murphy, and Mean bought up much of the peninsula that separated the bay from the lake, named it Laurelhurst, and then deliberately set about developing "the most aristocratic section of the city. In 1916 when the lake was lowered nine feet for the new ship canal and 610 acres of Union Bay

were suddenly reclaimed as land, Laurelhurst was still only sparsely settled. A few of the "people of good distinction" were living in tents. The university began reclaiming Union Bay's wetland in the mid-1920s with a garbage dump. By then the Laurelhurst neighborhood had begun to assume its still steadfast character as an affluent community of single family residences.

85 A Golf Course in Laurelhurst

*"Go take the wings of morning (or the legs
   of afternoon)
Some Saturday or Sunday fair—I hope
   you'll do it soon;
Take the Cable to the Lake and the
   Naptha to the Links,
And you will see our golfers—and be
   edified methinks."*

The first home of the Seattle Golf and Country Club was remote, but as the poet's couplet suggests, the route to it was as direct and effortless as a rhyme. A club member might leave work a bit early (very few of the link's elite punched time clocks), relax through the scenic ride on the Madison Street cable to the Lake Washington end of the line, and there board the naptha-powered Sunny Jim for an eight-minute cruise to the golf course landing. Then the effort began with a 100-foot ascent up the deep ravine to

the clubhouse, converted from an old farmhouse. This was followed by nine holes of caddie-assisted meandering over the hills of the future Laurelhurst Heights.

This was Seattle's second golf course. The first was a three-holed affair laid out in the mid-1890s in a Wallingford cow pasture. There the holsteins did the groundskeeping, and a tent was pitched for a clubhouse. The balls and clubs, imported from Scotland, were allowed through a confused customs only after being classified as "agricultural implements." (This classification was somewhat proper considering the size and character of the divots.)

In the summer of 1900 Josiah Collins, a local attorney of Scottish inclinations, returned to Seattle from a weekend of really civilized golf on a manicured course in Victoria. He was, in his own words, "so filled with the idea of a golf club in Seattle that I

went up and down the street trying to sell it."

Collins, one of the founders of the Wallingford cow pasture, was trying again. Fifty-four charter members responded to his enthusiastic recruiting and agreed to subsidize the rent and improvement costs on the already cleared 40-acre Laurelhurst site. The farmer wanted $175 a month for it, but when told it was for a golf course, instantly lowered the rent to $150. He too was a Scotsman.

The Laurelhurst course was short-lived, about eight years, but it was popular. A 1904 review reads; "Being peculiarly fortunate as regards climate, the enthusiasts can play the year around, and when eastern links are covered with snow, and clubs and caddies out of business, the game here is at the height of its popularity. A mild rain and unlimited mud are not counted as obstacles."

The greatest obstacle was the deep ravine that runs across the length of the historical

Laurelhurst in the distance from the Volunteer Park standpipe.   *courtesy, Old Seattle Paperworks*

scene. On the far side of this golfer's hazard is the clubhouse which in 1904 (a likely year for our photograph) included a pro-shop and a pro (another Scotsman), a small restaurant, and rooms for members to rent for a few days of uninterrupted golf. Apple and cherry trees surround the old farmhouse, and it was the cherries that President W. H. Taft remembered after forcing his abundant figure about this hilly course in 1908.[1]

That was the club's last year here. The links were sold and soon platted as Laurelhurst Heights. The 40 acres became part of what Laurelhurst's promoters called "the most aristocratic section of the city." The Seattle Golf and Country Club then moved to its new and present site in the Highlands. Many of its members, "the aristocrats' aristocrats," built their homes there in the region's richest neighborhood, four miles north of Ballard.

The old Volunteer Park bandstand. Fremont and Ballard in the distance across Lake Union.

86 Volunteer Park Voices

In 1887 Leigh Hunt came to town to take control of "Seattle's loudest voice: the Post-Intelligencer." Within the year, the new owner and editor was also hearing voices in the woods east of town. While trailblazing along the ridgetop that is now Capitol Hill, Hunt, as the story goes, "fell into a deep communion with nature and under the enchanted spell of her visible forms." When he then stumbled upon a few marked graves in a small city-owned clearing, a voice said to him: "Dispose of the dead elsewhere; this ground is reserved for the enjoyment of the living."

"Elsewhere" turned out to be, conveniently, only a few hundred feet north in today's Lakeview Cemetery. The city council soon agreed with the voices of Leigh Hunt, deciding to "dispose of the dead" there. It was amazingly the fourth move for many of these pioneer bodies.

In the historical panorama we can see Leigh Hunt's land for the living as it was 30 years later. In this 1917 scene, Volunteer Park rests in its well-groomed elegance much as the Olmsted brothers designed it in their early-century master plan. But at the time of Hunt's inspiration, this then wild 40 acres was only in its third year of covering bodies which had been transplanted here in 1884 from the city's first common cemetery at what is now Denny Park. David Denny had donated that original cemetery to the city in 1865. Slowly bodies from around the small town's numerous burial plots were gathered together there. It was their second disposal. Their third disposal freed Denny Park to become Seattle's first city-owned reserve for "recreation and living repose." Today it is also the administrative center for the park department.

Through most of Volunteer Park's first decade, it was called simply City Park. Then in 1901 P.I. theater critic J. Willis Sayers returned from volunteering in the Philippines during the popular Spanish-American War and proposed the commemorative name change. The city council soon agreed with Sayers, the Seattle Times future managing editor. (With the coming of more involuntary wars, the name's origin was soon forgotten by most park users.)

In 1901 Volunteer Park was just beginning to get the lavish attention it has steadily received ever since. In that year the 20-million-gallon reservoir was completed. Six years later the standpipe, from which these photos were taken, was constructed to improve water pressure for the mansions along 14th Avenue's "Millionaire's Row" and the rest of the hilltop homes.

By then, 1907, the Olmsteds' plans for their "jewel of the Seattle park system" were being traced in the earth itself. The park was laboriously pruned of its wild appearance of common second-growth fir trees and given an ordered variety of blue spruce, Port Orford cedar, flowering cherries, clipped lawns, and exotic shrubbery.

The two structures in the historical scene were not constructed until 1912. The crystal

palace-styled conservatory, showing upper right at the north end of the Olmsteds' concourse for carriages, was purchased prefabricated and put together by park employees. On the far right and running out of the scene is the north wing of the park's latticed pavilion. In its wisteria-and-hydrangea-draped center was a bandstand and to its east a semi-circular concert grove.[1]

Summer music has been a regular part of this park since 1911. In 1915 the concerts were moved from the grove to the large sloping lawn on the left. In 1932 the old pavilion and its grove were razed for the construction of the then strikingly modern art-deco Seattle Art Museum. It was a rare departure from the Olmsteds' plan.

In the early 1950s Willis Sayers returned with the other volunteer veterans from their forgotten war to place a plaque reminding all of the origin of the park's name. It was dedicated to the "volunteers who liberated the oppressed peoples of Cuba, Puerto Rico, and the Philippine Islands." It was a different sort of message than that heard by Leigh Hunt in the summer of 1887.

Lincoln Playground

Boys and girls together beside the Broadway Playfield's wading pool.

courtesy, Municipal Library

87 The Liberated Playfield

This 1909 scene of dancing and teeter-tottering upon the lawn of the Broadway Playfield is free of boys. That's probably because then, as one witness wrote, "the boys still retain that lordly disdain of petticoats which holds them aloof from the skirted performers." Indeed, this open display of the physical exhuberance of girls was in 1909 startling.

In the summer of that year, Broadway Playfield (then still called Lincoln Park) got its first regular supervisor for girls, Christina Kanters. (During the school year she taught physical education at the University of Washington.) That's probably Kanters on the far left of the historical scene under the bonnet and with her hands full. The park department reviewed her work as of "high grade and parents can safely trust their children at Lincoln Park during the hours of Miss Kanter's supervision."

Ms. Kanter was a worker in the field of what was called the Playground Movement. In 1909 its local supervisor, Howard Stine, announced that it was "sweeping with increasing velocity from one ocean to the other! Make room for the children." For the first time in Seattle parks, this emphatically included the girls.

That summer the Seattle Park Department reported that of the daily average of 850 "young folks" who played upon the apparatuses of Seattle's first four playfields, "550 were girls ranging in age from 4 to 14 years." This nearly two-thirds majority marked a revolutionary turn of events and drew radical comments from the boys' side of the playfield.

One male reviewer wrote: "There is an element of the pathetic in the play of the girl who has little control over her body, who scarcely knew she had such appendages as arms or legs until open air play became suddenly fashionable. Pathetic because it reveals the effect of that centuries old neglect of invigorating exercise which public opinion of the past held to be womanly. Such an elevating, normal, elemental craving for natural play by all humanity, whether male or female...has been fashionable now for just about five years of the four centuries white man's America has been in existence."

It was also five years earlier, in 1904, that the Olmsted brothers, that famous white male landscaping team from Brookline, Massachusetts, submitted to Seattle's all-white male park board their first plans for

The Broadway reservoir with the German Reformed Church beyond.

Lincoln Park. For a base fee of $300 they proposed a plan which purposely made "no provision for the more vigorous forms of play." It was, in fact, "particularly designed to make baseball impractical." In less than one month, however, this attack on the manly American pastime was thoroughly reversed.

Lincoln Park's baseball diamond—now still at the park's southern border along E. Pine Street—was graded in 1907. By the next spring, the Broadway High School team was competing for playtime with the Seattle Church League, the Mail Carriers League, the Wholesale Auto Parts League (Broadway was then becoming "Auto Row"), and an assortment of independent leagues. Still, all those wearing gloves were boys.[1]

But the next year, when the playground movement hit Lincoln Park, it was ready with swings, rings, jungle gyms, teeter-totters, and Christina Kanter. The feminine majority responded, and at least one "older boy" reporter admired those hundreds of "unafraid maids whose romping figures signify an entirely new order of sensible, capable, emancipated womanhood."

The landmark steeple over the girls' heads, tops the German United Church of Christ. Dedicated November 18, 1906, it is Seattle's last parish with a German-only liturgy. In 1984 the congregation was 103 years old.

courtesy, Catholic Archdiocese of Seattle

88 The Day the Dome Fell

Throughout the Sunday afternoon and early evening of January 30, 1916, 3,000 skaters slid on Green Lake while an equal number huddled around bonfires that ringed the lake. At 1 o'clock on the following afternoon, the Times weatherman made his last temperature check for the evening edition. The thermometer read 27 degrees. It had been snowing since 10 that morning and the forecaster was probably proud to report: "Today marked the close of the coldest month in the history of Seattle."

The next day the Times reported that it had snowed for 27 hours without interruption. This pile up marked the end of the popular slipping on Green Lake and the beginning of it everywhere else. In response, the Humane Society called for the sharp shodding of horses to prevent their falling. It also announced a general "feed-the-birds plea." And the Time's forecaster confidently predicted more snow.

And he was very right. The Wednesday afternoon final weather check found "the greatest fall on record for any similar period"—almost three feet in two days. This made for the kind of sensational weather that was a relief from the "partly-this-and-partly-that" hedging of meteorologists on Puget Sound. The schools were closed, street cars stuck, and the suburbs abandoned.

This "Big Snow" was indeed the big news of the day, and the Wednesday Times banner headline read "More Snow Predicted." The news included the collapse of the roof of the West Seattle Christian Church. That was at 1:30 in the afternoon, about 103 minutes before the cave-in of another Christian canopy. This second fall was the blizzard's most spectacular effect.

The front page of the Thursday Post-Intelligencer was topped "Cathedral Dome Falls." Since the morning paper had all night to dramatize the disaster, their description sounded a bit like a report from the front lines of World War I. "A roar like the boom of a heavy gun brought priest and layman to the cathedral. They saw a huge jagged hole where the massive dome had soared and poured great clouds of mortar dust and flying snow. The view within looked like the scenes of destruction brought by the cannons in Belgium. Through this the blizzard poured its white clouds, and rapidly drifts began to sift over sacred images and objects of great beauty in bronze, onyx, and marble."

The Thursday evening Times editorial response was fittingly touched by both remorse and hope. "Disaster to an edifice of this character constitutes a public loss. Great churches are part of the intimate life of the city. To the great many thousands in Seattle this mishap yesterday comes as a personal loss as much as if the individual had owned the stately pile himself....St. James will undoubtedly rise again in the not far distant

future mightier, more attractive, and more inspiring than in the past.''

Thirteen years earlier, in 1903, Bishop O'Dea moved his diocese from Vancouver to Seattle. With a leap of faith and a promoter's talent for raising money, the bishop built the grandest cathedral in the Northwest and dedicated it on December 22, 1907. Its twin 175-foot towers and octagonal dome, topped by an electric cross, dominated the city's skyline from First Hill.

Covered with copper, the dome was supported by four steel trusses of which the south one had an undiscovered flaw. With the estimated added weight of 30,000 pounds of wet snow, it buckled, neatly folding the whole dome 120 feet to the santuary's mosaic floor. Air pressure popped most of the cathedral's windows, and the pulpit and altar rail were crushed. The bishop, offering an ironic prayer, "thanked God" that no one was worshipping in the cathedral at 3:13 that Wednesday afternoon.

However, the fate of 500 white leghorn fowls was not so providential, when the roof of the Wilkens and Brian chicken house at the Ronald Station on the Everett interurban collapsed.

Perhaps it was in unconscious mimicry of both the cathedral and the chicken coop that on Thursday, February 3, the Times weatherman reported: "The backbone of the storm was broken during the early morning hours, and dawn found clear skies and warmer atmosphere.''

Saturday Seattle got its first mail from the east in five days. On Sunday, 19 snow-stalled trains reached the city. By Monday all the streetcars were again running on schedule; but on Tuesday the week of the Big Snow was followed by one of avalanches. The softened and exposed ridges along Sunset Hill, Magnolia, Queen Anne, and West Seattle began to slip in places, taking a dozen homes and two lives.

When the St. James Cathedral reopened for worship March 18, 1917, it was domeless. Although the sanctuary was less "mighty," it was more "inspiring," for the poor acoustics of the cathedral had been improved with the new cover. With this alteration, Gregorian chants and Latin oratories could stir the worshippers spiritually without the threat of the roof falling in.[1]

89 A Block of Hotels

The block of elegant brick that variously fills the center of the historical scene includes four hotels, two bars, two tailors, and one cafe. This early century setting extends north on First Avenue from the Hotel Ramona at Seneca Street to the Hotel Diller at University Street. Now 77 years later only the Diller remains but minus its projecting cornice and decorative chimney pots. These were prudently removed after the earthquake of 1949.

The Diller was one of the first brick buildings completed after the fire of 1889. Demand for masonry with which to rebuild a fire-resistant city was so great that a number of structures, including the Diller, were built of imported Japanese brick. The Diller opened its doors to first-class guests on June 6, 1890, exactly one year after its proprietor Leonard Diller lost another hotel, the Brunswick, to the Great Fire.

Leonard Diller's first hotel was the Old Town in Tacoma. He had followed the Northern Pacific to that town in 1873, the year that the railroad announced its decision to terminate on Commencement Bay. After the expectant Tacoma boom quickly fizzled, Diller moved on to Seattle and managed, in succession, two hotels: the Desmond and the Brunswick. Hotel Diller was next—his fourth. It was constructed on the site of the family home. Today, the Diller family still manages their namesake hotel.

The Diller had direct access down the University Street overpass to the depots and docks along Railroad Avenue.[1] Through its first years, the hotel enjoyed a mild success serving this water front clientele. Beginning with the gold rush of 1897, it was a wild success. The Hotel Diller was headquarters for many of those who actually struck it rich. It was in the midst of this manic economy of high tabs and filled rooms that Leonard Diller died in 1901.

By 1906, the year of our scene, there were, perhaps, too many hotels—seven of them on this one block. On the east side were the Ramona, Yates, Yellowstone, and Diller, and across the street, the Seneca, Victoria, and Arlington. There were many more up and down First Avenue.

"First Class" consumption had long since moved up to Second Avenue. There in 1907 the Savoy opened and the New Washington neared completion; both were glamorous skyscrapers. Many of the smaller hostelries along First Avenue began to let housekeeping

The Diller Hotel.

courtesy, Lawton Gowey

Rates 50c to $1.50.
G. A. WILLIAMS, Manager.
(Formerly of Tacoma.)

The Arlington Hotel
Corner First Ave. and University St., next to Postoffice, Seattle

ELECTRIC LIGHTS,
BATHS, ELEVATOR AND
STEAM HEAT.

The Arlington Hotel at First and University. Across the street from the Diller.

rooms. The Avenue was settling into its "second class" domesticity: a home for merchant marines, secretaries, fishermen, waitresses, and clerks. Two world wars added shipbuilders and sailors on the move.

After the last war, First Avenue became "Flesh Avenue"—a gaudy strip of neon sin lined with bars, porn and pawn shops and other down and out alternatives to modern middle-class amusements like department stores, drive-in banks, and first-class hotel-motels. Now a few remnants of this kitschy decor still line the sidewalk: two cut-rate music stores, one loan office, one t.v. repair, a passport photographer, a trick shop, but now, only one porn shop. The Avenue is changing.

When Leonard Diller arrived here from Tacoma in 1875, Seneca was a ravine and First Avenue had a bridge over it. Within one year the city's first regrade smoothed out First between Yesler Way and Pike Sreet. The Seneca Street drop-off was filled in. Now many "social regrades" later, First Avenue is being fitted with condos, luxury hotels (like the new Hilton which will soon be ascending across the street from the Diller), and cosmopolitan speciality shops.

In the old Hotel Diller's lobby is one shop named simply T&N. Inside are Asian antiques, folk arts, and textiles. Next door, in place of the passport photos, the windows of Di' Medici and Ming are lavished with Chinese and Italian paperworks. With uptown shops like these, the urban nomads from Bellevue, Broadmoor, and the new Hilton across the street will not be window-shopping for cheap thrills or a loan.

90 The Elks Carnival

When the Saturday Times reported August 16, 1902 that the "Elks big show is now close at hand...An air of expectancy hangs over the city,' carpenters and electricians were still working on the grand Welcoming Arch at First Avenue and Columbia Street. There, the Times continued, the city would "witness the formal launching of the greatest effort ever put forth by this city to amuse the populace. Shortly before noon Monday, the first big parade will be formed at the old Elks headquarters, corner of First Avenue and Columbia Street, and with the beautiful and queenly Queen Florence will slowly take up the line of march to the grounds."

The grounds were part of the old university property which in 1902 was still the lush greenbelt of Denny's Knoll. For the Seattle Fair and Carnival it was elaborately transformed into a walled garden filled with exotic villages, stages and tents, rows of booths, one big ferris wheel, and two more arches. Admission was 10 cents. Everything was in purple and white, the Elks' colors, including Florence Walker as she led the opening day parade to the coronation stand at Third and Union.[1]

There, the Times prediction continued, "the crowning of Seattle's first and only queen will occur in the open air and in full view of her many thousand loyal subjects. She will throw wide open the gate of festivity and Seattle will be plunged into a mad whirl of gaiety for 13 days." F.C. Eagan, who was in charge of the coronation exercises, promised "a spectacular event that will make the palmy days of Nero look like a game of marbles on the village green." Seattle was surrendering itself to the Elks. "Everyone and everything is now subordinate to Elkdom!" the Times reported.

The Times also made notice that on Tuesday, or Seattle Day, after a "parade of floats which in number and royal splendor will far outshine anything ever seen in this city," the city's Mayor T.J. Humes "will formally present the City of Seattle as a gift to the Elks." And the Benevolent Order, which had its beginnings in New York City shortly after the Civil War as the Jolly Corks, a social club for theater people, took the city for two weeks.

On Wednesday, Fraternal Day, the Times reported that 50,000 persons watched the Seattle Day parade run its course from the Welcoming Arch at First Avenue and Columbia Street. On Thursday, it reviewed the two-mile-long Fraternal Day parade of 7,000 multi-colored members of different orders as "the biggest street pageant that any city in the Northwest has ever had the pleasure of witnessing."

The parades kept on coming. There were 10 other days and they all had them. But not on Sunday which was reserved for rest or the more uplifting attendance of morning church and the afternoon balloon ascension at the Meadows race track. (In the "then" image the Kinnear Park electric trolley exiting from the Welcoming Arch has a poster for the balloon ascension tied to its front bumper.) There was Canada Day, Organized Labor Day, Puget Sound Day, and, of course, Elks Day.

Following the parades was a sensational mix of circus and vaudeville acts, concerts, sideshows, a wild animal show, and a tamer menagerie which included "dreamy, big brown-eyed camels" you could ride for a fee, an elephant named Regina with tusks tipped by golden balls, and, strangely for a city which for five years had been lucratively promoting its familiar proximity to the Klondike, there were "exotic dogs from faraway Alaska." Such was the atmosphere in which "care and confetti have been thrown to the winds, and there is no rule but the Abbot of Unreason."

"There were hundreds of other pesky contrivances on the grounds, and if anyone missed getting something thrust into his face, it was not the fault of those who carried them." This included "the small boy with the dynamite case that caused women to scream as if shot." The Times warned that the carefree crowds should be careful not to "allow their children to visit the carnival grounds with hair hanging in a braid." Someone with heavy shears was removing them.

On the fair's last day, Military Day, there was "one big battle of confetti."

Another publication, the Commonwealth, commented "so beautiful are the arches that have been erected, that it is with sorrow one thinks of their soon-to-be destruction. The designs are of striking excellence, and the electric lighting is such that at night they look, if possible, better than during the day." The arches were torn down at the end of the fair.

The contemporary early evening emptiness of the First and Columbia corner was chosen to contrast with the 1902 carnival corner filled with its grand Welcoming Arch.

The Elks arch at night, looking north on First.

a busy night at the Dream

91 Clemmer's Dream

On September 3, 1932 Seattle's "pioneer showman" James Q. Clemmer rolled up the sleeves of his tuxedo and mounted a soapbox outside the Fifth Avenue Theater which he managed. Above him stretched a bright red banner reading "Jim Clemmer's Campaign Headquarters."

In this depression election year in which radio charisma propelled Franklin Roosevelt's promises of "a new deal for every American" far ahead of Herbert Hoover's monotone assurances that "prosperity is just around the corner," the showman Clemmer was running not for an office but in the Fox Theater's coastwide contest for the "most popular manager in the West." Both FDR and JQC won.

Jim Clemmer beat out 200 other west coast managers by hawking the most advance sale tickets to the Fifth Avenue's coming show, Will Rogers' new talkie, "Down to Earth." Clemmer personally peddled these admissions to the multitude of happy customers he'd been entertaining, by then, through 24 years of pioneering film-playing in eight Seattle theaters.

The first of these was Clemmer's Dream. In 1907 the 26-year-old newlywed brought his wife over from Spokane to live in and manage a recent family acquisition, the Kenneth Hotel. The Kenneth was one of the first and also most pleasingly ornate stone structures put up after the fire of 1889. Its very narrow but tall seven-story facade sat at the First Avenue foot of Cherry Street.[1]

Within a year Jim Clemmer converted an abandoned bank lobby on the hotel's first floor into his Dream Theater. It was one of Seattle's first photoplay houses and its "most spacious and best equipped." In our historical photograph we see the Dream's marquee in one of its several incarnations.[2] Clemmer was constantly making improvements, both outside and in, and the best of these was the organ.

The Dream's Wurlitzer was said to be the first organ installed in any motion picture theater anywhere. And both the organ and Clemmer were fortunate to have "Ollie on the Wurlitzer" Wallace improvising his dramatic accompaniment to sentimental films like the one advertised above the Dream's entrance, "A Brother's Devotion." Oliver G. Wallace was one of those Seattle phenomena that after a hometown nurturing

Signage on the west side of First Avenue seen over the shoulder of the Pioneer Square totem pole. Part of the Kenneth Hotel sign is evident just left of the "Free Museum."

went on to great things elsewhere. With Wallace it was to Hollywood and a career of writing scores for many of Walt Disney's films including "Dumbo" and "Peter Pan."[3]

Another of Clemmer's Dream Theater innovations was probably the first "talking" motion picture. This it did literally. In 1910 Clemmer put actors behind the Dream's screen to mouth aloud the screen actors' mute lines. Predictably, after a week of this often too-comic dissonance, the noble experiment was shut up as an artistic howler.

The Dream Theater's fare was actually a 50-50 mix of one-reelers and vaudeville. Much of the latter was on-stage singing acts. The movie shorts included Italian dramas, French comedies, pastoral forest stories, and

from an American producer named Bison, the first of the cowboy pictures. Bison advertised that he still "employed men who have had actual experience in Indian fighting."

In 1912 Jim Clemmer sold the Dream and built the 1,200-seat Clemmer, "the nation's first grand theater devoted exclusively to photoplays." In the next 20 years he also managed the Winter Garden, Music Box, Blue Mouse, Music Hall, Paramount, and the Orpheum. When Clemmer and Roosevelt won by landslides in 1932, Clemmer was in his second term as manager of the lavish Fifth Avenue Theater. When he died in 1942, he was remembered by John Hamrick, the Fifth Avenue's owner, as "the best theater manager I ever knew."

92 Bicycle Row

February 18, 1901 a local bicycle merchant, Fred Merrill, staged what today we call a media event. He distracted the community and startled his competitors with a peculiar parade up Second Avenue, then Seattle's Bicycle Row.

The occasion is recounted in Frank Cameron's *Bicycling in Seattle, 1879-1904*: "Most merchants announced well in advance when a shipment of bicycles would arrive; it was cause for some excitement. Few could match Merrill. A shipment of 400 Rambler bicycles was loaded onto all the express wagons available and moved to his store in a parade led by a brass band and two carriages, one for Mr. and Mrs. Merrill and one for other company officers."

Cameron is pictured here in the contemporary photograph. The location of the "now" image is the same as the "then"—one half block north of Spring Street on Second Avenue. Cameron poses as part of a different sort of bicycle delivery: 15 bikes and riders from Bucky's Messenger Service. The deliverers pedal a total of 500 miles a day, courageously darting through traffic that's

not always willing to share the road with bicycles. Cameron is Bucky's repairman. He is a complete cyclist; he rides them, repairs them, and researches them.

The historical photograph shows a part of the parade, and that may be Merrill in the lead carriage at the far left. The carriage pauses beside his storefront—with the sign

for "Ideal Bicycles"—to pose with a few of those hired wagons for an unidentified photographer.

In 1901 there were more than a dozen bicycle shops on Second Avenue between Marion and Pike Streets. No doubt in February they were all preparing for the spring rush on two wheelers, but none with the showy delivery of

Scenes along the Lake Washington bicycle trail.

the man in the rented carriage.

The city's first bicycle was brought from San Francisco in 1879 by the book merchant W.H. Pumphrey for the son of a local bookkeeper named Lipsky. Indeed, little Lipsky's toy required the resilience of youth because the ride was very bumpy. The tires were hard, there were no brakes and, of course, no paved streets.

The flexible pneumatic tire, and a softer ride, first arrived in 1893 in time to test the city's first paved surface: an experimental block of bricks on First Avenue S. between Washington Street and Yesler Way. By 1896 there was still only a single mile of paved streets in Seattle, including those Second Avenue bricks supporting Merrill's parade. Cameron estimates that in 1896 there were only about 300 cyclists in Seattle. One year later there were 3,000. In 1897 in Seattle your first dream was to strike it rich in the Klondike, but you might settle for a bicycle.

All those bicyclers formed an effective lobby. The Queen City Cycle Club originated in the Argus offices in 1896 and a year later it became the Queen City Good Roads Club. The Argus ran a regular bicycle column which promoted the "wheeling" scene. With funds from licensing, benefit races, and pledges, bicycle paths were built first around Lake Union and then through a scenic 10 miles to Lake Washington—a portion of that path is today's Interlaken Boulevard at the north end of Capitol Hill.

By 1901, the year of Merrill's parade, there

were more than 10,000 local cyclists. Many wore bloomers, called the "national riding costume" for women. Bicycle racing for men and women was a popular sport, and the city's planked and cindered tracks were busy with both local contestants and touring professionals. Club retreats took off on weekends for West Seattle, Edmonds, Snoqualmie Falls, and even Tacoma.

Bicycles were even manufactured locally. Brands included, predictably, the "Queen City," the "Rainier," and the "Seattle." This city was also an exporter, and a few of

Merrill's 400 Ramblers were bound for China, Japan, and even for the gold fields of unpaved Alaska where the buyers expected to cycle over nuggets.

The bicycle bust followed the boom. By 1907 what Cameron calls the "decade of the bicycle" was over. Of the 23 merchants that sold cycles during the boom, only two remained in 1907. Many dealers went on to automobiles. The sales were less seasonal and the buyers, though often out-of-shape, were usually well-heeled.

93 Post Office Steps

In the early 1900s the federal government spent six years building Seattle its first "truly monumental post office." It opened in 1908, 56 years after the first letter reached Seattle by canoe.

When the site was chosen in 1901, it was a victory for the "uptown boys" over the downtown men. At that time Third Avenue and Union Street was far from the civic center. But the feds in their wisdom, looked into the city's future and bet on its "northerly expansion." And most of the city agreed, by then moving or regrading what was said to "stand in the way": Denny Hill. So while the P.O. was going up, the hill was coming down, and both were on the north side of town.

The construction of the post office began in 1903 with the site's grading; however, by 1905, it was only as high as its cornerstone. The lead box of memorials hidden within it included a sketch of the new post office. The artist's rendering showed no steps. These were added in 1907. That year Third Avenue was itself regraded. This put the post office's front door about four feet above the new sidewalk, which was a stroke of luck.

For half-a-century "meet me at the post office steps" was a common prelude to some downtown adventure. Many of these meetings were strictly practical but others were romantic. For instance, during war years when patriotic opinions about sailors pick up some, the post office steps were a serviceman's best chance for a pick-up.

The post office was made of a spongy Chuckanut sandstone that steadily absorbed the city's soot. Throughout the years, its monumental columns along Third Avenue were elaborately streaked by splashes from the pigeons that roosted in the Corinthian capitals.

But while the proud building eventually transformed into a "grim and ancient landmark," its front steps remained one of the city's most intimately human places. This coziness was enhanced when Third Avenue was widened in 1929 and its sidewalks narrowed. Pedestrians were often pushed into unscheduled meetings on the P.O. steps. Some probably liked the impromptu meetings but others did not; complaints followed.

On August 15, 1940, the Times announced "Those Post Office Steps on Third—They'll Be Gone Soon." The feds were promising to close the Third Avenue entrance and so remove the steps. But nothing happened. Sixty-five months later on January 15, 1946, the steps surfaced again in the Post-Intelligencer: "It's Those P.O. Steps Again!... The trysting place for young couples, meeting place for women shoppers... variously labeled as nuisance, pedestrian hazard, and traffic bottleneck, the steps have been damned but never doomed."

And the meetings and gripes continued until April Fool's Day, 1958 when Tacoma's demolition expert Lige Dickson began three months of dogged pounding on a sturdy post office that took six years to build and too long to raze for a profit. Also flattened were the steps which for 50 years were a kind of front porch to the city. [1]

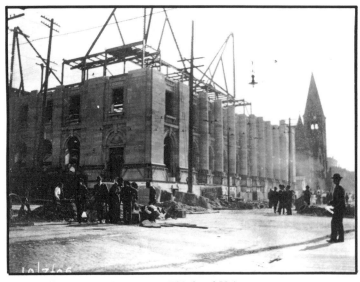

Post Office construction scene at Third and Union.

94   The Four Forms of Fourth Avenue

Every few decades with the help of earthquakes, fires, nervous engineers, and metropolitan dreamers, west coast cities like San Francisco, Vancouver, and Seattle are "made over." These two glimpses north up Fourth Avenue from Cherry Street show a startling reincarnation.

Actually, Fourth Avenue has had four transformations. Our historical photograph shows it passing into its third form, and our contemporary view reveals it moving well into its fourth. In the former, Fourth Avenue is losing its residential emphasis. The sides of the street are being furnished with institutions, like the Carnegie Library and Rainier Club in the scene's center, and hotels, like the Stander and Lincoln on the left. In the latter, this avenue is now fast becoming Seattle's deepest urban canyon with its slick sides of glass and polished metal.

The historical photograph was taken about 1905 by Arthur Warner a short time after the library, club, and hotels were built. By then the street had already lived through its first two forms. In the early 1860s Fourth Avenue was cut out of the virgin forest, some of which returned from Yesler's mill as

planks for building the few modest homes that soon irregularly lined the sides of this stump-strewn path. Fourth ran from the tideflats on the south to as far north as Denny's Knoll (not Hill). There it stopped at a white picket fence—a small swinging gate counterbalanced by horseshoes opened to the grounds of Washington Territory's university, for years the city's and Fourth Avenue's most distinguished landmark.[1]

Fourth Avenue's second form was also residential, but with more lavish homes that faced a street which although unpaved was given a regular width, curbed against sidewalks, lined with utility poles, and lit at the intersections. The duplex on the right of the older view counts as one of these classier second-stage residences. The tower behind it is attached to one of this street's distinguished mansions, the home of pioneers Agnes and James Colman. Like the McNaught mansion, whose tower is seen in the distance beyond the library, the Colmans' spacious Latinate-Victorian showpiece was built in 1883 and remained through the turn of the century a symbol of Fourth Avenue's domestic elegance.

However, entering their third decade these grand homes became vestiges of an earlier urbanity. In 1903 the imposing McNaught mansion was moved across Spring Street to make room for the Carnegie Library.[2]

In 1907-08 a metamorphosis occurred to the street itself which dramatically fashioned it into its third form. The Fourth Avenue regrade resulted in some casualties and many alterations. Denny's Knoll was cut through and the old landmark university first moved and then leveled. Practically every structure along the new grade required either new steps to the old front doors, as with the library, or new front doors into their old basements, as with the hotels. *(See feature 34.)*

The city engineer's longing to make "the crooked straight and the rough places plane" resulted in some very deep cuts. For instance, our contemporary photograph at Cherry Street was taken some two stories below Arthur Warner's location in the historical view. The incision at this intersection was 24 feet. By 1911 a bricked-over Fourth Avenue showed the same unruffled grade that made it the preferred course for the bed races of the 1970s.

Fourth Avenue north from the Yesler Way overpass after the 1908 regrade.

Agnes Colman continued to live in her towering home until her death in 1934. By then her mansion, the last sign of the elegant eighties and roaring nineties, was thoroughly surrounded by retailers and restaurants. Today that era of conservative cosmopolitan taste is recalled only by the Rainier Club, the single structure which survives from the "then" into the "now." The five-story Rainier Club houses 57,000 square feet of plush sitting rooms, coat-and-tie dining rooms, and other elite areas only its restricted membership knows.

When the Columbia Center is completed as the crowning touch to Fourth Avenue's fourth form, it will fill the old Colman mansion site with more than a million and and a half square feet of office space stacked 76 stories high.

In some future decade or century when the Columbia Center's 954 feet are dismantled by God, man, or nature, Fourth Avenue will be passing into its fifth form.

courtesy, Historical Photography Collection, University of Washington

95 The First Baptists

In the winter of 1870 Rudolph Weston, a blacksmith living in Olympia, made the cold trip down Puget Sound to visit a group of Seattle friends. The Rogers, Holgate, and Hanford families (local names that still sound familiar) waited for the gentle patriarch they called "Father" Weston to come, not to shoe a horse or turn a wrought iron gate handle, but to baptize Christian Clymer and his wife. This blacksmith with the long white beard was the Sound's first Baptist minister and those who greeted him at Yesler's wharf were Seattle's first Baptist congregation.

For the Christian Clymers the occasion included a real test of faith, for Seattle's first Baptist immersion was completed that cold February day in Elliott Bay at the foot of Columbia Street.

The first Baptist on the bay, not in it, was John Holgate. By staking a claim in the Duwamish Valley in 1850, he also was the first non-native to mark his intent to make his home on land now part of Seattle. This was a full year before those other parties of Protestants landed on Alki Point and the

Duwamish delta.

John Holgate was the brother of Abbie Hanford and the son of Elizabeth Holgate. It was Abbie who in 1866 moved with her husband Edward into a home at the northeast corner of Fourth Avenue and James Street, and it was Elizabeth who later bought another lot in the same block and donated it to the young congregation. Both of the historical views show the second Baptist church built on this lot and the second Hanford home on that corner.

The first Hanford home here was the site of both the first Baptist get-together on December 21, 1869 and the congregation's first regular service on New Year's Day 1870. The original church was dedicated in 1872 and from that time to this, the crises and triumphs for these Baptists were much like those of other frontier faiths growing up and surviving into the modern and increasingly secular American West.[1]

1869-1870 were good years to start a church, especially in Seattle. The city at last had incorporated itself and elected a mayor and council. Real estate prices were climbing fast because there were buyers. David Denny was platting his North Seattle claim, and a Portland real estate partnership, Russell and Ferry, were circulating a flier which read in part: "For sale, fifteen hundred acres near Seattle" which the firm first named "the future Queen City of the Pacific."

The name stuck and within the year an entourage of top Northern Pacific officials were in town looking for a railroad terminus.

And the city was becoming sophisticated. When the first circus appeared here in 1869 and advertised itself as "the largest and best troupe of daring riders, accomplished gymnasts, agile acrobats, witty clowns, and boneless contortionists ever brought together in any one establishment," a local editor, reviewing the circus' performance as "tame and insipid, and almost entirely devoid of merit," proved he was not living in an uncritical hicktown.

In 1869 the consistent sources of "entertainment," sacred and profane, were in the churches and saloons, and also, of course, between them in the eternal struggle between virtue and vice.

Actually in those years before all the diversions of electrified mass culture, the social side of the church as a place to spread Christian charity into hay rides, sewing circles, and new friendships was as important, perhaps, as saving souls. All of which also helped in times of economic and personal panic which was soon to come to the nation in 1873.

But all the churches, Presbyterian, Methodist, Catholic, Congregational, Episcopalian, and Baptist included, all of whom had either started congregations or built sanctuaries in the early 1870s, continued to grow. In 1875, Seattle First Baptist Church began trying to pay an $800 yearly salary to its first long-term pastor the Reverend J.A. Wirth.

Wirth's first spiritual service was material. He installed a gas heated baptistry in the church which the congregation, Christian Clymer and his wife still included, declared "a great convenience compared to the cold waters of Elliott Bay."

In 1894 the congregation moved one block west to the Seattle Theater at Third and Cherry where the stirring sermons of their sixth pastor, Dr. W.F. Taylor, were drawing crowds much too large for the little church a block away on Fourth. However, here the sacred and secular forms of enthusiasm were a little close for comfort, and the congregation made plans for a new church home on the same lot as their first. They opened it in December 1898 and worshipped in chairs

1906 view to the east from the top of the Alaska building. The Baptist church is near the photos center.

borrowed from a Jewish synagogue.

This is the church we see here. By 1908 the deep and close cuts of the Fourth Avenue regrade forced its abandonment. Like many other central city congregations, First Baptist sold its original site for a good price and moved up on First Hill to its present home at Harvard Avenue and Seneca Street.

The contemporary "civic temple" that now fills the old Baptist site is the Municipal Building, Seattle's city hall that looks like a Holiday Inn. The plans for this unfortunate example of the "forward look" were bought in the early 1960s from a Texas architectural firm that had a specialty in designing hotel-motels. The Queen City can change its nickname overnight, but it cannot so readily build traditions. And the Emerald City did not begin to build for posterity when it constructed its present city hall.[2]

courtesy, Seattle Public Library

96 A Dragon on Fifth Avenue

The Welsh, Romans, Germans, Babylonians, Japanese, English, and Chinese have something in common besides their humanity—a fascination for dragons. Indeed, this beast with lion's claws and serpent's tail is stirring in the oldest stories of many more cultures, East and West.

In the Western World, slaying a dragon is the single most crowning achievement for any hero. Down through legendary history champions like Apollo, Hercules, Perseus, Beowulf, St. George, and Siegfried have been rescuing damsels from the fiery embrace of dragons and carrying away treasures from their fierce protec tion. In Shakespeare's Macbeth, dragon scales were a favored additive for witches gruel.[1] Through centuries of Christian art, sin was symbolized as a winged crocodile—a type of dragon.

But in the East, the dragon is a different mythical beast. It is the most persistent symbol of vital power, fertility, and well-being. It is also a vegetarian. In our historical

The Dragon on the conventional Second Ave. parade route.

photograph of the Chinese dragon dance, we see the lead bearer carrying a staff tipped with a symbolic fruit. The dragon wants it and will dance through many city blocks to get it.

Here it is on Fifth Avenue with its tail still crossing Pine Street. This is a long way from the International District where the great dragon was released ritually on Chinese New Year to dance amid fireworks and the persistent beat of drums and cymbals through the streets south of Jackson.

The event pictured here is part of another celebration: the city's 1909 Alaska-Yukon-Pacific Exposition. This is, perhaps, China Day. The half-year-long fair had many such days given to different groups who were expected to put on a special show and help draw the crowds.

But there is no crowd and, indeed, the question is: what is this dragon doing on Fifth Avenue? It "should" be on Second Avenue. In 1909 Second was Seattle's parade street. It was not planked but bricked and impressively

"canyoned" beneath sky scrapers like the still standing Alaska Building, Savoy Hotel, and New Washington Hotel (today's Josephinum).

We might also ask what the man in the Caucasian costume at right is thinking. Could he be confusing this happy procession of the Asian monster with the fire-breathing history of its European cousin? Or could he be carrying beneath that derby another kind of demon—that old mean stereotype of the Chinese "coolie boy"?

This crude image of the opium-eating heathen, who worked more for less and then gambled it away, was the stock response to these Asian immigrants. By 1909 it had resulted in more than half-a-century of exploitive treatment. First, the Chinese were used as cheap labor to mine the gold and coal, build the railroads, and do domestic service. Then when the work was scarce, they were peculiarly taxed and prevented from owning property, gaining citizenship, and sending

for relatives and wives. Often they were railroaded out of town—from Tacoma in 1885 and Seattle in 1886—on the very rails they had laid.

Here on Fifth Avenue, some of them are back. Both their costumes and cut-back hair lines are from the Ching Dynasty, which in 1909 was in its 265th year. It had two years to go. In 1911 demonstrators in the International District replaced the dynasty's dragon flags with the new republic's single white star floating on a field of blue and red. (This was a design inspired by the Stars and Stripes.)

The contemporary scene is changed in every detail but one. The Westlake Public Market, behind the dragon's head, has been replaced by Frederick and Nelsons. Across Pine, the Olympic Stables and behind it the Methodist Church have left for Jay Jacobs. But the building, which in 1909 held the Hotel Shirley, is today still a hotel.

The dragon, of course, can still be seen dancing every Chinese New Year. But not on Fifth Avenue.

Hing Wo Laundry on the right and Yesler's mansion on the left.

97 Hing Wo's Hing Wa Hand Laundry

In 1909 a local photographer named Lee did a lot of freelance shooting for the Seattle Engineering Department. Here is one of Lee's city scenes.

Perhaps his intended subject is the street itself, Fifth Avenue, in its semi-liquid condition. Or did the city engineers want a photograph of the laundry? Whatever, these subjects fit one another quite well (like a foot in its galosh), for after crossing such a street one would surely need a laundry.

According to Kit Freundenburg of the Wing Luke Museum, Hing is probably the name of the washman who owned this laundry. And it's a good-sized laundry with two floors of outdoor drying racks in the rear, a sideyard of firewood, and a heaping coal bin attached to the front wall.

Inside, Hing and probably three or four other "sojourners" are sweating long hours over steaming pots and fire-heated flatirons. Hing probably lives upstairs, a floor also used for drying laundry when it was raining or freezing outside.

Hing opened his laundry at 513 Fifth Avenue in 1899. It was one of 25 Chinese laundries in the city. During the next ten years, the size of the city more than doubled and so did the number of its laundries. In 1909, Hing's was one of 55 Asian laundries in a Seattle which after a decade of wild growth was very dirty and in need of a good hand washing.

In 1908 Hing added a new sign above the door and changed his laundry's name from Hing Wo to Hing Wa. Asian-American scholar Dr. Doug Lee offered a possible explanation for this change. Hing traded his clan name "Wo" for "Wa," the new revolutionary name for China. And Hing's politics succeeded. In 1911 the republican revolution succeeded in closing out the 267-year-old Ching dynasty.

But Hing apparently was not a revolutionary sojourner ready to return home. The laundry stayed put until 1932 when it moved one block north to 606 Fifth Avenue. Its last move was in 1960 when the new owner, Wee Mar, took the Hing name to 908 Stewart Street, one block north of the Greyhound Depot. The following year, Wee Mar gave the business—no longer a hand laundry—his own name. 1966 was the last year for the Wee Mar Cleaners.

These hand laundries were one of the very few chances for Chinese self-employment outside of Chinatown. This was especially true in 1909 when Hing Wo was doing his own work in his own Hing Wa Laundry.

98 The View Up Madison

In 1888 Arthur Churchill Warner carried himself and his camera to the top of Mount Rainier. The naturalist promoter John Muir had invited him along to record Muir's intent to go the limits for nature. Warner's climb also was an intrepid first for national landscape photography.

Years later, Warner photographed another "hill," the cityscape up Madison Street's north side between Second and Fourth Avenues. The local landmarks here were less imposing than "The Mountain," and one could ascend this "path" in the clattering ease of a cable car.

The first landmark, the house that's somewhat hidden behind the bank and a covering of ivy, was only a quarter century old when Warner recorded this turn-of-the-century view. It was then already a souvenir of domestic elegance in a neighborhood turning to commerce. But in 1876, when Dr. Gideon Weed built this mansion, it was the local "better home"; Weed was not only the town's health officer but also its mayor. The doctor's residence was the "scene of many brilliant social affairs." They were also sober ones for Weed was an avid prohibitionist.

Eventually, he sold his home to the local entrepreneur John Leary who probably kept a few spirits around the house including his primary vice, the "Seattle Spirit." Bill Speidel in his *Sons of the Profits* claims that Leary once concluded a public speech with the rousing but hardly inspired line "Give me Seattle or give me death!" He got both, including the town's mayorship in 1884. He continued to make speeches and money until 1905 when, like Weed before him, he retired to California for his health and died there. Leary's Times obituary stated that, since his arrival in Seattle in 1869, "it is to be doubted if there was a single large transaction made that did not bear the imprint of John Leary's hands upon it."

Another view of the Leary mansion

The Third Avenue Theatre.

Further on up Madison at the northeast corner of Third is Warner's next landmark: the Third Avenue Theater. It was actually two theaters side by side. Patrons were first required to pay a 10-cent admission for an hour of variety and "polite vaudeville" including "juggling, legerdemain, optical illusions, Punch and Judy, and interesting works of art." The audience would then pay again and reseat itself in the main theater where on a larger stage a variety of farce and melodrama framed spectacular scenic effects including heroic 15-foot leaps into tanks of "real water," animals on stage, and dangerous devices like buzz saws threatening heroines.

Still this was a "family house" and its first impresario, John F. Cordray, posted rules which read, "No intoxicating liquors sold or permitted about the building and the eating of peanuts is prohibited."

Through 1899 the dramatic noises on stage were answered by those across the alley where the nine stories of Seattle's "first apartment

hotel," the Lincoln, were being hammered together. The Lincoln's ordinary masonry construction was described 20 years later, in the era of reinforced-steel skyscrapers, by the local fire marshal as "little else than a lumber yard with four brick walls around it." But for two decades those white bricks gleamed before they glowed.

In the early morning of April 6, 1920, night clerk A.A. Wright heard a dull thud "like something was falling." Immediately smoke was pouring up the elevator shaft and Wright's hands "flew to the plugs on the switchboard." Thus began what later that day the Times reported were "spectacular rescues and thrilling escapes in the presence of a horror-striken crowd that alternately cheered and groaned. The fire broke out again and again, flames shooting skyward, and brought a gasp of astonishment from the seething crowd that pressed forward to the ropes in an endeavor to get as close as possible."

The roof garden of the Lincoln Hotel.

For Fred Hamilton, the local confectionaire of Seattle's Puss'n Boots, and his daughter, Grace, the "thrilling escape" ended in death after a panicked plunge from the top of the west wall, shown in Warner's view.

Now all that survived of Warner's landmarks was the one that moved, the Madison Street Cable Railway. The Weed-Leary mansion and the theater were both victims of the 1907 regrading along Madison and Third[1] and the railway itself was changed somewhat, for after 1907 the block between Second and

Third was no longer the third steepest in the cable industry after 1907. From its commercial start in 1890, the Madison line was the most successful in town, as it still was in 1940 when the city shut it down.

The "now" view up Madison from Second also has its landmarks, principally the Sea-First Building in the place of the old theater and hotel. But the human scale has been sacrificed to corporate height, imposing in its way but hardly noticed unless you crook your head back. For that effort one might prefer to look at "The Mountain," Arthur Warner's 1888 landscape, which is still around to view and climb.

99 Luna Park Lunacy

Where West Seattle drops its northern face into Puget Sound, a tideflat continues for a hundred yards or more. Here for centuries an aquaculture of mussels and clams thrived in a deposit of Duwamish silt cleaned by the tides. It was, naturally, a favorite place of the natives. All this changed in 1906.

West Seattle residents understood that their exposed Duwamish Head with its shallow tideflat was a tough location for ship-tending piers, and in 1906 their city council agreed it was the perfect place for "the greatest outdoor amusement park in the Northwest." The pile driving began for an acre or two of thrilling rides and gaudy amusements.

In the spring of 1907, Seattle looked across Elliott Bay at a Duwamish Head with an altered profile. At night the tideflats would sparkle with thousands of lights that lined the Chute-the-Chutes Water Slide, the Figure Eight Roller Coaster, the Giant Swing, Canal of Venice, Merry-go-round, Salt Water

Natatorium, and Dance Palace. With Luna Park the West Seattle City Council had found another way, besides the ferry from Marion Street, the trolley along Railroad Avenue, and the real estate atop the bluff to get Seattle to West Seattle. However, there was yet another attraction: the best-stocked bar on the bay.[1]

Luna, the name for the Roman goddess of the moon, makes one think either of romance or lunacy. It was the latter that disturbed the residents of West Seattle. The spirits that escaped from their "longest bar on the bay" threatened to drive them crazy with drunken revelers running the length of Alki Beach. The citizens of West Seattle accused their council of planning a beachhead of bars for "the boozers from Seattle" and thereby turning their "Coney Island of the West" into the "Sin City of West Seattle." When the council conceded and voted no more bar building, the citizens soon went further and voted no more council. The 1907 election count was 325 to 8 for annexation to Seattle.

In 1907 Seattle was in an expansionist mood, annexing Ballard, Columbia City, Rainier Beach, as well as West Seattle. It was also in one of its moral moods, electing for mayor a judge named Moore who promised to close the town to unnatural vices and open it to municipal ownership of those "natural monopolies" like water and light. This is just what the citizens of West Seattle landslided for: better city services and an administration with a moralist's nerve to fight vice.

But like the phases of the moon, Seattle's moral moods waxed and waned. In 1910 Seattle allowed its new Mayor, Hi Gill, to once again open up the city. This, of course, now included West Seattle, Luna Park and its one long, well-stocked bar.

Almost as soon as Gill took office, a group calling itself the "Forces of Decency" tried to take it back by recall. These progressives, prohibitionists, and newly enfranchised women voters were aided by the muckraking reportage of the Seattle Post-Intelligencer. One P.I. story was headlined "Many Drunken Girls and Boys at Luna Park."

The January 31, 1911 accusations claimed that at "the Sunday night dances at Luna Park...girls hardly 14 years old, mere children in appearance, mingled with the older, more dissipated patrons and sat in the dark corners drinking beer, smoking cigarettes and singing." Against this spirit of righteousness, his honor Gill temporarily lost his honor in the February recall election.

Gill is best remembered for allowing his chief of police Wappenstein and a few of the latter's shady cronies to build a 500-room

Grace McAdams, right, and friends gamboling on Alki Beach with Luna Park behind.

brothel on the side of Beacon Hill. In this, Luna Park was implicated. Its manager W.W. Powers, a Gill supporter, was also, the P.I. reported, "the owner of 50 shares of stock in the corporation organized to erect a brothel on a public street at 10th Avenue S. and Hanford Street."

Two years later in 1913, Luna Park was closed. Three years later, Gill was once again elected mayor of Seattle.[2]

Our view of Luna Park looks west from atop the Figure Eight roller coaster. The merry-go-round's onion-domed round house is easy to identify. In the distant center of the photograph is the Bath House. The water was cold and salty. An indoor balcony circled the pool at the level where the roof line meets the great arching domed windows. From there one could enjoy the swimming without getting wet.

In 1931 you could still go swimming at Luna Park but the Merry-go-round, Figure Eight, Sunday dances, and Infant Electrobator were long gone. In April of that year, the Natatorium also was gone, torched by an arsonist.

Now the stubby remnants of those Luna Park pilings, which once supported a popular culture of dime sensations, show themselves only at low tide mixing with kelp, clams, barnacles, and human waders. Up the beach on the Alki strip, one can visit, or more properly "cruise" what is still on hot summer days one of the most popular outdoor amusement resorts in the Northwest.

Posing on the Luna Park pier.

courtesy, Seattle Engineering Dept.

100 Six Bridges to West Seattle

The contemporary photograph was shot at 11:30 in the morning of November 10, 1983. At that moment 140 feet overhead, the inaugural ribbon was being cut atop the new high bridge to West Seattle. And through the opening rushed the storm-tossed music of the Sealth High School Band, the wind-lifted cheers of West Seattle boosters in their red and white Hi-Yu uniforms, and the "ultimate solution" to 132 years (less about 68 hours) of the often frustrating task of getting to and from West Seattle. (This problem could be said to have begun in the early morning of November 13, 1851 with the landing of the original settlers, the Denny, Boren, and Low families at Alki Point.[1]

This high bridge (the western approach cuts across the top of the "now" scene) is the most recent of six bridges that have crossed the Duwamish here at Spokane Street. The historical scene was photographed from near the western end of the second bridge (and the "now" takes the same line of site). Designed in 1910 and built shortly thereafter, it was given no name but "temporary" in the

engineering department's original plans. All of the first five bridges were, obviously, temporary, and it's both an engineering and philosophical certainty that the sixth will also be.

The first bridge was simply a swinging gate in the long via duct built about 1900 along the future line of Spokane Street from Beacon Hill to Pigeon Point. It crossed above the tideflats and shifting sand islands that irregularly formed the Duwamish River's estuary into Elliott Bay. Grand plans to build the "world's largest man-made Island, Harbor Island" and dredge a wider, deeper, and straighter Duwamish resulted in Temporary Bridge No. 2—the one pictured.

Bridge 2 is a swinging bridge. It opened to commerce on the West Waterway by pivoting on a central turntable. But in doing so it also shut off the water supply to West Seattle. The pipes are evident to either side of the roadway. Thus, bathing West Seattle citizens understood that when the bridge was closed, they would temporarily suffer for the

long range good of Duwamish Valley commerce.

Partly hidden behind streetcar 689 is the often rowdy barroom business district of Riverview. The ridge behind it is Pigeon Point. Knowing the date of this scene, February 27, 1918, we also know that its rural qualities are deceptive. Directly behind the engineering department photographer, things are quite frantic. There on Harbor Island the largest government contracts in the region's history were financing the construction of thousands of WWI steel-hulled ships.

The third bridge was much like the second only a little higher and longer. It too swiveled for ships (but no longer carried West Seattle water) and was also labeled on its 1917 plans "temporary." [2]

On November 30, 1924, a Miss Sylvia Tell led a group of interpretive dancers from Cornish Arts School to the top of the then brand-new steel bascule bridge for some christening choreography. The crowd expected for the

official December 21st dedication was more than the bridge could handle, so the entire show was first broadcast the night before on Radio KFOA. The ceremony, both in the studio and on the bridge, was a mix of inspirational music, including a rousing rendition of "Ole South" by the West Seattle Community Orchestra and, of course, speeches.

This was bridge number four, although it was named Bridge No. 1 to indicate its hoped-for permanence. Its other name, "North Bridge" declared that it was only half the story. Within five years Bridge No. 2, the South Bridge, was alongside it. Side by side for the next 48 years, they acted permanent until that lucky morning of June 11, 1978 when local hero-scapegoat, Captain Rolf Neslund, ploughed his gypsum ship, Chavez, into Bridge No. 1 and made it temporary too. [3]

Now a ride to West Seattle atop Bridge 6 has the high altitude ease of Cloud Nine. This is the kind of trip that is next to eternity. [4]

courtesy, Lawton Gowey

101 The Railroad Avenue Elevated

On September 4, 1919 the Seattle Municipal Street Railway completed the building of its elevated line above Railroad Avenue. The event was remarkably subdued. There were no brass bands, no speeches amplified by public spirit, and no ceremonial first rides. Only a short bit buried on an inside page of the Times noted "Cars on Elevated." The reporter speculated that once the somewhat wobbly operation proved safe, the streetcars would be running up to speed and that then the trip to Alki and Lake Burien would be cut by as much as 15 minutes.

When the line was first proposed in 1917, it was not designed to get West Seattle residents home from work a quarter hour sooner. It was promoted to beat the Kaiser.

When the U.S. entered the First World War in April 1917, Seattle's southern harbor was already mobilized and setting speed records in shipbuilding. But while the workers were fast on their jobs, they were slow getting to their war work. The then privately owned street railway system was delapidated, and its service to South Seattle inadequate.

Encouraged by the federal government's Emergency Fleet Corporation, Mayor Hiram Gill proposed that the city build its own elevated service to the shipyards. In 1918 he put the plan to a vote. The voters chose the elevated but not Hi Gill who lost his reelection bid to a gregarious politico named Ole Hanson.

The ambitious Hanson took up the task of forwarding both the trestle's elevation and his own. The new mayor boarded the civic bandwagon for municipal ownership of the entire street railway system. This was put to a vote and the enthused citizens agreed to the purchase price of 15 million, or three times the deteriorated system's appraised worth. Armistice Day came only one week after the November 5th election, and when the international hostilities subsided, the local ones heated up.

Without war orders the once frantic south bay shipbuilding took a dive. Layoffs and wage cuts followed. The trestle which was still under construction began to loom as a white elephant. It, like the shipbuilders it was built to transport, was not so needed.

The waterfront strike, which followed in January of 1919, soon spread city-wide to a four-day general strike. Mayor Hanson characterized this "revolution" as a "treasonable Bolshevist uprising." His "heroic struggle" against these "red forces" got him a lot of world press, and the mayor was briefly catapulted into the national limelight. It also deflected local criticism against him as the highest-placed early proponent of the debt-ridden and still delapidated Seattle Municipal Street Railway.

His honor liked both the publicity and the protection from public criticism so much that he resigned, took off on a national lecture tour, and in a moment of gracious megalomania made himself available for the Republican presidential nomination. In a no-contest, the almost equally anonymous Warren Harding beat him out of it.

The older photograph was probably taken shortly before the elevated line was completed on September 4, 1919. Both the special car and the tracks have workmen on them, and the motorman seems to be posing. On the left, some of the men lined up under the old J & M Cafe's Washington Street entrance may be idle shipworkers seeking work

through the C.M. & St. P. Employment Agency in the little Collins Building just left of street car No. 103. Now both the Milwaukee Road and its employment agency are long gone.

On October 12, 1929, or only ten years and eight days after it was completed, the

Railroad Avenue Elevated was condemned and sold for salvage for $8,200. By then Ole Hanson had long since moved to southern California and founded a new town, which would many years later put his name in touch again with the presidency. He named his seaside community San Clemente.

courtesy, Historical Photography Collection, University of Washington

102
The General Strike

At 10 a.m. February 6, 1919, 60,000 Seattle workers laid down their tools and returned home where they helped with the baby, washed windows, cut firewood, and stayed quiet.

The Union Record, the "Voice of Labor," (and then Seattle's largest newspaper with a daily circulation greater than that of the Times, P.I., or Star) advised prudence in all-

caps: "SHOW YOUR LOYALTY TO THE CAUSE OF LABOR BY STAYING AT HOME: AVOID CONGREGATING IN CROWDS, AVOID DISCUSSION THAT MAY LEAD TO DISORDERLY DISPUTES: OBEY ORDERS."

It is this warning to "AVOID...CROWDS" that makes this historical picture a puzzle.

The photograph is from the University of Washington's Historical Photography Collection. A short caption on the back of the original print reads "February 7, 1919 [the second day of the strike], looking west on Pike Street from Ninth Avenue." This placing is almost right, but not quite.

The view actually looks north down Seventh Avenue, across its intersection with Union Street, towards the Waldorf Hotel,

now Waldorf Towers, at Pike Street. If the caption's timing is right, then this gray winter scene is one of the very rare photographs of the General Strike. Yet these men have not stayed at home.[1]

And it is mostly men in this picture. However, they do not seem in the least bit disorderly. Dressed in the era's uniform of starched shirt, hat and tie (in 1919 you would as easily wear a tie fishing or to a picnic as to church), these men look loosely lined-up. Most are just standing around with their hands in their pockets, avoiding the rope that is strung across Seventh Avenue.

These are hardly the gestures and dress of revolutionaries motivated by the "Hell inspired doctrines of Lenin and Trotsky" as Seattle's mayor "Holy Ole" Hanson charged on the third day of the strike. And by the

strike's fourth day, Hanson was, perhaps, already daydreaming about the national tour he would soon make, lecturing on how he had beaten the Bolsheviks with 1,500 deputies and tough talk.

The fifth day was the strike's last. What had begun as a massive act of sympathetic support for the thousands of shipyard workers who had struck two weeks earlier in January ended on February 11, without any employer concessions. What followed was a run of press sensationalism, intensified class resentment, political opportunism (Hanson made a 1920 bid for the Republican presidential nomination), and a ruinous combination of post-World War One depression and inflation. But the strikers had at least proven that they could stop business-as-usual and still supply local babies with milk, hospitals with clean linen, doctors with petrol, the hungry with stew, keep the peace, and stay quiet.[2]

103 Return of the 63rd

The day is Wednesday, March 12, 1919. The silent film "The Forbidden Room" is in the last day of a four-day run at the Colonial Theater on Fourth Avenue between Pike and Pine Streets. The film stars Gladys Brockwell who plays a "girl stenographer saving a big city from looters and plotters." Brockwell's performance, however, probably will be missed and the theater empty for tonight the city itself will be the show as it celebrates the homecoming of "Seattle's own regiment, the 63rd Coast Artillery."[1]

The photograph was taken in mid-afternoon and the parade of local heroes through downtown has just ended. Uniformed men and celebrating citizens are mingling in the streets and rehearsing, perhaps, for the night's street dance in Times Square. At 8 p.m. fireworks will be set off from the roof of the Times Building and the newspaper's next-day reporting of the celebration will continue these pyrotechnics:

"Nothing in the successions of explosions that made the day the 63rd came home a day to be remembered with such historical red letter days as Armistice Day (and night), the Great Fire, the first Klondike gold ship, and the opening of the Exposition was more characteristic of the atmosphere of benevolent and jubilant dynamite than the merry street carnival and pavement dance last night that made Times Square a mass of swaying, noisemaking, exuberant humanity...

"Fireworks at the Times Building represented literally the figurative fireworks that found expression in every other event of the dizzy program which piled sensation on sensation until the city's homecoming soldier sons admitted they scarcely knew whether they were coming or going...

"From the roof of the Times Building rockets soared screamingly upward and flared out in fantastic shapes and lights and showers of fire...Meanwhile bands—four of them—were making the night melodious with war tunes and the jazziest of jazz music—and throngs were dancing, looking skyward as they danced, and not bothering to apologize for bumps."

It is doubtful that even Gladys Brockwell's melodramatic heroics could soar so high.[2]

Grace McAdam (behind "The Bon') marching in a World War I parade.

courtesy, Oregon State Historical Society

104 Hooverville

In the winter of 1934 a University of Washington sociology student paid $15 for a squatter's shack a few blocks from Skid Road. Donald Francis Roy moved in not to lighten the cost of housing but to write a master's thesis he would title "Hooverville, a Study of a Community of Homeless Men in Seattle."

Roy's thesis is remarkable not only for its daring research but also for its style. A profile of the sometimes sarcastic and often sympathetic and playful Roy comes as steadily from his writing as has its scholarly influence on every bit of informed writing since on the local effects of the Great Depression.

In a style not very academic, Roy's introductory paragraph concludes: "From the sandy waste of an abandoned shipyard site, almost in the shadow of the multi-story brick-and-steel sanitaria of indisposed business was swiftly hammered and wired into flower a conglomerate of grotesque dwell-

ings, a Christmas-mix assortment of American junk that stuck together in congested disarray like sea-soaked jetsam spewed on the beach. To honor a distinguished engineer and designer, this unblueprinted, tincanesque architecturaloid was named Hooverville."

Before he could get started with his research, Roy's $15 home required some "aggressive adaptations." He placed "a curse upon the rat that gnawed under the flooring at night," let go his assistant "who snored vigorously from 11 p.m. to 8 a.m.," and vowed to get "an occasional night's rest in an uptown hotel."

His shack's homemade stove leaked so that in a single night "one could quickly smoke a winter's supply of fish." Consequently, Roy vowed to eat "at least one meal a day in a restaurant."

Our mid-1930s panorama of Donald

courtesy, Seattle Engineering Dept.

Roy's community was photographed from the roof of the B.F. Goodrich Rubber Company building at the northwest corner of what were then Connecticut Street and Railroad Avenue and are today Royal Brougham and East Marginal Ways. In this view we see a little more than half of the 500 shanties Roy described as "scattered over the terrain in insane disorder... In this labyrinth the investigator wandered for days, pacing off lengths and widths and distances from this to that and achieved, after a great sacrifice of leather, a fairly accurate map."

Roy used this map-making venture to develop rapport with the residents. With the help of Hooverville's "mayor" Jesse Jackson, he divided the shacktown into 12 lettered parts. Each residence was then identified by a letter and number whitewashed beside the door.

With the "college boy's map," the mayor explained, relief payments could be more readily delivered, new residents and drunk ones would have a better chance of finding their way home at night, and, with addresses, the residents could register to vote. Of

course, the map also would help the "college boy" begin his census and write his thesis.

Using a conversational style that was a "combination of aggressiveness and seeming indifference," Roy interviewed 650 residents. He developed what today is called a "demographic profile" of what he called "Mr. Hooverville, Seattle's candidate for all-American oblivion."

Mr. Hooverville was "jobless, propertyless, familyless. Savings spent, he came to Hooverville in the fall of 1932 to make that community his home." He was primarily a "rustler," scrounging for materials to build and maintain his shack and "bumming food from grocery stores." He was white, single, over 40 and a "shovel stiff," or unskilled laborer. Roy also counted seven women, 120 Filipinos, 25 Mexicans, and 29 blacks, one of them Hooverville's "sheriff."

Roy noted that Hooverville was a rare social "air pocket" in which the normal impersonality of city living had not "choked out the flowers of open, unaffected friendliness toward fellow men. This spirit of camaraderie is carried over racial barriers.

The attitudes of the Negroes, particularly, showed an utter absence of feelings of resentment or inferiority toward whites."

Hooverville was only one of several such local shantytowns. "Louisville" on Harbor Island was another of about the same size, around 1,000 residents in the dead of winter. And there were hundreds of other smaller sites dotting the tidelands, abandoned industrial parks, railroad sidings, and the banks of the Duwamish River. Rudimentary squatting had been a regular practice in any idle area since at least the Crash of 1893 and still is today.[1]

With wartime prosperity and the expansion of shipbuilding came the sudden destruction of both Louisville and Hooverville, even before Pearl Harbor. Many of the residents got jobs. Many others simply moved up river and rustled new shacks.

Donald Roy's thesis was completed in 1935, so it says nothing about the fate of his neighbors. Nor, for that matter, does the University of Washington have any records of whatever happened to Donald Francis Roy.[2]

105 The Commission District

The lanky lettering atop the second story windows in the historical scene's center reads "RYAN and NEWTON," and below the signage continues "Commission Merchants, Fruits and Produce." Company prexy T. Frank Ryan and treasurer Jasper Newton started their vegetable brokerage here at the southwest corner of Marion Street and Western Avenue in 1904 in the area that for years was called the Commission District.

This was the territory of "middlemen" who early every weekday morning directed their lucrative ritual of food transfer. Farmers would unload the fruits of their toil at prices they could barely afford. Then produce brokers, like Ryan and Newton, would in turn sell the produce to local grocers at prices marked up from 50 to 100 percent. It was a system that put expensive vegetables on citizens' tables and resentment in their hearts.

But this land of what was variously called the "food products trust," "Western Avenue Combine," or home of the "Western Avenue offenders" was originally no land at all.

This same perspective taken only 20 years earlier would have looked out from this spot across saltwater, past the stern of the wrecked bark Windward and towards the hooked end of Yesler's wharf. This is a neighborhood created in a hurry after the fire of 1889, atop its ashes, landfill, and planked over pilings. The Windward is still here, only submerged mid-block beneath Western Avenue's intersection with Marion (our "then") and Columbia Street to the south. *(See feature 39.)*

At the lower right, a dapper man embracing a loosely wrapped package and a woman in white, challenging the droppings and dust, cross Post Avenue. Today this narrow street, or alley as it is called further north, no longer cuts through here. Post was spanned in 1931 when the now old Federal Building was built across it. The "now" scene was taken from its windows.[1]

The solid stone face of the Colman Annex fills the upper left-hand corner of "then." It is almost brand new; its eastern granite was originally shipped around the Horn for construction of the old post office at Third and Union. After a federal appraiser judged the stone too soft for government use, it was bought up cheap and used to complete both the Colman Building and its annex. For years, Society Candies were made here. Today, it's a parking lot.

Looking from the "now" into the "then," it is probably not the buildings but the line-up of patiently waiting teams that first draws our attention. Familiar as we are with the horsepower of Celicas, Polarises, and Scirroccos, most of us have lost the horse sense to distinguish between Clydesdales, Percherons, and Shires.

The building just to the right of Ryan and Newton's commission house is the north end of the original post-fire Colman Dock. And to the right of that is the ferry slip where the excursion steamers to West Seattle and Alki Point took on their weekend crowds. A Post-

1912 view north on Western Avenue from Marion Street.

courtesy, Seattle Engineering Dept.

Intelligencer story boasted in 1905 (about the time of this photograph) that "the enormous Sunday business done by these boats puts to shame the crowds in New York bound for Coney Island, or the noon rush in the subway." *(See feature 2.)* In 1907 the names of Ryan and Newton were removed from their building. Newton, the moneyman from Spokane, pulled out, and Ryan slipped to vice-president in the reorganized and renamed company of Hull and Hamlet. The business stayed put and along with the rest of this Commission District continued to attract what the Argus called "the clouds of popular disapproval" and "the storm of the press."

These rumblings resulted in the 1907 creation of the Pike Place Market, an unusually friendly place where farmers and families could buy and sell freely and cheaply.

By 1903 T. Frank Ryan was back in business for himself as a banana specialist. The offices of his Banana Express Company were in the Globe Building, the present-day Alexis Hotel.[2]

courtesy, Oregon State Historical Society

106 Pike Place Public Market

"The Market is yours. I dedicate it to you and may it prove of benefit to you and your children. It is for you to protect, defend, and uphold and it is for you to see that those who occupy it treat you fairly.... This is one of the greatest days in the history of Seattle.!"

And it was, for with these opening remarks from city councilman, T.P. Revelle, the November 30, 1907 formal dedication of the Pike Place Public Market quickly climbed to its fitting rhetorical heights.

This classic market scene was photographed sometime before that November inauguration. A short while after, a long shed with 75 stalls for selling produce was constructed along the west side of Pike Place, north from the Leland Hotel. The corner of the hotel is seen on the left, but not the stalls. They were, however, in place for the November dedication.

The photograph also was taken sometime after August 17 of that year, the day the first farmer H.O. Blanchard rolled in at 9 a.m. after a long ride from Renton. His wagon was filled with produce and soon it was all sacked and sold to an eager crowd big enough to buy out a fleet of wagons.

Blanchard made his trip in defiance of the food brokers down on Western Avenue, or Produce Row, who were threatening to boycott him and any other producer who went around them directly to the consumer. There were rumors of sabotage and intents to flood the proposed market with badly bruised fruits and decaying vegetables. Still disgusted with the middlemen's mark-ups and reading public opinion correctly, Blanchard and eventually many other farmers made the air around Pike Place redolent with the aromas of flowers, pears, sweet carrots, and horses.

So sometime between the informal and formal openings of the market—perhaps in September—the photographer, O.T. Frasch, sighted his lens down Pike Place. What he captured was the human warmth of a busy scene lit by an early afternoon sun. A mist is still on the bay, but the farmers are in shirt sleeves, and the normally overdressed shoppers look a little too snug.

Across the street and behind the billboards for Headlight Overalls and the "Largest Theater West of Chicago"—the Coliseum then at the site of the present County Court House—are the last plaster traces of the ornately top-heavy Hotel York. *(See feature 47.)*

Not an old building, it had to come down when, in 1905, it was discovered that the Great Northern tunnel being bored directly beneath its foundations was causing vibrations. Today occupants of the Corner Market Building can feel the trains rumbling below.

T.P. Revelle's speech, the Times reported, was met with "thunderous applause" from the crowd that had begun to assemble from early morning until it "filled the street."

Today Pike Place still is congested with most varieties of produce and people. Unfortunately, automobile emissions have replaced the smell of horses.

A retrospective gaze from this year of the 75th anniversary of the market's founding (and the 11th anniversary of its "saving") probably will share the vision of the "father of the market" and grand uncle of County Executive Randy Revelle that November 30, 1907 was indeed "one of the greatest days in the history of Seattle!"[1]

107 The 'National Pastime'

By quitting business early he
May miss both wealth and fame
His wife may scold
His meals grow cold
But he saw the baseball game!

In 1894 when the weekly Argus published this bit of verse at the top of its sports page, baseball already was becoming the "National Pastime." Many men not only watched the game but also played it on a variety of fields and sandlots. Many a church, company, and ethnic club, in addition to schools and athletic clubs were fielding their own teams. Indeed, it was one of the few ways that race, class, and creed had of mixing. Doctrine was easily transcended in "good sport," and upward mobility neglected for circular mobility around the bases.

By 1910, the year Stewart & Holmes Drug Company team was photographed, Seattle baseball mania had spread from sandlots to more than 16 playgrounds. Amateur leagues had uniformed teams obeying the hand signals of serious-looking managers in suits and ties. The local model was D. Edward Dugdale, known as Dug. His professional team, the Seattle Turks, had in the year of Seattle's Alaska-Yukon-Pacific Exposition, 1909, fittingly won the Northwestern League pennant.

But 1910 was a different sort of year. Already in June the Times unhappily reported that an upcoming game in Dugdale Park at 12th Avenue and Yesler Way did not look promising for lifting the hitless locals out of the cellar. And it didn't.

A few months later a sportswriter wrote: "Frankly, it was a rotten season. Not only did it deserve to die but it deserved to have somebody hit it in the head with a club along about the time the cows were standing knee deep in June and alfalfa."

Dugdale responded with familiar-sounding managerial optimism: "Seattle is not a cellar city and next year we should have a team that will set the pace. This dust in the face business don't go."

Back in 1877 community pride in its ball team had been a good deal more steady. One thousand fans spent their Fourth of July out on Duwamish Flats rooting Seattle's first organized team, the Alkis, to victory over a visiting Victoria nine. There was no baseball field as such, only a somewhat improved field near the track of a jockey club.

Dugdale Park at Rainier Ave., and McClelland Street.

Not until 1890 was a regular baseball field built at Madison Park. In 1898 a YMCA park was added at 13th and Jefferson, in 1903 a recreation park at Fifth and Republican—part of the present Seattle Center grounds—and in 1907 Dugdale Park, in which Dug was winning and then losing the pennant.

By 1913 Dug and his team's success had grown too large for the "Band Box Park" at 12th and Yesler and so they moved on to the new and improved Dugdale Park at Rainier and McClelland. It was there in 1924 that Seattle won its first Pacific Coast League pennant. In 1932 the park was destroyed by fire, and the team (then called the Indians) played at Civic Field, at the foot of Queen Anne Hill, until 1938 when the new Sick's

Stadium was completed at the old McClelland site. New owners named the team the Rainiers, and it promptly rewarded fans with the 1939 pennant.[1]

Those Pacific Coast League decades of the '40s and '50s were for many the years of "real baseball" with players like Jo Jo White, Fred Hutchison, and Edo Vanni.

The "now" image is of players at a Sunday pick-up game at Cascade Park. Although the ball may be bigger and the distance from base to base shorter, softball is still a great way to act out the dream of scoring the winning run and laughing at your opponent's first base overthrow. And evidently it is just as much—and for some more—fun when women also are making the hits and errors.

108 Golden Potlatch

This photographic record of the almost toylike shapes of Colman Dock and the graceful steamers that nestle to its sides has a peculiar intimacy. The friendly effect is heightened by the press of people that trustingly squeezes to the edge of the pier and swells the clock tower's balcony. Even the time is intimate. We can get as close to it as the exact minute. It is 25 minutes after one o'clock on the Wednesday afternoon of July 19, 1911.[1]

What the P.I. would headline the following morning as the "true thrill of science" was, at this precise moment, literally taking off from the mudflats of Harbor Island. There at 1:25 p.m. the "always punctual" Lieutenant Eugene Ely lifted his Curtis biplane up over Elliott Bay. Earlier, with the simple confidence one hopes for in a pilot, Ely explained to the press, "I like to fly as well as you like to see me fly." Now only moments later than the time recorded on our Colman Tower clock, 100,000 heads were stiffened with the "very contagious" condition of "aeroplane neck" as they followed heavenward "the famous aviator rise up out of the heat haze on the Bay and ascend into the cloudless skies."[2]

Eugene Ely's buzzing of the Seattle waterfront in his "latest achievement of man" was the highlight of the city's first summer festival, the Golden Potlatch. The hybrid name was chosen by contest and derived from the native ritual of gift giving called the "potlatch." The idea was for the city to give itself and its guests what the Reverend W.A. Major invoked as that "genuine frolic that never hurts a man...and destroys the poisons of blood and mind."

The "Golden" was added because of Seattle's enduring obsession with the gold rush of 1897. In 1911 the city advertised itself as "the fastest growing city in the world." It was the popular belief that the gold rush was responsible. Two years earlier, in 1909, local promoters had celebrated their successful hegemony over the Northland with the summer long Alaska-Yukon-Pacific Exposition on the University of Washington campus. *(See features 27, 28, 29.)* Predictably, the summer of 1910 was a letdown.

Therefore, on Monday July 17, 1911, or exactly 14 years to the day since the Post-Intelligencer headlines screamed "GOLD GOLD GOLD GOLD, Sixty-Eight Rich Men on the Steamer Portland," Seattle began six days of what the Duke of Proclamations decreed "Innocent

The Colman Dock's first clock tower after it was rammed by the Alameda.

Amusements."

Soon after Lieutenant Ely returned his Cutlas to the reclaimed earth of Harbor Island, all 100,000 heads also descended to the waters of Elliott Bay. Here "the King of Gold arrived from Mythland and the gold ship Portland repeated history and landed her sourdoughs in Seattle."

This King-for-a-week was outfitted in a rough black flannel shirt, rusty coat, and German socks he wore "ala Alaska," outside his courdoroy pants. "Sweating under the weight of an obese gold poke," he made his ritual landing on schedule at 2:10 in the afternoon. The King's gangway touched down at the Grand Trunk Pacific Dock, one slip north of Colman Dock.

Accompanied by an entourage of distinguished dukes and costumed attendants, the King and his Queen Daphne were driven through the crowds to their coronation. Here, Seattle mayor "Duke" Dilling announced: "May the arrival of your staunch ship Portland this day be the beginning of a second period of prosperity such as

was inaugurated by your first." Then followed two parades, one of floats through the city streets and another afloat in the bay. Both the H.B. Kennedy and the Athlon, carrying many of those celebrants who in our photograph crowd Colman Dock, probably joined the afternoon naval parade.

The Golden Potlatch was a potluck of symbols commemorating the sea, economic growth, pioneer nostalgia, sentimentality for native ways, and manly exhibitions of sporting life. It lasted awhile longer than the Colman Dock clock tower. On April 25, 1912 the entire front end of the old Colman Pier, including the tower, was rammed into the bay by the clumsy docking of the steel-hulled steamship Alameda.

Two years later, in 1914, the Gold Potlatch was retired until its depression-relieving revival in 1938.

World War Two put an end to these and many other innocent amusements. For nine years Seattle was without its summer celebration until the 1950 inauguration of Seafair.

courtesy, Old Seattle Paperworks

109 The Smith Tower

Before the mid-1960s, when the Seattle skyline began to sprout the modern American silhouette of glass, steel, and polymers, the city's front face looked much as it did on the Fourth of July, 1914, the day the Smith Tower opened to its awe-struck public.

Seattle had distinguished itself with the tallest building outside of New York. The building's promoters boasted that one could tour its 42 stories and 600 offices, pass through any of its 1,432 steel doors to gaze at the unparalleled view through a few of its 2,314 bronze encased windows and still feel secure that the 500 foot high edifice stood secure on 1,276 concrete piles reaching 50 feet below to the bedrock.

After the skeleton of structural steel was

topped off in February 1913, the terra-cotta skin began to steadily ascend its sides. The completed frame of the "monster structure acts as a guiding beacon to vessels in and out of Elliott Bay...The Queen City's noblest monument of steel is declared by seasoned skippers to be by far the finest aid to navigation ever placed on Puget Sound...now Seattle would be better advertised than any place outside of New York," wrote the Seattle Times.

This recurring comparison to New York extended to the building's namesake Lyman C. Smith, a New Yorker but from upstate Syracuse. In the early 1890s Smith made what was then the largest purchase of Seattle property in the city's history. It included the Second Avenue and Yesler Way site. By 1909

the armaments enterpreneur had beat his firearms into a typewriter fortune big enough to finance skyscrapers. During a 1909 visit, Smith unexpectedly met another eastern capitalist with similar ambitions. John Hoge was also in town scrutinizing his site at Second Avenue and Cherry Street, catty-corner to Seattle's first skyscraper, the Alaska Building. Both Smith and Hoge had monumental plans for enhancing what was already being called the "Second Avenue Canyon." Since each wished to build a little higher than the other, they coyly agreed that the Alaska's 14 stories was "about the proper height."

The dramatically different consequences of their will to build is apparent in the 1913 panorama of the Seattle skyline. The 18 stories of the Hoge are just left of center and

the Alaska Building. Hoge began his construction in March 1911 and set a world record for speed of steel framing. The skeleton was up in 30 days. Later that year Smith started his tower. By the time the photographer from the firm of Webster and Stevens climbed the coal bunkers near the foot of King Street and sighted the tower's newly completed frame, it was already a "beacon to the world."

For all the Smith Tower's steady grandeur there are plenty of ironies and oddities connected with its history. The darkest irony is the first. Smith decided to build a tower so high that there would be no danger of anyone, including Hoge, approaching it in his lifetime. Smith died before it was completed.[1]

The building project was announced in 1910, only after Smith received the assurances of the city council that they would not move City Hall from its site at Third and Jefferson Street, a half-block from the proposed tower. *(See feature 23.)* Both Smith and Hoge were anxious to stabilize land values in the southern business district. They were ultimately unsuccessful. Already in 1910 it was the commercial fashion to move north and away from the "old city center."

The building's first superintendent, William Jackson gave the tower its final topping in 1914 with an unplanned 20-foot flag pole from which the Stars and Stripes were waving for the Fourth of July opening. This is the same pole that years later flew another symbol for reasons more fishy than patriotic. Ivar Haglund, in 1976 the first local owner of the tower, insisted that the carp he was flying from the top of his tower was not a publicity stunt but an innocent public service for indicating the wet direction of Seattle's weather.[2]

The city's skyline, as it appeared in the spring of 1982, was photographed from the Port of Seattle's Pier 46, once the location of the old coal docks and now of containers. Orville Elden, a mechanic for the American President Lines, the pier's lessee, stands beside one of the cooling units that are regularly spaced between two rows of refrigerated containers. The composition like runway lights forms a line-of-sight that ends in the city's new corporate center. The Hoge and Alaska Buildings, although dwarfed, are still visible to the left of the light pole. The lights pin point the spot where the Columbia Center's 76 stories will eventually top off in 1984.

Comparing the 1982 and 1984 Seattle skylines.

110 From the 35th Floor

When in February 1913 the last rivets were punctured into its steel skeleton, the Smith Tower was, at last, "topped off." Residents, who normally would be gazing at the ring of sublime scenery that surrounds the city, had for more than a year been looking inward at the city's center and upward at the steadily scaling colossus of their very own "largest building west of" almost everywhere.

Now with 42 stories attached to the horizon, everyone could imagine a trip to the top. However, only a few like the Webster and Stevens photographer of this historic panorama could arrange an early ride up through the skinless structure to the exposed 35th-floor observation platform. The general public would settle for the photographic record of what they could not see until a year later at the July 4, 1914 official opening of the Smith Tower.

As the photographer was transported to

the top, in every direction the views were surprising. Especially to the north where, at the 20th floor, Lake Union suddenly appeared. Beyond that the developing suburbs stretched on to the forest. What the photographer finally framed from the 35th floor in the spring of 1913 can still be compared in a few details with what can be seen nearly 70 years later.

The roof of the Central Building is evident in the lower left portions of both views. More elegant remnants are seen in both on the lower right: the Rainier Club, built in 1904 and added onto later, and behind it the classical third home of Seattle's first congregation, the Methodist Episcopal.

Just right of center in the old view is Providence Hospital. First occupied in 1883, its seven-story, cross-topped central tower was a landmark until it was torn down in August of 1914. Today, the Federal Courthouse, which in the contemporary photograph can be seen

between the Bank of California and a hotel being built, The Madison, fills the hospital's old block facing Fifth Avenue between Madison and Spring Streets.[1] When the Federal Courthouse was completed in the early 1940s it was the city's first modern institutional structure. In the historical view, there are many more landmarks still remembered by thousands. We'll name and locate a few.

Starting with the old Carnegie Library, just left of center, we move west across the street to the Lincoln Hotel at the northwest corner of Fourth Avenue and Madison Street. The Lincoln and its roof garden were destroyed by fire April 6, 1920. *(See feature 98.)* Today the Seafirst Building fills that spot. The library with its classical facade was leveled in the mid-1950s. The new library is hidden behind the 23 stories of the white-ribbed Pacific Building in the foreground.

Across Spring Street from the old library, the dark bulk of the old McNaught Mansion is silhouetted against the back wall of the Metropolitan Theater's stage. The theater opened the night of October 2, 1911 with a

performance of "Jumping Jupiter," and in 1924 was surrounded and later absorbed by the Olympic Hotel. The recently renovated Olympic is seen in the contemporary photograph, just to the right of the Seafirst Building. *(See features 35, 36.)*

To the left of the Metropolitan Theater is the southern wall of the White-Henry Building. In 1914 the Stuart was added to fill the block, and later all was leveled for the Rainier Tower.

To the right of the theater and to the left of the chancel end of Plymouth Congregational Church is the old Hippodrome dance and exhibition hall at the present site of the Skinner Building. The church's white tower, which faced Sixth Avenue between Seneca and University Streets, is evident just above the center of the photograph. *(See feature 51.)*

There are at least seven other church steeples on the horizon. Most of them are attached to modest Gothic structures built to serve the working-class families that lived between downtown and Lake Union in the Cascade neighborhood. The most evident is the Immanuel Lutheran Church at Pontius Avenue and Thomas Street. It is silhouetted against the lake as is Cascade Elementary School just to its right. The school is gone but the church still stands and serves the inner city.

The Seattle Public Library at Fourth and Madison, circa 1906.

Across Lake Union the treeless streets of Wallingford line up as far west as Stone Way. There the old Stone Way Bridge connects across the lake with the boardwalk along Westlake. *(See feature 66.)* To the north, Stone Way, which still divides Wallingford from Fremont, extends past the forest of Woodland Park to the southern shores of Green Lake.

For half a century, until the Space Needle was opened in 1962, the Smith Tower was the axis for the ring of spectacular views throughout and surrounding the city. Some still prefer it.

111 Imogen

Self-portrait.

In 1913 the Town Crier, a Seattle weekly devoted to local culture, published a profile of Imogen Cunningham which included directions to her studio: "Walk north from Madison Street on Terry Avenue for a block and a half on the left-hand side of the street and you will notice a quaint little sign swinging out over the sidewalk and modestly challenging attention. It consists of a single artistic portrait under glass and the words in German lettering: Imogen Cunningham—Photographs."

Well, it used to say that. Today, if you follow those instructions you will find yourself near the center of Virginia Mason Hospital, walking down a first-floor hallway between the in-patient pharmacy and the Office of Materials Management.

Seventy years ago, however, Terry Avenue was still a regular sort of First Hill street lined with mansions, small hotels, a better class of boarding houses, and an occasional studio or small business.

The Town Crier's article continued to describe the Cunningham business: "Below the level of the street crouches the studio, a little old cottage which was once, no doubt, an ordinary dwelling but which has long since surrendered its soul to art and its body to the overwhelming embrace of the giant ivy that covers it completely."

This historical photograph of that scene is not by Imogen Cunningham but of her as she contemplatively inclines on her studio porch. The picture's qualities of soft focus and low contrast are photographic conventions which were popular at that time. They help evoke the charmed setting which gently envelops the backlit figure of the artist. She seems not to be posing but rather to have been furtively discovered by a photographer that is still anonymous.

This photo was included in the Henry Art Gallery's 1984 show of Imogen Cunningham's work commemorating the 100th anniversary of her birth. The exhibit was an elaborate revelation of artistic work that was energetic without being obsessive, ironic though hardly alienated, and more than occasionally irreverent.[1]

112 Seattle's Skyline

In early 1908 a now anonymous photographer took a camera to Duwamish Head and shot back at the city. Using a telescopic lens he required 14 negatives to cover the four miles of Seattle's waterfront from Smith Cove to Harbor Island. Both this "now" and "then" record the same part of that grand panorama: the six blocks between Spring and Washington Streets.

Although the monumental difference that 76 years can make is as unsubtle as the Columbia Center, there are many finer parts in the old scene that survive in the new. Single towers of both the twin-towered St. James Cathedral and the Church of the Immaculate Conception manage to peek through the screen of skyscrapers. Parts of Trinity Church and the Lowman, the Colman, the Alaska, the Central, and the Mutual Life Buildings are in both scenes.

The contemporary view was photographed on Friday April 27, 1984 at 2 o'clock in the afternoon. That was one weekend before Mayor Charles Royer announced his grand May Day plan for keeping the central business district "in scale." This, the mayor candidly explained, meant free of any more Columbia Centers.

Only twice before has this city's skyline been so dominated by a single structure. First in 1914 with the completion of the elegant Smith Tower, seen on the right of the "now." Then not again until 1968 when the dark bulk of the Seafirst Building, seen on the left, pushed its way toward heaven. Now, if Royer's plan succeeds, what may be called the "Sea-Center" will stay stuck up and out of scale for however long contemporary buildings are supposed to last.

Both scenes also show a ferry. The older one is coursing its two-mile trip from West Seattle to the slip at Marion Street. The newer one, also at Marion, is taking on commuters and tourists for what the state in 1984 promotes as the "greatest show on Puget Sound." *(See features 2, 99, 105.)*

This does not exhaust the two scenes' continuities; however, trying to discover the others may exhaust you. [1]

An aerial from above the Denny regrade with the long wall of the Alaska Way Viaduct and the construction of the Seafirst tower.

Notes

1 THE FIRST PHOTO

[1]This feature on Yesler's home and Clark's photography appeared in part as the second in the "Now and Then" series in Pacific Magazine on January 24, 1982. That Sunday I received a helpful phone call from an Oregon resident who was in Seattle visiting his son.

Father and son were arguing over whether or not I had made a rather gross error. The father gently suggested that my description of which of the two Clark photos of the Yesler home was shot first was haywire. The son defended me, perhaps believing in the infallibility of newspaper feature writing. Father knew best.

Indeed, this was my worst error in ten years of "reading" regional pictorial history.

I have three excuses. First I was misled. It was a common mistake, made many times before, and I kept to the tradition. Since this probably does not impress anyone, my second excuse refers to why it was a common blunder. In what is really the first photo of Seattle, a gravity-system waterworks on stilts comes down James Street and crosses in front of Yesler's home. It seemed natural to assume that such an "improvement" came later.

My third excuse is a confession. I was anxious. For years I have hoped to find a really good print of either one of these early Clark photos, and I never have. Frustrated by their rough and dim condition, I became nervous and uncaring. I avoided these photographs and never took the time to really look at them.

The father's evidence, once seen, was obvious and made my error as obviously gross.

2 HOW TO GET TO WEST SEATTLE

[1]In 1907 the ferry West Seattle took over primary service to West Seattle from the ferry (and city) City of Seattle.

3 THE SMITH'S STOCKADE

[1]Actually, Hanford's text is ambiguous regarding the exact site of Smith's harbor and his vision. The passage is on page 74 of Volume I of *Hanford's Seattle and Environs* and is too long to quote in full here. However, you are encouraged to check it out (from the library) and see what you can make of it. I am inclined to think that the "this harbor" Hanford refers to is Elliott Bay and not Puget Sound generally.

[2]The Smith Tower was built by a Smith of a different sort. There's more about that in features 109 & 110.

4 PRINCESS ANGELINE'S SHACK

[1]It is difficult even, perhaps, impossible to now place Angeline's shack. Descriptions of its location vary. A close reading of the featured photograph shows some of the waterfront in the gap just to the left of the shack. Using this pictorial clue and the best "average" on the various locations given at her time, I think my choice of a location for the "now" is close.

There's another wrinkle here as well. There are other photos claiming to be Angeline's shack, and they don't seem to be the same shack.

5 YESLER'S MANSION

The fire-ruined library.

The Coliseum Theatre filled this site for the years between the mansion and the courthouse.

6 SALMON BAY CHARLEY

[1]As of this writing, summer 1984, David Buerge's book on regional native history is still waiting to be published. The fruits of his elaborate research are available in several articles that have appeared over the last few years in The Weekly.

[2]After this feature first appeared in part in the Times I received a peeved letter protesting that my "now" photo was not of Lawton Wood but rather of Bay Terrace. Well, it was Lawton Wood and it still is on my big four-color Kroll's Map of Seattle. We might say that this is the Bay Terrace part of historical Lawton Wood or Lawtonwood (spelled both ways). But then both Lawton Wood and Bay Terrace are parts of the historical Stanley donation claim, or Stany, or Stanly, or Standy, who was illiterate and had a variety of spellings for his last name.

The man sitting in the "now" scene is Frederick Mann, former university architect at the University of Washington and more recently consultant to the Seattle Parks Department in its development of Discovery Park. He was my guide.

[3]The Daybreak Star Center was opened in 1977. Much of its design was patterned after the old Indian longhouse.

7 THE FIRST PANORAMA OF SEATTLE

[1]The other surviving Sammis photos are the portraits of Doc Maynard and Chief Seattle. When Sammis took his long exposure of Seattle, the chief had his eyes closed. In the many variations which have been retouched from this Sammis original, the chief's eyes are usually open. Should we say of the retouches or the retouchers, "eyes have they but they see not"?

8 COMMERCIAL STREET

[1]In the late 1880s Singerman's San Francisco Store grew so that it moved into its own building at Front and Columbia Streets. It was destroyed in the Great Fire of 1889, but Toklas and Singerman (which also became the store's new name) rebuilt again on the same spot.

[2]Main and First Avenue S. was the site of a riot during the 1886 attempt to expel Seattle residents of Chinese ancestry from the city. This sketch appeared in Harper's Weekly. The view is east on Main Street across Commercial (now First Avenue S.).

courtesy, Lawton Gowey

Post-fire Commercial Street.

9 THE BIG SNOW OF 1880

[1] These King Street coal wharves were for years a monumental feature on Seattle's waterfront. Other views of the wharves are included in features 10, 11, 18, 21, 38, 57, 104, and 109.

courtesy, Historical Photography Collection, University of Washington

11 KING STREET COAL WHARF

[1] For nearly twenty years, from 1877 to 1896, the King Street coal wharf was the most southerly pier on the waterfront. (I'm not counting the Stetson and Post lumber mill which was about a block further south and also a ways east, and so on the tide flats.) Throughout the 1880s and 1890s hundreds of photographers must have trecked out there for a shot of maritime Seattle, for there are scores of photographs that have survived including many others of the wharf itself. This one was shot in 1890 by F. Jay Haynes, the Northern Pacific's official photographer. (Haynes photos are the subject of features 4, 42, 46, and 77.)

[2] What I mean by "systematic filling" is large-mannered, single-minded filling. There was a lot of filling before 1896, but not of this sort. The original settlers' Seattle was a peninsula that hung like a tear drop south of Yesler Way to King Street. South and east of that to Beacon Hill were the tideflats some of which were filled in with dirt from the first primitive street gradings and with sawdust from Yesler's mill. This was effective but not really systematic. (See feature 57 for more on the tidelands.)

courtesy, Tacoma Public Library

13 JOHN COLLINS' OCCIDENTAL HOTEL

[1]Other views of the first Occidental Hotel are included in features 7 & 12.

[2]Those "wooden houses across James Street" can be seen on the right of the featured photo in the next feature, number 14.

[3]The tradition of the "Seattle Spirit" suggests that besides the four elements of earth, sky, water, and fire this city had a fifth element that worked the first four to local advantage. This quintessence was guided by a collaboration of Adam Smith's invisible hand and the Seattle Chamber of Commerce.

14 YESLER'S CORNER

[1]In the early 1970s a close friend of mine from college decided to lease and reopen the Merchants Cafe. Sensitive to its past, Richard Moultrie set about doing a renovation that preserved it. Dick asked me to help research the Merchants' history. Before that I had been downtown, perhaps, six times in six years, and maybe twice to Pioneer Square. Now I'm familiar with the entire central business district but I identify its parts by landmarks that are no longer there. In this sense I live in Seattle's past. So, whenever I get a chance in the present, I take time to thank Dick Moultrie for finding me a job in the past.

15 THE GREAT FIRE OF 1889

courtesy, Lawton Gowey

[1]The Opera House ruins.

[2]The most common metaphor for the fire was also animal, but a fantastic one. Seattle was said to have died that day, but like a phoenix rose from its own ashes.

courtesy, Old Seattle Paperworks

16 BRICK BUILDINGS AND BOX HOUSES

[1]Thomas Prosch's work has been most helpful. The typed manuscript of his turn-of-the-century unpublished "A Chronological History of Seattle from 1850 to 1897" has filled many of my features with the texture of his facts. And his two photo albums of classic Seattle cityscape have captions which are early ones and generally accurate. (Both the "Chronological History" and the albums are at the University of Washington Library Northwest Collection.

The figure of Thomas Prosch is included in feature 38 as one of the group of men standing around the steps of the Post Building at the foot of Yesler Way. The caption explains which one is Prosch.

[3]The 1889 panorama of temporary tents and post-fire construction looks south from Third Avenue and Cherry Street. It sights through the block that would later be filled by Cort's Grand Opera House and Seattle's first skyscraper, the Alaska Building. It is from the recently renovated Alaska's eighth floor that I shot the "now."

The Skid Road corner that once held Cort's Standard is now a parking lot and is hidden by the Interurban Building which fills the scene's center. Occidental Avenue is on the right where it begins at Yesler Way across from the building site of the Seattle Hotel.

In 1889 the tidelands south of King Street stopped both the Great Fire and, temporarily, the city. When Doc Maynard first platted his claim south of Mill Street in 1853, most of it, including part of Occidental Avenue was a salty swamp. The Standard was built on a fill which was mostly sawdust. The county's big house, the Kingdome, was built on a fill which is mostly Beacon Hill. The Dome which has been compared to a hamburger and Jello mold might also knowing its fundament is in the tidelands, be imagined as a scallop.

[2]The Grand Opera House and now the Cherry Street parking garage. A full house at the Grand Opera House.

17 THE FIREBOAT SNOQUALMIE

[1]Feature 24 tells the story of "Moran's Five Challenges."

The Grand Trunk Fire, July 30, 1914.

[2]An August 13, 1905 article in the P.I. lavished this romantic description on the then 15-year-old Snoqualmie: "She is tug-like in shape, black and tan in color, tough and sturdy in appearance. She is always at her post, and from her thick tan funnel the smoke is always rising...holding to the dock by two rope nooses, she swings with the tide and waits..."

"Watch her when the alarm sounds in Station Five! Hardly before the gong is still she has slipped her leash and darted from the dock. A fire along the waterfront! The fireboat's time has come...The crew jump to their places...They strap their sleeves to their wrists and button up their coats, for the fire boat is true to her name, and while in action one were just as dry under Snoqualmie Falls....From the nozzles' mouths there leap white and sparkling lines that carry death to flames. Now upon the deck there is in strictest truth, a young Snoqualmie. The wind tosses the spray back upon the boat, and the men are working in a mist."

18 HARRISON'S ROYAL ENTRANCE

[1]Here Harrison's steamer, The City of Seattle, is still a ways offshore.

[2]An early Leschi view is shown in feature 77.

The welcome arch in Pioneer Square.

19 THE RAINIER HOTEL

[1]Although I did write a feature on the Butler Hotel for the Times "Now and Then" series, it is not included here. It will appear in part in *Seattle Now and Then Again.*

The Denny Hotel is included in features 50, 51, and 53. The Seattle Hotel is shown in feature 32.

[2]*He Built Seattle* is the title of Robert Nesbit's excellent biography of Thomas Burke. Burke figures throughout this book; the little lawyer was so big in local booming and development that he's perhaps the best local evidence for the effect of individuals on the course of history. So here's his portrait. It's the best looking Burke I could find.

courtesy, Historical Photography Collection, University of Washington

[3]The Rainier Grand was one of a long line of hotels that ran up both sides of First Avenue. Feature 89 shows the hotel block between Spring and University Streets.

[4]Feature 98, "Up Madison Street," shows another of Warner's photographs and tells a little something about him.

courtesy, Mrs. Herbert Coe

⁵This back door winter view of Central School and the Rainier Hotel was taken sometime in the early 1890s.

21 A VIEW FROM PROFANITY HILL

¹ This scene of the post-fire devastation also looks down from First Hill. Like the feature picture in the main text, this photo shows the backside of the City Hall and the side view of Turner Hall. See feature 23 for a front view of both halls and a look up at First Hill as well.

22 TRINITY CHURCH

[1]When the cars of the James Street cable line began pulling up James Street on March 18, 1891 a lot of the swearing that went with Profanity Hill left it. Now lawyers and litigants could avoid this cursed climb to the Courthouse with a five-cent fare. Of course, this correction wasn't required of the parishioners enroute to church. But any rider, whether going to worship or to court could now recline and choose to either look right toward the masked figure of Blind Justice and her scales atop the drab west entrance to the Courthouse, (*See feature 23*) or look left into the translucent stained glass figures of the Angels of Mercy and Purity that hovered to either side of Christ in the windows of Trinity's west chancel wall. It was a dramatic choice.

By 1906 the cable riders also passed by what the P.I. called "these glaring and unsightly structures that lift their flaming fronts and tell their own story of aggressive insolence." These "blots of beauty" were the billboards we can see from on end at the left of this feature's view down James Street.

23 COURTHOUSES AND CASTLES

[1]The "Katzenjammer Castle" was named after the old comic strip whose humor extended to the buildings and contraptions that served its characters. The Seattle City Hall was discordantly strung together through 18 years of an expanding city and city government. The still standing 400 Yesler Building was built in 1908-09 to replace it.

[2]This gleaming front face view of Harborview Hospital was photographed soon after its dedication.

26 ROAD TO NOME

[1]It is a truism that as soon as the film leaves the hands of the photographer its record is softened by memory or fancifully rearranged by desire. If, later, we wish to determine the content of a photograph that has no caption, or confirm one that does, we first search it for a sign here or a landmark there that will give us the key to unlock its meanings. Or if we wish to relax this hide-and-seek, we may look for an expert. I found one in Jim Faber, who also posed for my "now" photo.

The old pier shed we can see over Faber's right shoulder is Pier 55. Before the wartime Army Corps renumbering of the water front wharves in 1944, it was number 4.

Jim Faber's book on Puget Sound steamships will likely be out sometime in 1985.

[3]Two other landmarks included in the feature photograph but not mentioned in the text proper are the Turner Theater Building, behind City Hall and the City Light substation at the brim of the hill on the south side of Yesler Way.

24 MORAN'S FIVE CHALLENGES

[1]Here the heroic builder perpetuates his identification with the city, or what's good for Robert Moran is good for Seattle.

[2]I have heard a rumor that Moran's organ played itself and that when he took to the console the self-motivated keys were hidden from the audience who could see only Moran's head bobbing and not his fingers flying.

If this is true, then Moran played his organ something like Jack Benny might be imagined conducting one of his benefit concerts. I'm thinking of the Los Angeles Philharmonic performing a Beethoven violin concerto with Issac Stern the soloist in fact but with Jack Benny claiming to be. Obviously, here too the audience would have to be either blindfolded or otherwise sight-impaired.

However, I've not uncovered any evidence that Robert Moran had such a sense of humor. This is only a once-heard rumor, and I would appreciate receiving a letter with evidence either way.

[2]The Victoria offshore at Nome.

25 OUTFITTING THE ARGONAUTS

[1]As of this writing, a joint venture between two local architectural firms, Olsen and Walker, and Hewitt, Dailey, and Isley are preparing to put up a new Olympic Block. The building will be part of a larger plan that will also renovate the City Club and Libby Buildings which are contiguous to the Olympic just south of First Avenue S.

The beach at Nome.

27 AYP'S ARCTIC CIRCLE

[1]The primary photo exhibited in this feature and the two following were all taken by Frank Nowell, the AYPE's official photographer. These are not.

[2]Another early appraisal of the AYPE was that it "put Seattle on the map." Now its sensation is largely forgotten. However, a brief time after Mt. St. Helens sensationalized this region, long-time Seattle Times newsman Don Duncan named his all-time "Washington's Top 10 News Stories." Besides the eruption Duncan's educated choices were: the Narrows Bridge collapse in 1940, the completion of the Grand Coulee Dam in 1942, the Great Earthquake of 1949, the Gold Rush of 1897, the Centralia Massacre of 1919, the Weyerhaeuser kidnapping of 1935, the Great Seattle Fire of 1889, the first flight of the Boeing 707 in 1954, and the opening of the Alaska Yukon and Pacific Exposition in 1909.

Curiously, Duncan ranked the AYP's news as greater than Century 21's. A comparison of their grand designs suggests why.

28 THE PAY STREAK

[1]This view looks across the Klondike Cirle from the Battle of Gettysburg to the Architecture Building.

courtesy, Historical Photography Collection, University of Washington

[2]A poem of the time played with the rumored habits of the Igorrotes:

Once there was a little puppy an' he wouldn't stay at home,
But alluz seemed determined to stray about an' roam:
An' once wheen he was straying they heard an awful yell,
An' a great big bared-legged Igorrote just grabbed him
  pell-mell
An' whisked him in the stew pan for he knowed what
  he's about,
An' the Igorrotes'll get yo' if yo' don't watch out.

An' mammy allerz tells me unless I'm awful good,
That some day I'll find Igorrotes a lurking in the wood.
I guess we all have trouble an' I'm frightened mos' to death
An' every time I'm naughty, I jes' hold my breath,
An' stop and look and tremble, peering all about,
For fear the Igorrotes'll get me ef I don't watch out.

29 TEMPLE OF TIMBER

[1]The Washington State Museum is now housed in the Burke Museum on the University of Washington campus, near the 45th St. entrance. The museum will celebrate its centennial in 1985. Events and exhibits are planned.

30 THE PRIEST AND THE PROSTITUTE

[1]Here's a view looking the opposite direction, or up Washington Street from Fourth Avenue. The counterbalance that ran here between Fourth and Sixth Avenues, although Seattle's first, was not its most famous. That was on Queen Anne Hill and it is shown in feature 61.

[2]A frontal view of the Montana Stables.

[3]Henry Broderick's reminiscences are used two other times in this book. *See features 16 and 94.*

courtesy, Seattle Engineering Dept.

31 PIONEER SQUARE

[1]A number of features included in this collection touch upon this phenomenon of the wandering business center. See especially features 12, 32, 50, 59, 93, 94, 103, 109, 110.

[2]The many thousands of negatives in the Webster & Stevens collection are now safely kept in the basement of the Museum of History and Industry where they are being catalogued, printed, and preserved.

32 A HUB OF THE PAST

[1]The number of times this "sinking ship" shows up in the text and pictures is a little embarrassing. It's an invitation to satire. My obsession with this garage was divined in this collage of it coming through the Montlake Cut. I made it for an early — mid-1970s — presentation of my "Work in Progress" on local pictorial history at the And/Or performance on Capitol Hill. The Denny Building is on the left.

The 1960s destruction of the Seattle Hotel.

[2]Bill Speidel considers Doc Maynard his alter-ego. Here he poses inside the Merchants Cafe with a picture of Maynard shot in 1865 or 1866 by Sammis. *(See feature 7.)* One of Sammis' studios was at this Yesler Way location. It's probable that his Maynard portrait was taken from very near where Speidel stands.

33 DEPARTMENT STORE SANTA

[1]Action in front of Garvey & Buchanan's department store.

courtesy, Museum of History and Industry

34 DENNY'S KNOLL

[1]Actually 1907 was a crashing year economically. The local regrade projects on Denny Hill and Fourth Avenue were acts of faith conceived in good times but underway in hard times. The 1907 recession inspired anxious memories of the 1893 Crash. Digging into hills and streets was a good way to relieve these flagging recollections.

The view south on Fourth Avenue from the roof of the university building in the mid-1870s.

[2]The same contemporary shot is used for both feature 34 and 35. The historical scenes were recorded from very near the same location.

[3]The columns.

courtesy, Old Seattle Paperworks

courtesy, Historical Photography Collection, University of Washington

35 YMCA:
A HOME FOR WORKING WOMEN

[1]This feature's photo appears on the cover of that YMCA publication. Inside, of course, are many other scenes from YMCA history,

36 DENNY HALL

[1]The Coe family is the source of both story and picture in feature 20.

[2]Another early record of Denny Hall.

37 DENNY'S BELL

[1]Perhaps the last time Denny's Bell was rung was when I took the "now" picture from its belfry. I hit it. The tone was still one of "quality" but not "power.' It was chained.

[2]David Denny's fate is briefly narrated in feature 60.

38 THE VIEW FROM BEACON HILL

courtesy, Historical Photography Collection, University of Washington

39 PIKE STREET COAL BUNKERS

courtesy, Seattle Public Library

[1]A late 1870s view of the Intelligencer Building at the foot of Cherry Street on Front Street, now First Avenue.

²This 1880 view of the Pike Street coal wharf from the King Street coal wharf shows its stubby remains.

²1888 was also the year that George Kinnear gave his park to the city, Robert Moran built his dry dock, Julia Kennedy was elected the first woman Superintendent of Schools, Central School burned down, the Rainier Club and Crescent Spices both got their start, and the year the first Yesler Way cable car began the line's half-century of service to Leschi Park. *(See feature 77.)*

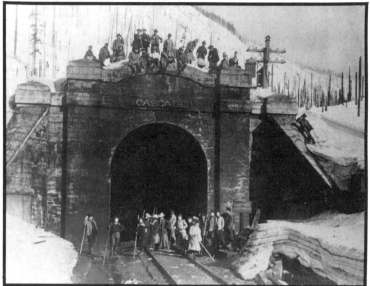

³The Great Northern did not come over Snoqualmie Pass but over Stevens Pass in 1893. See features 46 through 48. Actually, it tunnelled under the pass.

41 THE SEATTLE LAKE SHORE AND EASTERN

¹This turn-of-the-century sighting up First Avenue from Virginia Street shows both Dr. Root's tower on the right and the cut on First made during the 1899 regrade.

courtesy, Frederick Mann

42 THE RAVENNA NEIGHBORHOOD

[1] One plan for this neighborhood-busting freeway had it passing underneath Union Bay and then cutting through Ravenna.

43 'MAGNIFICENT STUPENDOUS SNOQUALMIE FALLS'

Photographer Will Hudson on the road to Snoqualmie Pass.

[1] In 1909 the Milwaukee Railroad completed its transcontinental through Snoqualmie Pass. That same year 150 reinforced automobiles from the East made it through the pass enroute to the Alaska Yukon and Pacific Exposition in Seattle. *(See features 27 through 29.)* In 1915 this Sunset Highway was opened to the family car.

Now every day thousands of travelers, preoccupied with getting either east or west, speed through the plateau above the falls, the site in the 1880s of the largest hops farms in the world. They hurry by those "magnificent stupendous Snoqualmie Falls," and rush beyond the valley below the falls where Carnation's cows still graze contentedly.

44 BALLAST ISLAND

[1]Seattle was actually incorporated twice: first in 1865 and then again in 1869. The unincorporation in between resulted from minor corruption within the elected council. A councilman gave himself an exclusive franchise to fish in Lake Union.

[2]It was only a very few years earlier that all this land, both within and without Seattle's city limits, was the same native land it had been for thousands of years before. When the European invasion of this continent which began in the 16th century at last reached the Northwest coast in the mid-19th century with its first flood of settlers, it brought with it the strange idea of ownership. Surveyors, lawyers, Indian agents, and other specialists were imported to institute the literally un-natural notions of artificial borders, land grants, acres, and water rights.

[3]This 1880 view of the rock pile on the wharf at the foot of Washington Street is Ballast Island in the making. See feature 10 for the panorama from which this detail is taken.

46 THE COLUMBIA STREET DEPOT

[1]The King Street Station in its early years. Now its classical lines have been severely cluttered by a communications disk. *(See feature 56 for an early view from the top of the station's tower.)*

45 DUGOUTS AT THE FOOT OF WASHINGTON STREET

[1]And there was an accident. At the last moment the races were moved to Pier 70. And there were other accidents as well. The photo exhibit never made it onto the Virginia V. Instead it was displayed on Pier 55. Of course, it's not an accident that I've kept the book's text close (but not exactly) to how it originally read in Pacific Magazine. I did it for the accidents.

That there have been maritime rowboat races at the foot of Washington Street is evidenced in this official Port of Seattle photograph.

[2]In 1898 the clapboard West Street House burnt to the ground taking lives with it. It was to that time the city's worst disaster.

[3]The Colman Building shortly after it was completed.

[4]Unfortunately James Hill was not around in the early l950s to sound a warning when the Alaska Way Viaduct was proposed, put up, and so cut the city away from its waterfront in a type of "aesthetic suicide."

The Empire Builder James J. Hill.

47 'LONGEST TUNNEL'

[1]When the two ends at last met in late October of 1904, the Seattle Times considered it one of the four great historical events of that year. The others were the building of the Alaska Building (now recently renovated), the launching of the battleship Nebraska *(see feature 24),* and the arrival to its Smith Cove moorage of the then largest ocean carrier in the American merchant fleet, the Great Northern's Minnesota. *(See feature 48.)*

[2]Sometime the joke is told "...from Virginia to Main." However, Washington Street is closer to the tunnel's southern portal and so closer to the truth but still a long way from it.

48 SMITH: THE MAN AND THE COVE

[1]In 1983, it seemed for awhile that the Navy was interested in getting Smith Cove back from the Port. The Navy's advances were, however, cooly met by Mayor Royer. The responses from the neighbors nearby on the Queen Anne and Magnolia Hills was downright chilly. They did not wish to live above what they called the "New Jersey of the West."

courtesy, Katharine Sparger

A close-up of the Minnesota and Dakota.

49 "THE GREATEST NAVAL PARADE EVER."

[1] Both of this feature's historical photos were taken not by a professional photographer but rather by a professional musician, a clarinetist in Pop Wagner's band. An odd circumstance about the crowd scene is that it was photographed from a ship in the slip where the presidential steamer Spokane would later dock. Perhaps, this vessel delivered Wagner's band and then backed out. The view of the flotilla was probably exposed at the last photo graphic moment the clarinetist could steal before he had to rush back to the band and take up its ceremonial music. (Other photographs by this unnamed clarinetist are included in features 47 and 65.)

[2] The Washington Hotel's lobby.

50 THE HOTEL ON DENNY HILL

[1] Tacoma's Tacoma Hotel seen from Commencement Bay.

[2] In 1983 when I originally wrote this I was thinking of the failed proposal for an art museum in Westlake Mall. However, there is a long list of frustrated opportunities for preservation and innovative use of old and cherished resources — buildings and hills included. To think that City Hall might have been moved from its travel lodge into the Smith Tower!

51 "THE LARGEST BRICK CHURCH"

[1] This article first appeared in part in Pacific Magazine on February 21, 1982. It was the sixth feature to appear in that weekly series, and I was still — sometimes — using the present tense. This tense suggests that in a photograph the past lives somewhat uncannily in the present. And so it reads theatrically. I abandoned it for the prosaic habit of referring to the past as the past.

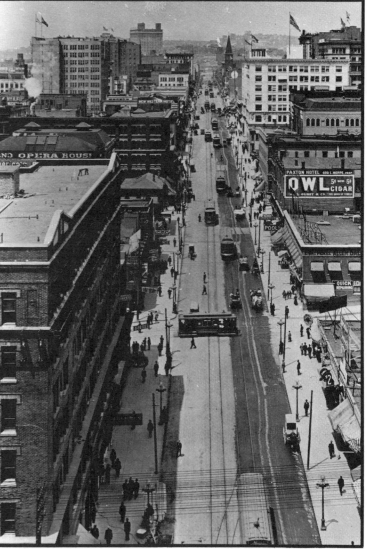

courtesy, Old Seattle Paperworks

52 SECOND AND BELL: REMNANT OF A LOST NEIGHBORHOOD

[1] Nick's Athens Cafe is now closed after several years of searching for a menu and decor that would suit a changing neighborhood clientele.

[2] I've wondered why this photo was taken. It's not a subject that promotes anything, just a rare view of the back side of Denny Hill. I think it is probable that the Webster and Stevens photographers took this shot as a last record of the old pre-regrade Second Avenue.

A 1930s view of the three gables at 2222 Second Avenue.

53 THE UPS AND DOWNS
OF SECOND AND VIRGINIA

[1]The view looking south on Second Avenue from Lenora Street shows from three sides how the pre-regrade intersection of Second and Virginia was in a depression.

The conveyor along Battery Street.

54 CLOSE ENCOUNTERS
ON THE REGRADE

[1]Actually, Hi Gill during his mayoral campaign flirted with the idea of regrading Queen Anne Hill into Lake Union.

[2]The best suggestion I received for what Curtis's uncanny regrade-scape was most like came from an opera fan. When Glynn Ross was still Seattle Opera's impressario, he proposed building a permanent outdoor setting for the opera's annual Wagner festival. The opera buff suggested that Ross's fantastic dream is almost all there in Curtis's regrade scene. Ross would have saved those buttes, added a few cushioned bleachers, curtains, and a fog machine and had the perfect setting for Wagner's Gotterdammerung or "Twilight of the Gods." The final scene in which Siegfried, Brunhild, and Valhalla are consumed first by fire and then by the rising tides of the Rhine River could be easily effected with a few pyrotechnics and the imaginative use of those water hoses.

55 THE CLIFF ALONG FIFTH AVENUE

56 THE JACKSON STREET REGRADE

[1]I don't mind aerobic exercises but I do not like climbing catwalks. Thus, I describe this ascent second-hand. My friend, Genevieve McCoy made the climb and took the picture.

[2]Now it is generally agreed that the removal of Denny Hill was a mistake. The jury, however, is still out on Jackson Street. This hill was more like a ridge, and the three-and-one half million cubic yards of hosed earth sluiced to the tidelands below did help raise 678 muddy acres two feet above high tide.

[3]Since Ms. McCoy took her picture in 1983 from the top of the campanile, the gabled structure which used to be the Baptist Church has been renovated.

The slice into the west side of Denny Hill is shown well in this view of the Second Avenue regrade taken from Second and Pike.

Holy Names Academy ruins during the Jackson Street regrade.

57 FILLING THE TIDELANDS

RALPH W. DEARBORN

[1]Dearborn was one of the big developers on the tidelands.

A rich mix of dredgings is pumped out onto the tideflats.

58 FRANK OSGOOD'S HORSE CARS

An early electric trolley on First Ave.

60 DAVID DENNY'S CLAIM

[1]David Denny's first residence was the roofless beginning of Alki Point's and so Seattle's first cabin. Alone and waiting for the rest of the Denny party to join him from Portland, he worked on the cabin until he injured himself with his own axe. *(See feature 3.)*

That was in 1851. Fifty years later he recalled in a Seattle Times interview that while waiting for his brother Arthur and the others, all he had to look at across Elliott Bay "where Seattle now stands, was an unbroken forest with no mark by the hand of man except a little log fort made by the Indians." What David Denny could not see, but would be happy to discover months later, was that behind that green curtain was a swale of naturally cleared lowland that led to a fresh water lake. That became part of his claim, and today part of the Seattle Center.

[2]The David Denny mansion at Mercer and Queen Anne Avenue.

[2]The counterbalance's underground tunnel and tracks.

[3]LaRoche also took this picture of the army mules mustered for the Phillipines insurrection. Queen Anne Hill is in the background.

61 THE QUEEN ANNE COUNTERBALANCE

[1]The sensitive reader will realize that the story of the lost mayor and the photographer's Queen Anne assignment have nothing to do with one another except that both occurred in remote north Seattle at about the same time. My weak pun on the photographer's "shot" is not a tie that will bind them. I simply like the story of the lost Humes and it's a digression I chose to include.

The counterbalancing truck.

Mayor Humes.

[3]A later view of a paved Queen Anne Avenue and its counter balance. The view looks north from between Mercer and Roy Streets.

[4]An egg, we can presume, Mayor Tom Humes would have relished on his second morning lost in the wilderness!

62 MANSION ON A PROPER HILL

[1]I have a recurring dream that I am climbing a wild Queen Anne Hill, and that near the top I come upon a large orchard. I can see the abandoned Queen Anne High School through the trunks and branches but I can never get to it.

Florence Blethen in the garden.

63 SEATTLE'S FIRST CHARITY

[1]The Leary mansion is shown in part on the left side of the historical photo in feature 98, "The View up Madison."

Gilbert Duffy on the sidelawn with the family samovar.

Edward Duffy   *courtesy, Gerald Johnson*

[2]The Seattle Children's Home on the present site of the Seattle Center's Fun Forest.

[3]The last "regular" job I had was at the Seattle Children's Home. In 1966 for half-a-year, I was a house parent to 12 adolescent boys. They wore me out. In the fall of 1966 I left the home to develop courses establishing the Free University in Seattle. That was the beginning of a life of random freelancing in education, media, music, and, for the last ten years, history. It's usually been easy, and I can often sleep in. But when I remember or pass by the home on the hill, I recall how emotionally demanding that work was, and I'm thankful that some have the heart and strength to keep doing it. It's really not at all "regular."

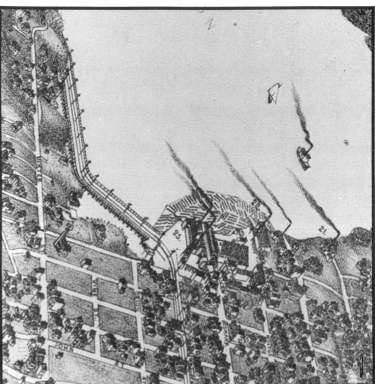

[1]Two other promotional views taken from LaRoche's prospectus for Griffith. The one shows the south end of Lake Union from Denny Hill and the other another portion of the "electric bridge" which ran along the west side of Lake Union to Fremont.

The second home on the hill.

64 THE ELECTRIC BRIDGE TO FREMONT

65 LAKE UNION'S SWIMMING HOLE

courtesy, *Historical Photography Collection, University of Washington*

[1]Here's the Elks carnival costuming. I hope you agree that the brother and sister look the same age here as in the lake shot. This parade scene was taken on Denny Hill near the old Dexter Street. The kids are in their Elks carnival costumes. The story of the Elks carnival is sketched in feature 90.

66 TAMPERING WITH LAKE UNION

Fremont Ave. bridge after break in Gov't. dam. 3-13-14.

The Fremont Bridge after the 1914 washout.

67 THE AURORA BRIDGE: SUNRISE AND SUNSET

[1]Another early view of the completed bridge.

68 WOODLAND PARK: FROM COUNTRY ESTATE TO AFRICAN SAVANNA

[1]In 1938 David Hancock acted like himself and resigned his post after the city — its voters — failed to correct the awful condition of the zoo's elephant house.

[2]This view of the south entrance to Phinney's Woodland Park shows its arch and the gatekeeper's cottage, the Phinney family's temporary home.

69 RAVENNA PARK

Another view of the Burkes' park.

70 GREEN LAKE WAY

[1]Don Sherwood was a draughtsman who, apparently, did not care for typewriters. Included in his files are handwritten thumbnail histories for nearly every park, playground, and parkway in the city. Although now deceased, he is memorialized in his collection. He is also frequently thanked by many a researcher, including this one. Most of this feature came from material Don originally gathered.

[2]This inviting view of the boathouse is also from the Sherwood file. Here the structure is still afloat and the lake at its old level.

71 GAS WORKS

[1]That in 1910 both aviator Hamilton and the photographer of the Lake Union Gas Works were up high is probably not sufficient reason to include them in the same article. Still, I have joined them that I might introduce this picture of a pre-crash Hamilton .

courtesy, Museum of History and Industry

[2]In the late spring of 1984 Gas Works Park again "resisted becoming a conventional park," when it was discovered that some of those hydrocarbons had leached into the children's sandbox. Mayor Royer closed the park for months of testing. Today, August 21, 1984, it has been reopened for less than a week. The kites are back on the mound but the kids are still kept out of the sand.

courtesy, Michael Maslan

[3]Two small photo albums recording the original 1906-07 construction of the gasworks have recently surfaced — with the help of Michael Maslan. Here is one scene from that album.

72 BALLARD AVENUE

[1]In 1976 this stretch was designated the Ballard Avenue Landmark District. That the name, attention, and protection which comes with it are all deserved is shown by how much alike are the Ballard Avenues of 1908 and 1984. Unfortunately, this preservation act came too late to save the landmark Ballard City Hall.

73 BALLARD SKYLINE

[1]In the week following the Sunday June 24, 1984 that this feature appeared in part in Pacific, I received a note and some snapshots from a Times employee. It read: "Dear Mr. Dorpat — regarding your article "Cedar Was Ballard's Business" — you state the mill fire was in 1964 — I took pictures that night as you can see — Notice the date on the photos! Thanks, Earl E. Shattuck, Times Receiving Dept."

I replied: "Dear Earl Shattuck, Thanks. I made the correction in the book's text. And thanks for letting me reprint one of your night-of-the-fire shots. "May '58" is clearly marked on the border."

[2]Attached to the Ballard Bridge near its southern end is a terribly exposed steel grill staircase. When you ascend these see-through steps from Fisherman's Terminal below, you are confronted with an unsettling sign at the top. It reads: "Stairwell not in service." It is for this reason that the "now" photo for this feature is credited to Dan Patterson a friend who owed me a small favor. I asked him to make this exposed exposure. I waited below with the light meter.

74 A DIFFERENT DUWAMISH

[1]The original print is faded. On the back, written with a light pencil and in an antique script, is inscribed "Mount Rainier." Since the picture's view looks south in line with "The Mountain," it is probable that when fresh this print also showed it, however faint.

[1]A view of the neighborhood atop the Boeing B-17 plant during the Second World War. The photo was taken from an airplane not from Catholic Hill.

75 CATHOLIC HILL

Another view of Catholic Hill in the distance with the brothers' school on top.

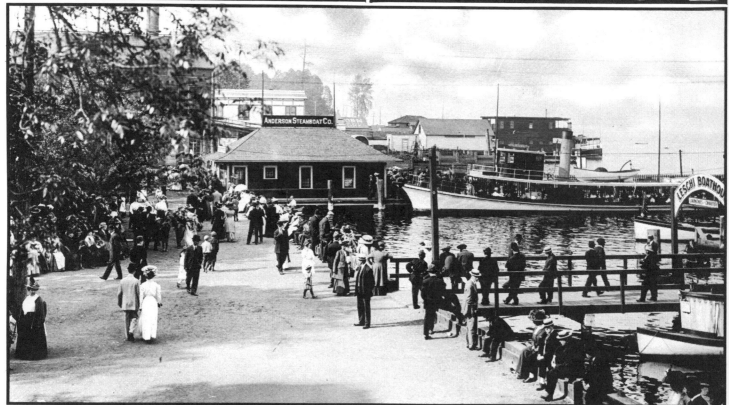

77 AT THE LESCHI END OF THE CABLE LINE

78 RAINIER VALLEY'S ELECTRIC RAILWAY

[1]Among the misfortunes predicted were that the tracks would electrocute pedestrians and horses, that the electricity would be eventually washed away from the wires by the Northwest rain, and that riders' watches would be magnetized.

[2]For a different view about whether Leschi was around during the Battle of Seattle, read pioneer Ezra Meeker's excellent book Pioneer Reminiscences on Puget Sound or The Tragedy of Leschi.

83 THE MONTLAKE CUTS

[1]In 1869 Harvey Pike ambitiously platted his Montlake property as "Union City," and began promoting his vision of linking the lakes. Although the canal was too much for him, a tramway was soon laid across his property. By 1872 coal was being barged up Lake Washington to Pike's isthmus and then trammed across his Union City to Lake Union and there loaded on scows and pulled by steamer to a narrow-gauged railroad at the southern end of the lake. *(See features 11, 38, 39, and 40 for more on transporting coal from the deposits on the east side of Lake Washington.)*

79 MORNINGSIDE

[1]It was Asa Mercer who is remembered for bringing single women west to meet the lonely bachelors of Seattle. In 1865 on his second expedition, Asa and his "Mercer Girls" wound up broke and stranded in San Francisco. Luckily, the already married John and Zeopporah Wilson were also on this waylaid trip and able to rescue the entourage with part of their life savings. It was for this loan that Mercer paid the Wilsons off in land.

[2]Our late spring of 1983 visit to Morningside was Harold Smith's last. He died January 25, 1984, two months before his 94th birthday.

84 RECEDING UNION BAY

[1]So am I.

85 A GOLF COURSE IN LAURELHURST

[1] This view of the course was photographed a few hundred feet south of the feature photo. This one is actually closer to the location from which the "now" photo was taken.

courtesy, Old Seattle Paperworks

86 VOLUNTEER PARK

[1]The old bandstand.

87 THE LIBERATED PLAYFIELD

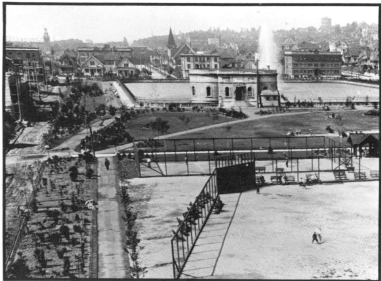

[1]The Lincoln-Broadway baseball diamond from the top of the Oddfellows Temple on Pine Street.

88 THE DAY THE DOME FELL

[1]Other scenes from the Big Snow of 1916.

89 A BLOCK OF HOTELS

[1]This view of the waterfront was shot from the back of the Arlington Hotel at the southwest corner of First and University. The University Street ramp cuts across the picture.

90 THE ELKS CARNIVAL

[1]Denny's Knoll is pictured in feature 34.

courtesy, Historical Photography Collection, University of Washington

91 CLEMMER'S DREAM

[1]The Kenneth Hotel at the foot of Cherry Street.

[2]Here is another of the Dream's faces.

94 THE FOUR FORMS OF FOURTH AVENUE

[1]See feature 34 for other views down Fourth Avenue.

[2]The Carnegie Library at Madison Street with the moved
McNaught mansion behind it and across Spring Street.

[3]Oliver Wallace at the Dream's Wurlitzer.

93 POST OFFICE STEPS

[1]Demolitionist Dickson's work.

courtesy, Seattle Public Library

95 THE FIRST BAPTISTS

[1]A view of the First Baptists' first church on this site can be glimpsed up Cherry Street in the 1880 snow scene in feature 9.

[1]Besides the dragon's scales, the witches' recipe required: fillet of a fenny snake, eye of newt, toe of frog, wool of bat, tongue of dog, adder's fork, blind-worm's sting, lizard's leg, howlet's wing, tooth of wolf, gall of goat, nose of Turk, Tartar's lip and more.

98 THE VIEW UP MADISON

[1]The Madison Street regrade.

[2]On the other hand, the Baptists did succeed in nurturing their tradition with the new church on First Hill.

96 A DRAGON ON FIFTH AVENUE

The dragon on Pike street just east of Fourth Ave.
courtesy, Old Seattle Paperworks

[1] The grand entrance to Luna Park.

courtesy, Oregon State Historical Society

CHARLES W. WAPPENSTEIN

[2]The best brief description of Hi Gill's career is in Murray Morgan's classic history of Seattle, *Skid Road*.

The Alki Beach bandstand.

100 SIX BRIDGES TO WEST SEATTLE

[1]While I was below photographing the line of the old bridge, a friend, Dan Patterson, was on top of the new bridge photographing scenes of the high bridge's inaugural. Here he caught the mayor entertaining the princesses.

[3]Bridges four and five side by side.

[4]For West Seattleites the bridge to eternity will be number seven. It is a toll bridge.

102 THE GENERAL STRIKE

[1]This 1919 scene can be interpreted very differently. The ornate building on the right with the central tower was the then popular Dreamland Dancing Pavilion. Built in 1908 as a roller skating rink it was soon converted for dancing. All these men could be waiting for their dates.

[2]Despite Hanson's armed deputies, during the strike police arrests dropped from a daily average of 100 to 30, and not one was strike related.

[2] Bridge number three.

Arming the deputies.

103 RETURN OF THE 63RD

¹This was the first "Now and Then" to appear in part in Pacific. The date was Sunday January 17, 1982. Like many of the other early articles, it was written in part in the present tense, as if the past subjects in the photograph were here with the reader. This, it has been noted mentioned in many places, is the peculiar, surreal, and uncanny paradox of photography.

²The "now" photograph was shot in the summer of 1981. Now, in 1984, the corner on the left — the northwest corner of Fourth and Pike — has been razed and with it the Colonial Theater-converted bank. The 1919 photograph was shot from the street. In 1981 I chose the sidewalk, because the cookie seller was willing to hold the older photo.

Spontaneous parade on Armistice Day, 1918.

1918 influenza epidemic masks.

WW1-era dress.

104 HOOVERVILLE

[1]Some other shanties during the Great Depression.

[2]After this feature appeared in part in Pacific I received a number of letters from persons who knew Donald Roy. I learned that Roy went on to teach sociology for many years at Duke University. There he was studying workers' attempts to unionize the textile mills in the South. Roy died recently before he was able to collect his research into a book. Some of Roy's students, I am told, have been organizing his material and preparing to publish it.

10544
10-27-31

105 THE COMMISSION DISTRICT

Post Street
looking North from Marion St. (On Bridge) 5-23-12.

[1]Post Avenue before it was spanned by the Federal Building.

[2]T. Frank Ryan made the right move. Bananas were very good to him. Ryan developed a thermometer that saved many man hours in monitoring the condition of bananas in shipment. Today his namesake company, Ryan Instruments, is a leading producer of industrial thermometers. Their home offices are in Kirkland.

106 PIKE PLACE PUBLIC MARKET

[1] This feature in part, and the "now" photo published here, appeared in Pacific in 1982. Now, in 1984, the market is 77 years old.

107 THE 'NATIONAL PASTIME'

The north side of Marion Street west of Western Avenue, circa 1909.

courtesy, Old Seattle Paperworks

courtesy, Michael Maslan

[1]The same Potlatch scene one hour later.

[2]Lieutenant Ely's Curtis biplane over Elliott Bay.

courtesy, Museum of North Idaho

Two scenes from early Seafairs.

109 THE SMITH TOWER

[1]The family's fate was further attached to the tower in 1915 when the Smith daughter was married in the Chinese Temple at the 35th floor observatory. That was also the year a one-armed parachutist leaped from the top and barely survived a windblown bumpy ride down the west wall of the tower. This illegal descent was followed by a risky ascent. The Times reported that "a human fly climbed the outside of the building from sidewalk to top to earn cigarette money for soldiers overseas." This fly was assisted by William K. Jackson, the building superintendent, who confessed at his retirement thirty years later, "We had to cheat a little bit to do it. I stretched ropes over cornices. He never could have climbed otherwise."

[2]The Smith Tower might have been City Hall. However, in February 1945 the City Planning Commission reported to Mayor William Devin that the building was "wholly un-suited" for municipal use. Today that report is recognized as an embarrassing bungle and missed opportunity. Seattle might have inexpensively acquired ($900,000 was the asking price) a headquarters whose elegant height would have saved the city the eventual double scar of its Public Safety Building and Municipal Building. *(See feature 95.)*

110 FROM THE 35TH FLOOR

[1]By now, the Madison Hotel is completed, as is the First Interstate Bank Building on the contemporary photo's far left.

Rainier Club at Fourth and Marion.

Providence Hospital at Fifth and Madison.

111 IMOGEN

[1]Using the house number, old real estate maps from the County Assessors Office, one other soft-focus photograph of the studio's back porch, and the spatial evidence of the sun's shadows, I determined that the position of the anonymous photographer behind the historical scene was near what is now a parking lot and hospital service entrance a little ways west of the hospital's main entrance on Seneca Street.

112 SEATTLE'S SKYLINE

[1]Now that you have come to the end (assuming you began at the beginning), I hope you will respond. Please write me a note with any criticisms, comments, corrections, or whatever you might have or harbor. Set the record straight or confuse it. Or if you have any photographs, memories, whatever you would be willing to share in future possible articles and books then let me know. For whatever reason, get in touch. Next to readers, I love letters. Send them to Paul Dorpat, P.O. Box 85208, Seattle, Wash. 98145-1208. P.S. You can also order more books through this address.

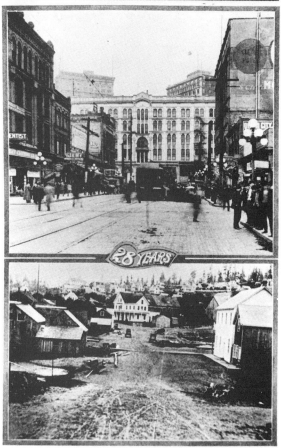

Seattle Contrasts was probably the first local treatment, in book form of the "now and then" convention. The title page does not show a date, but judging from the photos it was probably published in either 1911 or 1912. The timing is understandable, for Seattle had just passed through a quarter-century of growth in which its population exploded from under forty thousand to more than two hundred thousand. The contrasts were obvious and, in *Seattle Contrasts* they were celebrated.

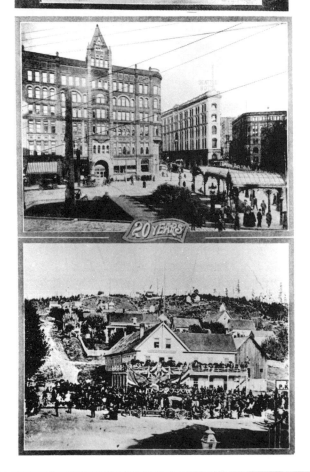

Index

No. 5. MADISON PARK, SEATTLE.

Matthews, Mark, 28, 69

Metropolitan Theater, 110

No. 15. PIONEER SQUARE AND TOTEM POLE, SEATTLE.

SEATTLE.—RESIDENCE OF HON. H. L. YESSLER.

TARTU PUBLICATIONS
P.O. Box 85208
University Station
Seattle, WA 98145-1208

(Signed copies of this book can be ordered from Tartu through the mails. Use the above address and send $17.95 for softcover and $29.95 for hardcover. The postage is included in the price. Please indicate if you do *not* want the copies signed.)